Youth in Transition

VOLUME V

*Young Men
and Military Service*

JEROME JOHNSTON
JERALD G. BACHMAN

SURVEY RESEARCH CENTER

INSTITUTE FOR SOCIAL RESEARCH
THE UNIVERSITY OF MICHIGAN
ANN ARBOR, MICHIGAN

ISR Code No. 3434

The research reported herein was performed pursuant to a contract with the Department of Defense. Contractors undertaking such projects under Government sponsorship are encouraged to express freely their professional judgement in the conduct of the project. Therefore, points of view or opinions stated do not necessarily represent official Department of Defense position or policy.

First Printing 1972

Library of Congress Catalog Card Number: 67-66009

ISBN 0-87944-122-4 Paperbound
ISBN 0-87944-123-2 Clothbound

Published by the Institute for Social Research

Printed at Lithocrafters, Ann Arbor, Michigan

To Pat and Ginny

PREFACE

This book is the fifth in a series of monographs documenting the Youth in Transition project, a longitudinal study of young men conducted by the Survey Research Center. Primary support for the project has come from the U.S. Office of Education, with some support also from the U.S. Department of Labor. The work reported in this volume received considerable additional support from the U.S. Department of Defense.

The present volume is concerned with military enlistment behavior, attitudes toward military service, and prospects for an all-volunteer armed force. In late 1968 the Department of Defense anticipated the need for information bearing on the feasibility of an all-volunteer force. Harold Wool, who was then directing manpower procurement policy studies, and Ralph Canter, head of manpower research, visited the Survey Research Center to explore the possibility of research dealing with these issues. At this time the majority of respondents participating in the Youth in Transition project were in their senior year of high school—an ideal time to ask about military plans and attitudes.

This was a fortunate matching of interests and opportunities, but it did not result immediately in a contractual relationship. Feelings about the topic of research were quite mixed, both within the project staff and throughout the Institute for Social Research. At campuses across the country students and faculty alike were actively protesting the involvement of their institutions in any form of war-related research. After considerable discussion and debate, we agreed to undertake a research project dealing with military manpower issues. We did so on the assumption that the research was important, not so much to the conduct of any particular war, but rather to the nature and shape of military manpower policy—a matter likely to have long-range impact on both youth and the broader social fabric. A further underlying assumption was the view that military manpower decisions ought to be made ultimately by an informed citizenry, based on the most complete information possible. It thus became important to highlight issues which might be overlooked by policy-makers in the press of providing immediate answers to immediate problems.

The major interest expressed by the Department of Defense was the use of longitudinal surveys to track the knowledge, plans and attitudes of high school youth concerning military service. Equally important was the discov-

i

ery of the relationship of these and other factors to voluntary entrance into military service. One of the contributions that we could make over and above providing information on these two questions was to point out more about the types of individuals who would and would not be attracted to a volunteer force. For example, in Chapter 13 we highlight the fact that using strictly monetary incentives may fail to attract a large and important segment of today's youth: the college-bound. We discuss two reasons why this could be detrimental to national policy. One, the college-bound are among the most capable individuals in terms of aptitude, and therefore are a desirable resource in terms of ease of training and ability to take and exercise responsibility. Second, they are likely to be the most committed to returning to civilian life. The results of these findings is our recommendation that new incentives be used to attract the college bound. It is this type of finding and recommendation, which goes beyond the immediate question at hand, that we feel represents a valuable contribution. To reject researching such issues because they are war-related makes it much more likely that policy decisions will be made which will later be deemed unwise after the results are seen.

A second matter that had to be considered at the time we negotiated a contract was the openness of the findings to public scrutiny. We took pains to insure that the research would not be classified and could be openly disseminated by us. The Department of Defense has proved to be very supportive of our efforts to disseminate results as we have found them. In the summer of 1970 we published and distributed more than a thousand copies of a preliminary report entitled, *Young Men Look at Military Service*. The following summer we presented many of our findings and ideas on an all-volunteer armed force at a national conference on "Youth in the Seventies;" a paper summarizing this material will also be published separately as part of a book of readings—*Youth in Contemporary Society*. The present volume represents one more example of the dissemination of findings which can be (and hopefully will be) read by citizens and military policy-makers alike, thus making possible active debate on the nature and structure of the armed force of the future.

The Structure of This Report. There are three parts to this monograph. The first part (Chapters 1-10) is a study of choice behavior of young men at the end of high school. It represents a search for the reasons why some young men choose to enlist after high school rather than take a civilian job or continue their education. The study should be of interest to the sponsors of this study, the Department of Defense, in their continuing effort to implement an all-volunteer armed force. But it is hoped that it will also prove helpful to guidance counselors and others who are concerned with guiding the choices that young men make at this time in their lives.[1]

The second part, Chapters 11-13, is an examination of some of the issues surrounding the debate over an all-volunteer armed force and an indication

----

[1]Chapters 1-7 and 10 served as partial fulfillment of the requirements for the degree of Doctor of Philosophy at The University of Michigan (Johnston, 1971).

of the feasibility of attracting volunteers to such a force using various incentives.[2]

The third part, Chapter 14, presents a summary of the findings as well as our view of the implications of this research for military manpower policy. It contains a number of specific recommendations which we feel should be considered in light of the findings. Those readers who wish to begin with an overview of the whole study should turn to this section first.

Acknowledgements

A project as large as Youth in Transition could not be undertaken without a large staff of dedicated and competent people. A group effort has been essential to collecting, managing, analyzing and interpreting the massive quantities of data involved. We are pleased to acknowledge the vital role these people have played in the production of the present study.

Among the many colleagues we are especially indebted to Martin Gold, for his guidance at every stage in the development of Part I. His insight and incisive comments have added immeasurably to the final product. David Bowers and Lloyd Johnston had many useful comments which affected the shape of Parts II and III. In the early stages of this study Bill Rodgers and George Levenson contributed much to the development of instrumentation. Garry Walz and Joe Johnston provided insights into ways of conceptualizing the problem of choice, and Frank Andrews, Patrick O'Malley, and Terry Davidson contributed their expertise in the use and interpretation of various statistical techniques. Harold Wool, who initiated this research, coordinated and interpreted the many informational needs of the armed services.

Diane Davidson brought order and calm to the project by orchestrating the great variety of tasks involved in producing the final product: submitting computer runs, typing drafts, drawing graphs, editing manuscript, and coordinating a number of other people in their jobs. Donna Ando filled Diane's shoes very capably when Diane left to take a new job as a mother. Pat Veerkamp, Pam Deasy, Kathy Farrell, and Reggie Gerstman all contributed their typing skills to the production of the final manuscript.

Many people who have served on the Youth in Transition project staff have been mentioned above; it is a pleasure to acknowledge all of them in the listing that follows.

Youth in Transition Project Staff *(Past and Present)*

Gayle Ackley	Lynn Bozoki
Donna Ando	Janet Bumpass
Allison Arscott	Robert Cope
Jerald Bachman	Diane Davidson
Joy Bingham	Terrence Davidson

---

[2]These chapters were adapted from a chapter which appears in a book concerned with youth in contemporary society (Bachman, 1972).

iv

John French, Jr.
Regina Gerstman
Swayzer Green
Penni Holt
Sally Iman
Mary Jacobs
Jerome Johnston
Joseph Johnston, Jr.
Lloyd Johnston
Robert Kahn
Rita Lamendella
Judith Long
Martha Mednick
Haydee Navarro

Roberta Niaki
Guttorm Norstebo
Patrick O'Malley
Karen Paige
Janice Plotkin
Philip Rappaport
Joel Raynor
Willard Rodgers
Susan Shapiro
Claire Taylor
Barbara Thomas
Elizabeth van Duinen
Patricia Veerkamp
Ilona Wirtanen

CONTENTS

TABLES

FIGURES

PART I

A STUDY OF CHOICE BEHAVIOR
AT THE END OF HIGH SCHOOL

CHAPTER 1

INTRODUCTION

This chapter introduces the study described in Part I. The reader who wishes an overview of the whole study should turn to Chapter 14, Summary and Policy Implications.

This is a study of choice behavior of young men at the end of high school. It is a search for the reasons why some young men choose to enlist after high school rather than take a civilian job or continue their education. This problem has obvious implications for an all-volunteer army, but it has broader significance as well. While the primary focus is on the specific choice of enlisting, this choice has many similarities to the other options available. Military service is temporary in nature for all but a few who persist beyond the first tour of duty. But college and other forms of advanced education are also temporary activities; and few young men who enter the job market immediately after high school persist at their first jobs. What is unique about military service is that, for many, it is not strictly speaking a choice at all, because the draft "forces" many young men to enlist. But there are involuntary aspects of other choices as well. Few young men who enter the labor market choose the job they would most like; the "law" of supply and demand eliminates many desirable jobs from the possibilities considered. Similarly with the college bound. Many go to college simply to avoid the draft [1] (in this study 20 percent mentioned avoiding the draft as a reason why they chose to continue their education); still others are faced with having to choose a school that is not their first preference, because of institutional selectivity or personal financial limitations. These and other similarities suggest that the present investigation has broad significance for understanding not only enlistment decisions, but choice behavior in general among young men leaving high school.

In looking for explanations of choice behavior, several families of factors are examined. These include a young man's culture, family background, school performance, attitudes about jobs and war, and his position on three factors which were hypothesized to be particularly central to an enlistment

1

decision: self-perceived "fit" with service life, vocational indecision at the end of high school, and status with respect to the draft. Also examined are influence patterns of parents, siblings, peers, and school officials.

The study is based on data from a longitudinal study of young men, called Youth in Transition (YIT). This is a nationwide study of adolescent boys who entered tenth grade in public high schools in the United States in Fall, 1966. The initial sample included 2213 boys. There were four data collections, one each in tenth, eleventh, and twelfth grades, and one a year after high school. Youth in Transition has among its purposes the examination of various background and school factors relating to the development of occupational plans and later occupational attainments. However, this particular phase of the project, exploring specific choices at the end of high school—especially the choice of military service—was conceived several years after YIT began its data collections. At the time, most boys in the panel were in the middle of their twelfth grade. Accordingly, the present study draws on two types of variables. One is a set of measures collected at the end of twelfth grade and one year later, all of which are specifically designed to investigate end-of-high school choice behavior; the other is a large data bank of related measures from the parent project. These were collected at various times over a span of nearly four years. This large data bank presents a unique opportunity. Certainly, one of the limitations of research in vocational development is the plethora of studies based on small specialized samples and limited in scope to only a few potential correlates of the choice process. While such a large data source is an advantage, it must be noted that YIT was not designed to test a particular theory of vocational development or choice, so the available measures do not fit neatly into a single unifying theoretical framework.

Conceptual Framework

To impose some order on this research a broad conceptual framework was constructed which guided both the selection of variables to be examined and the order in which the analyses would be performed. This framework shows the influence of a number of theoretical orientations which are described below.

Choice of a post-high school activity has not by itself been the focus of previous research. Instead, it has been viewed as just one step in a larger domain of interest, vocational choice or vocational development, where vocation denotes the occupational attainment, such as doctor or construction worker, of an adult. The shape of the present conceptual framework reflects this influence of vocational development theorists.

The problem of explaining vocational choices has been approached from a number of different perspectives, none of which has purported to explain the behavior entirely. Some of these orientations are elaborated in Chapters Four through Seven. They are described at a general level here.

One of the oldest theories of occupational choice is trait-and-factor theory. This theory considers that individuals are in effect "keyed" to one or a few "correct" occupational positions, and if one knew enough about an individual's traits—especially his aptitude for various tasks—the "correct" few occupations could be discovered prior to the individual's entry into one of those occupations. This approach received its biggest boost during World War II from the task of matching men to jobs in the Army. More currently, the view is associated with the work of men like Thorndike (1959) and Flanagan (1964). The theory has not been particularly successful in differentially predicting the choice of one occupation over another, although it has been somewhat more successful in predicting to the level (status) of jobs attained. Since the latter is also related to educational attainment (and thus to the choice of college over military service), this theoretical orientation led to the inclusion of measures of intelligence, social class, and cultural and family traits as potential predictors of the choice of enlistment.

In the 1950s vocational researchers became disenchanted with the pure trait-and-factor approach. There evolved what Katz (1963) has called neo-trait-and-factor theory, with Super and Bachrach (1957) as its chief proponents. In many ways it is not a theory at all, but rather a number of theories which, taken together, underscore the fact that there are a large number of forces in addition to an individual's stable traits which must be considered in explaining a choice. These include cultural forces and so-called "deeper motives." Another contribution was the recognition that occupational choice has to be treated developmentally, ". . . not as an event occurring at a point in time and explainable by determinants which can be observed adequately at that same point in time, but rather as a process which takes place over a period of time, and which is best explained by a combination of determinants which themselves interact, are modified, and thus developed over time" (Super and Bachrach, as quoted in Katz, 1963, p. 13). Having said this, Super and other exponents of this approach have not yet detailed how the multitude of intra-personal, inter-personal, and sociocultural forces are interrelated.

One aspect of this approach which Super has singled out for special emphasis is the importance of an individual's self-concept as a determinant of choice behavior. Briefly, self-concept theory views vocational development as a process in which an individual develops a concept of himself which he refines through role-playing and ultimately implements in the choice of a job which he feels matches his traits, abilities, and interests. An important element in this process is compromise, which occurs whenever it is recognized that a particular concept of self is unrealistic or disfunctional.

Super's theory has influenced this study. A number of self-concepts are related to enlistment choice to see if they have any explanatory power. One of these is the concept of self as a military "type" of individual; the other is the concept of self as a student qualified for advanced education after high school.

Another aspect of Super's theory (and Tiedeman's as well) that has been influential is the conception of an occupational choice not as a single event,

Table 1-1

Variables Examined as Potential Predictors of the Choice of
Enlisting After High School

I. Motives or Dispositions to Enlist

Perceived "fit" with (affinity for) military service life
Vocational indecision
Draft status (draft avoidance)

II. Conditioning Factors

Background
    Cultural
        Race
        Geographical region
        Urbanicity
    Family
        Broken home
        Family size
        Parental punitiveness
        Social class and richness of home environment
        Father's military experience
        Brother's military experience

Influence sending
    Anticipated response of parents, peers, friends, and school
        officials to possibility of enlisting

Aptitude
    Intelligence (GATB Test)

School factors
    Average classroom grades
    Attitudes toward school
    Rebellious school behavior
    Educational attainment (dropping out)
    Failing a grade prior to high school
    High school curriculum

Attitudes toward jobs

Political attitudes
    Toward Vietnam
    Trust in government

Economics
    Area Unemployment
    Area Wages

---

but as a succession of choices, each of which is influenced by earlier choices, and each of which influences subsequent choices. Added to this is Katz' (1963) emphasis on the importance of different factors at each choice point, especially the individual's value structure. This has resulted in examining the impact of a number of events, attitudes and values that are considered to have occurred or been particularly salient at the time of making the choice. These include high school academic performance, senior year attitudes toward jobs, and anticipated draft status.

In addition to the influence of several comprehensive theories of vocational development, a number of small studies of choice behavior suggested several isolated correlates of choice which were investigated and are reported here. These include race, geographical region, modeling of parents, and influence sending from friends and relatives.

The net result of considering these various orientations is the set of variables summarized in Table 1-1.

Analysis Strategy

In addition to suggesting which variables ought to be examined, theory also suggested a very simple organization of the variables for analysis. This is shown schematically in Figure 1-1. First of all, Super's theory suggested that there might be two central motives or dispositions for enlistment: perceived self-fit with a military-type job and indecision over future plans. A third disposition that seemed equally likely to be central to the decision was draft status from which one could infer the motive of draft avoidance. These three dispositions are the first measures to be related to the criterion. This is represented by Arrow A in the figure.

The remaining variables cannot be thought of as being immediate causes of behavior such as the choice of enlisting or not, so they are classified as conditioning factors. These factors can be collapsed into four categories as shown in Figure 1-1. For each category, the central question is how the measures within the category relate to the criterion.

In this study almost all of the predictors are correlated to some degree. For this reason there is nearly always some "overlap" in prediction between any two variables; thus there is overlap among variables within a category and also among variables in different categories. Only one kind of overlap is of interest in this study: the overlap between the motive set of measures and each of the four sets of conditioning factors. In Figure 1-1 this is represented by Arrow B. The purpose of analyzing this type of overlap is to see how much of the effect of the conditioning factors can be viewed as operating *through* the motives and how much is *unique*. Since the motives are considered the most parsimonious explanations of enlistment behavior, they are the preferred explanations of the behavior. When a conditioning factor overlaps with a motive it will be interpreted as having its effect through its impact on the development of one of the motives.[2]

FIGURE 1-1

Model for Analyzing Unique and Overlapping Effects of Predictors

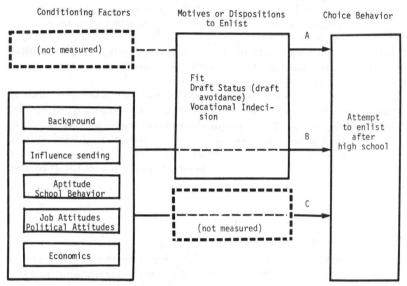

Arrow A: Effects of dispositions that are independent of the effects of the measured conditioning factors.

Arrow B: Joint or overlapping effects of conditioning factors and dispositions. These are interpreted as the effects of conditioning factors operating through the dispositions as intervening variables.

Arrow C: Effects of conditioning factors that are independent of the effects of the measured dispositions.

Some Notes on Statistical Procedures

Of necessity, a study such as this contains a large quantity of statistical data. In order to analyze the large number of variables some fairly sophisticated analytical procedures have been used in addition to the more familiar procedures such as one-way analysis of variance. However, at the same time, an attempt has been made to make the findings understandable to those with limited statistical training. Several things have been done to facilitate this. One, an effort has been made to give the reader a "feel" for what size numbers have been interpreted as important by the authors. Another is that the results of the analytical procedures are discussed in as non-technical terms as possible. This is done both in the body of each chapter and in the summary at the end of the chapter. At the same time, the more statistically experienced researcher will find complete tables with figures and summary statistics which he can interpret for himself.

In the remainder of this chapter several topics are discussed which are related to the presentation of the findings. These include the general format for each chapter, including conventions used in dealing with data in this study, and a description of each of the statistical procedures used for analysis.

Chapter Format and Conventions. Each of the main analysis chapters (four through seven) focuses on a set of predictors which were hypothesized to relate to the choice of enlisting after high school. The major portion of each chapter is devoted to an examination of the bivariate relationship of each of these predictors to the criterion. The last section of the chapter describes the multivariate relationship between the predictors taken as a set and the criterion. In each case the criterion is the percent of the sample that tried to enlist.

For bivariate relationships the format is to present a table such as the one shown in Table 1-2. The rows show different categories on the predictor

Table 1-2

Sample Table Showing a Bivariate Relationship

Region	Percent of Sample (N=1719)	Percent of Category That Tried to Enlist
1 West	16%	16.8%
2 N. Central	32	11.5
3 N. East	23	11.5
4 South	29	9.1
	100%	

Grand Mean = 11.6%
Eta = .064
Eta-square = .004

variable, in this case region of the country. For each category there are two pieces of information: (1) the percent of the total *sample* that fell into that predictor category (e.g. 16 percent of the 1719 boys lived in what is here called "the West") and (2) the percent of the *category* that tried to enlist (e.g. 16.8 percent of the Westerners). The summary statistics are presented at the bottom of the table.

Predictor variables can be either categorical or continuous. The first type is ideal for data presentation; a reader can easily scan the small number of categories to look for patterns of enlistment. For a number of reasons it was desirable to treat the interval scales in the same way; i.e., reduce each of them to a small number of categories. This permits easy visual comparison of effects across both predictor types. It also makes possible the use of a single multivariate analysis technique—one which can operate using both types of variables. This technique is called Multiple Classification Analysis and is described below.

The continuous scales typically encountered in this study are indexes formed by the combination (usually a mean) of two or more item-level responses. For example, Vietnam Dissent is an index which was formed by taking a mean of each individual's responses to six separate questions about the Vietnam War. The resulting range of scores was collapsed or bracketed into seven categories. The collapsing was done using equal-sized intervals, with the middle category capturing the mean of the distribution. Often, the two terminal categories (one and seven in this example) include a larger interval in order to accommodate some of the extreme cases on a distribution.

Missing Data. In large-scale survey research there is typically a small amount of missing data associated with each measure. It results when a respondent inadvertently skips a question or gives a response that is sufficiently unclear that it cannot be properly classified. The phenomenon is largely random, with different people comprising the missing data category on each measure. Those with missing data by definition cannot be classified on the measure of interest, even though their criterion score is known. For this reason, it is desirable to eliminate from the analysis of any one measure (but not from the study entirely) those respondents with missing data. This has no effect on the findings as long as it is valid to assume that the missing data cases are a random subset of the sample. In this study this assumption was assumed to be valid if the mean enlistment rate for the missing data cases was within 1½ percentage points of the mean for the entire sample. Accordingly, when this is the case, missing data cases are not included in the tables. If the mean departs from the grand mean by a larger amount, the information is reported.

Measures of Association. The most common measure of association between two measures is the product-moment correlation, or Pearson's r. This measure is appropriate when the predictor being examined is a continuous, normally-distributed variable which relates to enlistment in a linear fashion. However, these conditions do not hold for many of the measures under investigation. Some predictors are categorical, like race and geographical region; by definition these are not normally distributed or continuous. Other variables which do meet these restrictions do not relate to enlistment in a linear fashion. These include such important measures as draft status and classroom grades. Accordingly, a universal measure of relationship was needed for this study which could be used with every type of predictor. Eta (η), or the correlation ratio, is just such a measure. It is analogous to r in many ways and to some extent it can be interpreted similarly. Bachman's earlier description of the measure, put in the context of YIT analyses, will be helpful here.

Eta is analogous in some ways to r, and to a degree it can be interpreted similarly. The most important differences are (a) Eta can be used with categorical variables, thus making it particularly appropriate for such predictors as race or geographical region; (b) it is not restricted to linear relationships. Another difference between Eta and r is trivial but potentially confusing: Eta has a range from zero to 1.00; it never takes a negative value when describing a relationship. In general, the absolute values of Eta and r are practically identical, when applied to interval or ratio scale data, whenever the association between predictor and criterion turns out to be linear; when the association is non-linear, Eta is larger than r. This means that Eta is better suited for many exploratory analyses, because of its ability to detect linear and non-linear associations equally well. Another advantage of Eta is that it works for a wider range of predictors, since any continuous variable can be made categorical but many categorical variables cannot be treated as continuous (Nunnally, 1967).

(Bachman, 1970, p. 7)

For the reasons noted above, eta is used almost exclusively in reporting bivariate relationships between predictors and enlistment behavior.

The format of most of the tables (see sample Table 1-2) is identical to that for an analysis of variance. The predictor is used as the variable of classification and the percent enlisting from each class on the predictor is the dependent variable. The mean percent enlisting from each class on the predictor is presented along with the grand mean, eta and eta-square values. The eta indicates the strength of association between the two measures, and the eta-square indicates what proportion of the total variance in enlistment behavior can be accounted for by the particular predictor.

Statistical and Substantive Significance. Statistical significance is as important in survey research as it is in other forms of research. It is an indication of whether or not the relationship that is observed is haphazard or is the result of some systematic variation. However, when sample size is as large as it is in a survey study like the present one, many relationships meet the criterion of statistical significance without being substantively significant. For example, in the set of family background measures, the relationship of "parental punitiveness" to attempted enlistment is statistically significant, but the pattern of association is uninterpretable. To deal with this problem, judgements are made on the importance of a relationship—the "substantive significance"—using a two-fold criterion. The eta value must be statistically significant; in most cases this corresponds to a value of .07 or higher.[3] In addition, the predictor must show a meaningful pattern of relationship with enlistment. A third rule of thumb is that substantive significance begins when a measure can account for at least one percent of the variance in the criterion. This corresponds to an eta of .10 or an eta-square value of .01. In each case, all of the data are presented so that the reader can make his own judgment.

Rare Events and Use of the Gamma Statistic. One other statistic is occasionally used to summarize a bivariate relationship. This is gamma (γ), a measure of association in ordered classes (Hays, 1965, p. 655). It is used in this study instead of the Pearson *r* to summarize the relationship between ordinal scales that are being combined into a single summary measure. Like the Pearson *r*, it has a range of -1.00 to +1.00, but the interpretation is somewhat different. Technically, gamma is a measure of ordered predictive association between two variables. It was chosen over other rank-order measures because of the fact that it ignores "ties" in rankings on the two variables—a common occurrence in studies of rare events. Table 1-3 provides an example.

Table 1-3

Sample Data Illustrating the Use of Gamma statistic

		Y Expected in 12th Grade to Make a Career of Military Service	
		NO	YES
	1 Poor Fit	191	0
X Self-Perceived Fit with Military Service Life	2	403	1
	3	563	14
	4	366	20
	5 Good Fit	85	15

Gamma = .72

5302

The "No" column on the Y-variable shows a large number of tied rankings of respondents, yet the overall distribution indicates that there is some monotonic increasing relationship between self-perceived fit with military service life and the expectation of making a career of military service: the higher the perceived fit, the greater the likelihood that an individual will expect to make a career of military service. This is captured in the gamma of 0.72.

Multivariate Prediction: Multiple Classification Analysis (MCA). It was noted earlier that an objective of this research is to look beyond the bivariate relationships and discover the impact of a number of predictor dimensions taken together. Such analyses require the use of a multivariate technique. The one that has been found to be most useful in this study is called Multiple Classification Analysis, or MCA. A brief overview of this technique follows.

MCA was described in considerable detail by Bachman in Volume II of the Youth in Transition series (1970, pp. 62-75), and a complete description of the MCA model and the corresponding computer program is provided by Andrews, et al. (1967). Much of the following introduction is adapted from a briefer summary presented in Volume III (Bachman, et al. 1971, pp. 46-48).

MCA permits predicting to a criterion dimension such as attempted enlistment after high school using a number of predictor dimensions simultaneously. It computes a multiple correlation coefficient, R, which when squared provides an estimate of the total variance in the criterion explainable by all predictors operating together. It may be helpful to think of MCA as a form of multiple regression analysis that has a good deal of extra freedom. Most important, it treats predictors as nominal scales. For some dimensions, such as region or high school curriculum, this is essential. For others, it means that a curvilinear relationship does not get forced into a straight-line "compromise" estimate. In addition, MCA can handle a wide range of interrelationships among predictors, another important feature in dealing with highly correlated dimensions such as background factors and intellectual ability. Finally, MCA can handle missing data on any particular predictor simply by treating absence of data as another predictor category. This means that not all information on an individual is lost simply because he has missing data on one of the predictor dimensions.

Like other forms of multiple regression, MCA assumes that the effects of predictor variables are combined *additively;* i.e., it assumes that there is no interaction among predictors. This assumption is of critical importance, for it means that either the investigator must assume that no appreciable interaction exists (based on other findings, theory, or intuition), or he must search the data for such interactions prior to final application of the MCA technique. The problem of interaction is taken up and discussed in each chapter as MCA is used for that particular set of variables. When interaction is discovered, it can be incorporated into the MCA model by first creating a "pattern variable" out of the interacting measures. This is described in Chapter Four.

MCA is the procedure used to detect overlap among predictors. This can be done in two ways. The first involves the comparison of two summary statistics for each of the predictors. One is eta-value, or the correlation ratio. As described earlier, this indicates the strength of association of the predictor with the criterion. But this measure includes the unique effect of the particular predictor, plus the effect of that predictor that results from its correlation with other predictors in the equation. The other summary statistic is an estimate, termed beta, of the separate effect of each predictor as if it were uncorrelated with all other predictors—i.e., with other predictors "statistically controlled." To the extent that the eta and beta values differ, this is an indication of how much the particular predictor overlaps with other factors being considered.

The other way of detecting overlap is used when the question is in this form: How much additional variance can be accounted for by school factors *over and above* what is already explained by the primary "dispositions" to enlist? In this case a comparison is made of the Multiple R^2 for the dispositions considered by themselves and tne R^2 for an analysis in which both the dispositions and the school factors are included. The difference in Multiple R^2 for the two runs indicates the amount of overlap. As indicated earlier this kind of overlap will be interpreted as one of the conditioning factors affecting the dispositions, which in turn affects the enlistment choice. This will become clearer as specific examples are considered in later chapters.

Summary

The focus of the present study is on the choice of a post-high school activity by young men, especially the choice of enlisting in military service. This study is part of a larger longitudinal study of adolescence called Youth in Transition. Using data from this study, an examination is made of the effects of a large number of factors on the decision to enlist. The particular variables chosen for analysis and the order in which they are considered derives largely from the theoretical orientation of Donald Super and self-concept theory. The influence of a number of other theorists, dealing with less comprehensive theories, is also apparent.

The analysis strategy is to look within categories of variables; first at the bivariate relationship of each variable to enlistment behavior, then at the multivariate relationship of the entire category of variables to the criterion.

---

[1] This study was conducted during the period just prior to the inauguration of the lottery system.

[2] An example might be helpful here. It turns out that intelligence predicts to enlistment. This is an interesting finding in itself, but it does not indicate how intelligence affects the choice of enlistment. Checking the overlap with the motives shows that intelligence has its impact through its effect on draft status, which in turn is very strongly related to college entrance. Thus, it was concluded that intelligence affects choice of advanced education which in turn affects whether or not an individual chooses to enlist.

[3] This assumes a design effect between 2.3 and 2.8 and a sample size of N=1799. See Appendix F.

CHAPTER 2

THE YOUTH IN TRANSITION PROJECT

The data for this report come from a large study of adolescents, the Youth in Transition project, being conducted at the Survey Research Center, University of Michigan. This is a longitudinal study, supported by the United States Office of Education, which has followed a sample of young men from the start of tenth grade (Fall, 1966) to the time when most of them have been out of high school for about a year (Summer, 1970). It includes among its most basic purposes the study of attitudes, plans, and behaviors, particularly those relating to educational and occupational aspirations and achievements. In keeping with these purposes, the study was expanded in 1969, with Department of Defense support, to include special emphasis on military plans and attitudes. A complete description of the purposes and procedures of the Youth in Transition project may be found elsewhere (Bachman, et al., 1967); however, it will be useful here to mention a few highlights of the study design.

Youth in Transition began data collection in the fall of 1966, using a national cross-section of about 2,200 tenth-grade boys located in 87 public high schools. There were four data collections from this panel. These are summarized in Figure 2-1. The initial measurement (Time 1) consisted of individual interviews and group-administered tests and questionnaires conducted in the schools. About four hours were required for each boy to complete the various instruments. A second measurement (Time 2), conducted in neutral sites away from the schools, took place in spring of 1968 as most of the boys were ending eleventh grade. This shift away from the schools to neutral interviewing sites was done on the assumption that more school dropouts would participate if they did not have to return to the site of their earlier failure. At Time 2 both the interviews and questionnaires were administered on a one-to-one basis.

The data collection in spring of 1969 (Time 3) occurred when most of the respondents were nearing high school graduation. Two questionnaires were administered in small groups of less than ten by trained Survey Research Center interviewers. One questionnaire contained a standard set of repeated measures; the other contained a new set of questions on plans and attitudes toward military service. Each instrument took approximately one hour to ad-

13

Figure 2-1

THE YOUTH IN TRANSITION STUDY

Overview of Research Design

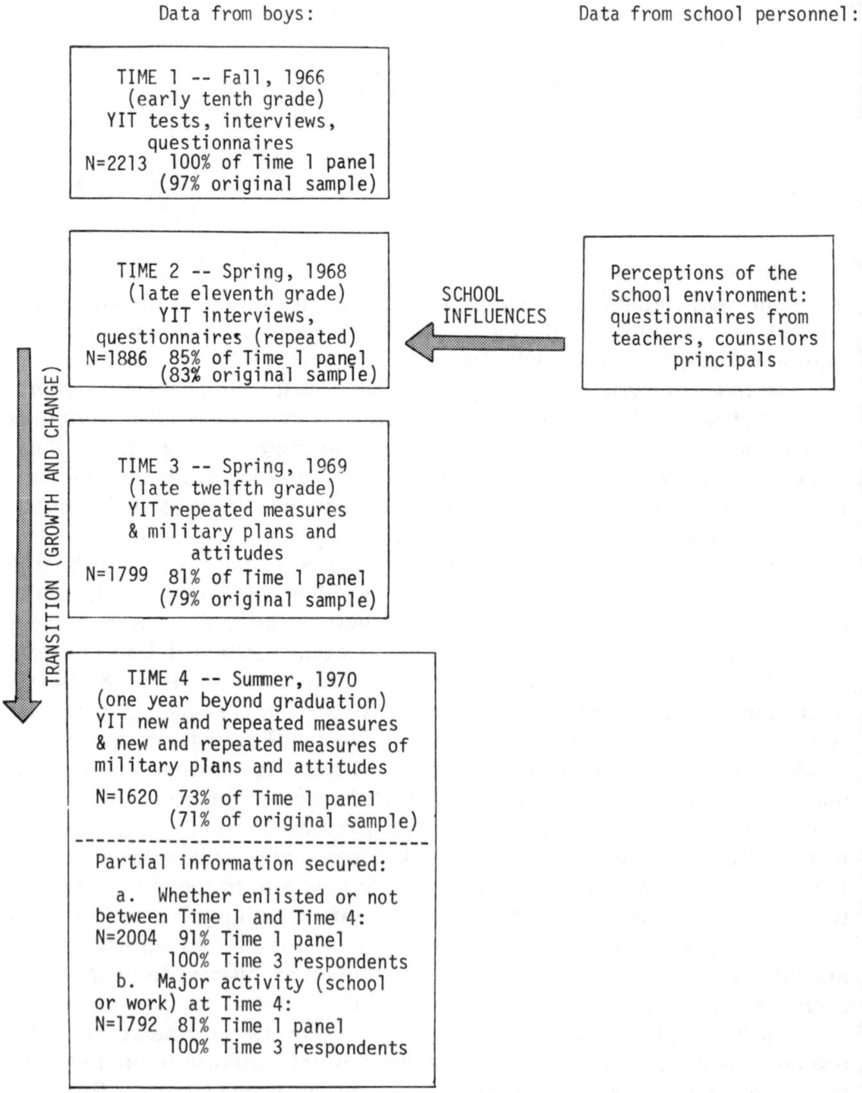

Data from boys: Data from school personnel:

```
┌─────────────────────────────┐
│ TIME 1 -- Fall, 1966        │
│ (early tenth grade)         │
│ YIT tests, interviews,      │
│     questionnaires          │
│ N=2213  100% of Time 1 panel│
│     (97% original sample)   │
└─────────────────────────────┘
```

```
┌─────────────────────────────┐        ┌──────────────────────────┐
│ TIME 2 -- Spring, 1968      │ SCHOOL │ Perceptions of the       │
│ (late eleventh grade)       │INFLUENCES│ school environment:    │
│ YIT interviews,             │◄═══════ │ questionnaires from      │
│ questionnaires (repeated)   │        │ teachers, counselors     │
│ N=1886  85% of Time 1 panel │        │ principals               │
│     (83% original sample)   │        └──────────────────────────┘
└─────────────────────────────┘
```

TRANSITION (GROWTH AND CHANGE)

```
┌─────────────────────────────┐
│ TIME 3 -- Spring, 1969      │
│ (late twelfth grade)        │
│ YIT repeated measures       │
│ & military plans and        │
│         attitudes           │
│ N=1799  81% of Time 1 panel │
│     (79% original sample)   │
└─────────────────────────────┘
```

```
┌─────────────────────────────┐
│   TIME 4 -- Summer, 1970    │
│ (one year beyond graduation)│
│ YIT new and repeated measures│
│ & new and repeated measures of│
│ military plans and attitudes│
│ N=1620  73% of Time 1 panel │
│     (71% of original sample)│
│ ----------------------------│
│ Partial information secured:│
│   a. Whether enlisted or not│
│ between Time 1 and Time 4:  │
│ N=2004  91% Time 1 panel    │
│        100% Time 3 respondents│
│   b. Major activity (school │
│ or work) at Time 4:         │
│ N=1792  81% Time 1 panel    │
│        100% Time 3 respondents│
└─────────────────────────────┘
```

minister. Since these group-administrations occurred outside of school and "after hours," each respondent was paid five dollars to cover his time and transportation costs. Participation in the third data collection was secured from 1799 boys, representing 81 percent of those who began the study in fall of 1966, or 79 percent of the original sample.

The last data collection (Time 4), one year later, consisted of individual interviews with respondents. There were two interview booklets and three self-administered questionnaires. Average administration time was over three hours. Respondents were paid ten dollars this time, taking account of the fact that many of them had to take off up to five hours from paying jobs to come to a neutral site to participate in this interview.

More than any other data collection, extensive (and costly) efforts were made to secure participation from as many panel members as possible. Former respondents who had moved were contacted if they lived within 50 miles of a Survey Research Center interviewer. Those in military service stationed at bases in the United States were contacted even though they were beyond the Center's usual 50-mile limit. Those stationed overseas were sent questionnaires and special self-administered forms of the interviews. As a result, complete interviews were obtained from 1620 young men; this represents 71 percent of the original sample. Overall, this represents a very high rate of retention. In survey research, typical non-response figures for a national sample of households range from 15 to 20 percent for a single non-repeat interview. The Youth in Transition study has a rate of 29 percent at the end of a four-year period.

Only a small portion of panel losses from this study was due to refusal to participate. More frequently, losses were due to the inability to locate some of the respondents who had moved, or an inability to collect data when respondents moved to locations out of range of the Survey Research Center's field staff. It is clear from preliminary analyses that losses occurred more frequently among those panel members who dropped out of school; thus it must be noted that the sample at Time 3 and Time 4 tends to underrepresent high school dropouts. At the same time, there is some under-representation of those with characteristics that are associated with dropping out: low socioeconomic level and low intelligence scores. Non-black minority groups also were lost from follow-up interviews at a higher rate than either whites or blacks. This has inevitably introduced some bias into the sample; thus descriptions of the distribution of these particular subgroups in American society represent underestimates. However, these losses do not appear to have altered the composition of the subgroup from which they come; e.g., those dropouts who remained in the study during all four years are not very different from those who did not participate after the initial data collection. This was demonstrated in the YIT study of dropouts (Bachman, et al., 1971). In this study, three major analysis groups were distinguished: high school dropouts, high school graduates with no further education, and graduates who continued their education after high school. It was possible to classify both respondents and non-respondents into the appropriate analysis group, on the basis of interviewer reports on non-respondents. Using data from the initial interview, participants were compared with non-participants. The authors concluded that:

> In general, the initial scores for intelligence, socioeconomic level, etc., obtained at the start of tenth grade are about the same for those dropouts who participated at Time 4 as for those non-participants who were identified as having dropped out. This conclusion for [dropouts] also applies to [high school graduates with no further education and graduates who continued their education after high school]. In other words . . . within each analysis category there is little difference in background and ability between those who continued their participation through Time 4 and those who did not. (Bachman, et al., 1971, p. 19)

One other thing should be noted about non-respondents; this concerns some valuable information that is available on them, even though they did not participate in some of the regular interviews. At each data collection interviewers were able to gather current activity information on a large number of the non-participants. As a result, criterion information on enlistment behavior is available for all of the Time 3 participants. For the original panel, criterion information on enlistment behavior at some time after the beginning of tenth grade is available for 2004 cases, or 91 percent of the original panel.

FIGURE 2-2

Survey Research Center's Random Sample of the United States

Note: Each point indicates one sample unit.

Some Characteristics of the Youth in Transition Panel

What are the young men in the Youth in Transition (YIT) panel like? Where are they from and what are they doing now? The answers to these and similar questions provide a necessary backdrop for interpreting the findings of this study. On the one hand they demonstrate the representativeness of the YIT sample; on the other, they provide a context in which to interpret their enlistment plans and behaviors.

Respondents are scattered throughout the 88 Primary Sampling Units (PSU's) that comprise the Survey Research Center's sampling frame for national studies. As Figure 2-2 shows, there are PSU's located in every region of the country. The PSU's range in composition from farm districts and small towns to large metropolitan areas, so a range of urbanicity is represented also. Racially, the sample approximates the national average for blacks; approximately 11 percent are black. Another 1.7 percent are from other minority groups including Spanish, Mexican, Puerto-Rican, Cuban and Portuguese.

Upon leaving high school these young men selected themselves into one of three major environments: post-high school education, work, or military service.[1] The pie chart in Figure 2-3 illustrates the distribution. By one year after high school one-half of them were in some form of further schooling; most of these were in college as opposed to technical or vocational school. Another third were in the labor force and 14 percent were on active duty in one of the regular branches of service, the Reserves or the National Guard. The remaining five percent were either doing nothing at all or continuing their high school education.

Before looking more closely at the military service group, it is helpful to be reminded that this sample is a grade cohort and not an age cohort. This is important, because Defense Department enlistment figures and related statistics are usually presented by age-groupings and may lead some readers to be somewhat surprised at the large percent who enter service. In June of 1969, the end of senior year, 86 percent of the boys were 18 years old or younger; old enough to enlist but not old enough to be drafted. During the following year about 70 percent reached draft age. This is shown in Table 2-1.

In Table 2-2 the military service experience of this cohort is shown in more detail. Both successful and unsuccessful attempted enlistments are shown. Successful enlistment attempt should be self-explanatory. An unsuccessful enlistment attempt is defined as a boy trying to enlist but being turned down for a physical or mental deficiency. Both types of enlistment are of interest, because the focus of this research is on the choice that a young man makes. Rejection is beyond his control and in no way alters the events or personal characteristics that led to the choice.

In Table 2-2 there are four groups with military experience that are always excluded from analyses in this study. These include (1) those who were drafted, (2) joined the National Guard or the Reserves, (3) entered a military academy, or (4) were found to be in service, but could not be accurately cate-

FIGURE 2-3

Status at Time 4 -- One Year
After High School

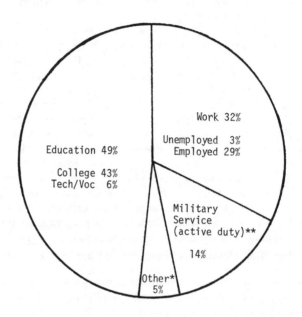

5475

*Other
    3% Still in high school
    2% Doing nothing, and not actively seeking employment

**Military service (active duty)
    9.3% Enlist after high school
    2.5% Enlist before completing high school
    1.1% Drafted
     .2% Military academy
     .6% On active duty, but how entered is unknown
    __.6% Active duty training for National Guard or Reserves

   14.3% TOTAL (See Table 2-1 for additional data on military
                 experience of YIT panel)

NOTE: N=1792, the number of Time 1 (1966) respondents for whom
there was complete status information at Time 4 (1970).

TABLE 2-1

Age Distribution of the YIT Panel

Age	Percentage Frequencies (N=2213) June 1969	June 1970
17	31%	1%
18	55	30
19	13	55
20	3	13
21 or older	--	3
	100%	100%

gorized as enlisted or drafted. The rationale for eliminating these groups is that the meaning of their behavior is unclear in the context of a study of enlistment behavior. Those who were drafted are not in service of their own choice. Whether or not any of them would have chosen to enlist in the absence of a draft is unknown. The motivation of those who selected the National Guard or the Reserves is equally unclear. For most, it is suspected that they are not militarily inclined, and that their motivation was to avoid having to serve as a draftee in a regular branch of service. Selecting a military academy is a slightly different type of choice than enlisting as a regular. In many ways it is more like the choice of college than military service. For this reason and because of the small number in this category (N=3), it was decided to eliminate them from analyses.

The resulting criteria for this study are shown in Table 2-3. The major criterion of interest in this study is attempted enlistment after high school. *Throughout the text, any references to "enlistment" or "attempted enlistment" include both successful and unsuccessful enlistment attempts unless otherwise stated.* When this criterion is being used, the underlying sample size is 1799 (the number of Time 3 respondents), minus 80 (those who were drafted, etc.), or N=1719.

Included among the predictors of enlistment behavior are a number of measures taken from the Time 1 data. These include such concepts as race, intelligence, socioeconomic level, and family size. When these are used, parallel analyses are shown for both the major and minor criteria shown in Table 2-3. The minor criterion codes the same behavior—attempted enlistment—but broadens the group being examined to include high school dropouts, many of whom enlisted but did so prior to the time when their classmates graduated from high school. Frequently this criterion shows a very different relationship with the more stable characteristics than the major criterion shows. The differences often lead to a better understanding of the real relationship of a predictor to enlistment. For example, in predicting to the major criterion it appears that blacks enlist at a rate that is one-half that of whites. Is this to be believed? Are there really racial differences in preferences for the

TABLE 2-2

Master Table of Military Service Experience of the YIT Panel -- A Tenth Grade
Male Cohort -- Over a Span of Four Years (1966-1970)

Category	Frequency	Percent
ENLISTMENT ATTEMPTS		
Between T3 & T4 (post high school)		
Successful **	179	8.9%
Attempted, but rejected	21	1.1
Prior to T3 (dropouts only)		
Successful **	56	2.8
Attempted, but rejected	24	1.2
Drafted (21), National Guard or Reserves (40), Military Academy (3)	64	3.2
Missing Data -- entered the service but don't know whether drafted or enlisted	15	0.8
Total involved in military service or attempted service	359	18.0
Total with no military service (includes 48 in ROTC programs. See Appendix A)	1645	82.0
Total	2004*	100.0%
Data on military experience missing	209	
Total Time 1 sample	2213	

5426   5475

*The sample size used for this Table is considerably higher than that for Figure 2-3. The reason for this concerns the availability of information about non-respondents from the original panel. Interviewers tried to collect Time 4 activity information on them at a point in time when it was very difficult to locate these individuals. However, at the time they conducted the 11th and 12th grade interviews, they were able to classify many non-respondents as having enlisted or tried to enlist at those times. These boys could be classified as having entered the military, although their activity at Time 4 could not be stated with confidence.

**See Appendix G.

TABLE 2-3

Criteria for the Predictive Study
of Enlistment Behavior

Category	Frequency	Percentage
The Major Criterion: Attempted Enlistment After High School		
Tried to Enlist	200	11.6%
Did Not Try to Enlist	1519	88.4
Total for Analyses using major criterion	1719	100%
Rejected for enlistment analyses*	80	
Total Time 3 sample	1799	
The Minor Criterion: Attempted Enlistment at Any Time After the Beginning of Tenth Grade		
Tried to Enlist	280	14.5%
Did Not Try to Enlist	1644	85.5
Total for Analyses using minor criterion	1924	100%
Rejected for enlistment analyses*	289	
Total Time 1 sample	2213	

*The Major Criterion is limited to Time 3 respondents; the Minor Criterion to Time 1 respondents, N=2213. Eliminated from both samples are those respondents (N=80) who were drafted, joined the National Guard or the Reserves, entered a military academy, or were in service, but it is not known whether they enlisted or were drafted. For the Minor Criterion, another 209 cases were eliminated on whom there was no military experience information by Time 4.

service? Yes, if it is clear what the criterion is: enlistment after June of 1969—the point when most of the sample graduated from high school. When the minor criterion is used, the rates for blacks and whites are identical. Blacks do not enlist at a lower rate; but they do enlist earlier than whites, because a higher proportion of them drop out of high school, enlisting shortly afterwards. Using both criteria helps to tease out such relationships.

Summary

This chapter introduces the reader to the Youth in Transition Project and the boys who comprise its panel of respondents. A description was given of the purposes of the project, the nature of the sample, and the field procedures used to collect data from this panel over the course of four years. Following this, a description was given of the post-high school activities that these young men chose. Particular attention was given to the military service choices and to a description of the major criterion for the study, attempted enlistment after high school.

---

[1]For convenience, the panel is described as though all of them had successfully completed high school. In fact, some 13 percent dropped out of high school prior to graduation and another three percent remained in high school after June of 1969 to complete work on a diploma. Figure 2-3 uses the entire Time 1 panel as its base; thus, it shows the Time 4 environmental status of high school graduates, high school dropouts, and those held back but still in high school.

CHAPTER 3

PLANS AND LATER ATTAINMENTS

The particular post-high school activity (work, military service, advanced education) which a young man attains after high school is easily observed. Much more difficult to detect is when and why the choice of that activity gets made. Is the decision made close to the point of transition into the activity, or has it already been made by the beginning of high school? Is there a common time when most young men commit themselves to a choice or does it vary depending on the person and the activity chosen? These and other related questions will be addressed in this chapter. The types of information that will be examined are (1) plans during high school for a post-high school activity and (2) attainments one year after high school.

The data for this discussion come from the coding of a series of questions on occupational plans. At Time 1 and Time 2 respondents were asked the following interview question: "What sort of work do you think you might do for a living?" This was followed by a series of questions eliciting the steps they thought they would follow to get into the occupation of their choice. One of these steps was the first major activity planned for after high school. The activities included:

1. Get a job
2. Enlist in military service
3. Go to technical/vocational school
4. Go to college
5. Unique plan ("go to Greenwich Village") or plans unclear and cannot be categorized

At Time 3 respondents were asked directly about their post-high school plans. "What about your plans for this coming fall (1969)? Pick out the *one* plan that will most likely work out for you." Following this statement was a list of activities, including the first four above and two more:

6. Continue high school
7. No definite plans; just wait and see what happens.

23

These same categories were then used to classify respondents' major activity during the year after high school.[1] Those who were drafted or who joined the National Guard or Reserves of a particular branch were all placed in a separate category, so that "entered or attempted to enter military service" included only those who tried to enlist in a regular branch of the military. These procedures were used to construct parallel measures for plans in tenth, eleventh, and twelfth grades, and for behavior measured one year after high school.

How is an individual's statement of plans for the future to be interpreted? In this study the assumption is made that a statement of plans indicates the expectancy and value that a person attaches to a particular high school activity. That is, in stating his plans for the future, an individual is indicating the net result of his taking into account both preference for a particular activity and the likelihood he attaches to attaining it over other alternatives. The discrepancy between plans and later behavior is interpreted as an indication of the realism of prior plans. This discrepancy will be referred to as the consistency (or inconsistency) of plans with behavior.

Most of the comparisons that will be made in the following discussion will be made among only three categories of activities: job, enlistment in military service, and education. These three categories distinguish among three very different kinds of post-high school attainments. While this simplification is helpful, it is also potentially deceptive. The three categories reflect varying degrees of specificity. "Education" covers a very broad range of alternatives, ranging from Harvard to technical trade schools. "Work" is similarly very broad in what it includes. But "enlist in military service" is relatively specific, even though there are a large variety of activities and specialties which an enlistee can pursue. Keeping in mind the differences in specificity will be helpful in interpreting the discussion that follows.

Predictability of Behavior from Plans

Table 3-1 shows how the sample distributed on post-high school plans at each grade level of high school. In addition it also shows the percent of each plan-group that followed through on their stated plans. This latter figure can be thought of as an indicator of "slippage" between behavioral intention at one point in time and the realization of that intention at a later point in time. The causes for slippage or the lack of it are not treated here; only whether or not it exists.

Looking at tenth grade plans, it can be seen that fewer than two-thirds of any plan-group followed through on their plans three years later. Education had the highest follow-through rate with 63 percent. Work was somewhat lower with 55 percent. Military service, albeit a highly specific plan relative to work or education, had a much lower rate of follow-through; only one-third of those who planned in early tenth grade to enlist, did so shortly after high school. A useful index of follow-through is provided by taking a weighted average of the three plan-groups. This comes out to 60 percent.

TABLE 3-1

Predictability of Post-High School Behavior
From Plans Stated in Tenth, Eleventh, and Twelfth Grades

Plans for Post High School	Percent of Sample (N=1580)**	Percent of Plan Category that Followed Through on Plan	
EARLY TENTH GRADE			
Work	20%	55%	WTD
Mil Service	5	34	AVG
Education	68	63	60%
Other	7	*	
	100%		
LATE ELEVENTH GRADE			
Work	17%	55%	WTD
Mil Service	9	37	AVG
Education	72	65	61%
Other	2	*	
	100%		
LATE TWELFTH GRADE			
Work	12%	77%	WTD
Mil Service	9	63	AVG
Education	64	76	75%
Other	15	*	
	100%		

5396   5387

**This is the number for whom there is complete data on plans at all three points in time as well as attainment at Time 4.

*"Follow-through" rate cannot be calculated for this group.

The distribution of the sample into the three plan-groups at the end of eleventh grade was very similar to that for tenth grade; and the rate of follow-through was almost identical, averaging out to 61 percent.[2]

At the end of twelfth grade, close to graduation for most respondents, the distribution in plan-groups was slightly different. There were somewhat fewer intending to get jobs or pursue further education, but this has largely to do with the addition at this time of a new category, "no plans." This unfortunately allowed the boy who was undecided about his next step to avoid specifying his most likely choice. For those who made an explicit choice, the rate of follow-through was somewhat higher. The weighted average was about 75 percent. While this is higher in comparison with the rate for plans expressed earlier in high school, it is surprisingly low from another standpoint. These plans were expressed within two to four months of the time when most of the sample began to implement their choice. Given the broad range of activities that are included in these three plan categories, especially education and work, it is somewhat surprising to discover how much slippage there was between plans and behavior.

Earlier Plans of the Time 4 Behavior Groups

At Time 4 there were many more respondents in the work and military service categories than suggested earlier plans. For example, in twelfth grade, 12 percent of the sample planned to get a job after high school. Only three-quarters of this group, or 142 boys, were actually on a job during the following year, but the total number who took jobs after high school was 503. The difference between the two numbers (503—142 = 361) is accounted for by boys from other plan groups switching into the job category at Time 4. In this section, the Time 4 behavior groups will be examined to discover what proportion of them were composed of boys who planned to be in that group vs.

TABLE 3-2

Percent of Post-High School Behavior Group
For Whom Behavior is the Fulfillment of
Earlier Plans

		Percent of category with high school plans consistent with post-high school behavior		
		Consistent for:		
Behavior at Time 4	Frequency	Grades 10-12	Grades 11-12	Grade 12
Job	503	1%	10% (1+10=11%)	19% (1+10+19=30%)
Military Service	187	1%	9% (1+9=10%)	39% (1+9+39=49%)
Advanced Education	837	72%	10% (72+10=82%)	8% (72+10+8=90%)
Other	53	--	--	--
	1580*			

5387   5396

NOTE: "Grades 10-12" indicates that respondents had high school plans consistent with post-high school behavior in all three grades of high school. "Grades 11-12" indicates consistent plans in 11th and 12th grades, but not 10th. "Grade 12" indicates that respondents had consistent plans only in 12th grade.

*This is the number for whom there were data at all four points in time.

"switchers" from other plan groups. Then, those who tried to enlist will be analyzed in greater detail to see from which plan groups they came.

Consistency of Plans and Behaviors. Table 3-2 reverses the information in Table 3-1. The first column shows the distribution of the sample by activity at Time 4. The second column shows the percent of the behavior group that had plans consistent with that behavior during all three grades of high school. For example, 503 boys were working at Time 4. Of these, only one percent planned in all three grades, 10 through 12, that they would enter a job after high school. Column three indicates the percent that had consistent plans in 11th and 12th grades. Column four shows the percent that had consistent plans in only 12th grade.

The most important information from these analyses comes from cumulating these figures across rows. This results in a total percent that had consistent plans at any grade level. For example, the number who had consistent plans from grade eleven until the time they entered their post-high school activity includes both the number consistent in grades 10 through 12 as well as those who were consistent in just grades 11 and 12. These cumulative totals are also shown in the table.

Almost three-quarters of those who entered some form of advanced education anticipated back in tenth grade that they would be following this course of action; and they consistently expressed this choice during tenth, eleventh and twelfth grades. The percent increases if only 11th and 12th grade plans are considered, and it gets as high as 90 percent if only 12th grade plans are considered.

The findings for the advanced education group are in striking contrast to those for the work and military service groups. Only one percent of the job group consistently planned to get a job in grades 10 through 12, and only 11 percent had consistent plans in eleventh and twelfth grades. Thirty percent of them knew in twelfth grade that they were going to end up on a job by one year later. Expressed another way, 70 percent of those who had jobs at Time 4 had some expectation at the end of senior year of high school that they would be doing something *different* from taking a job! This lack of realism is amazingly high, and suggests that a number of events important to the choice process must occur between late senior year and entry into a post-high school activity.

A very similar picture appears for those who tried to enlist in military service. Very few of them had long-standing plans consistent with their post-high school behavior. Only one percent planned in grades ten through twelve that they would later enlist; and only 10 percent accurately forecast in eleventh and twelfth grades what they would do. By the end of twelfth grade, one-half of them anticipated that they were going to try to enlist after high school.

It is clear that the point at which a decision gets made about a post-high school activity varies depending on the activity being chosen. The decision to go to college or pursue some form of advanced education is made very early by most young men, although some do switch into this plan in eleventh and twelfth grades. But the choice of working at a civilian job or enlisting in mili-

FIGURE 3-1

Enlistees: Point in Time When The Choice to Enlist
After High School Became A Firm Commitment*

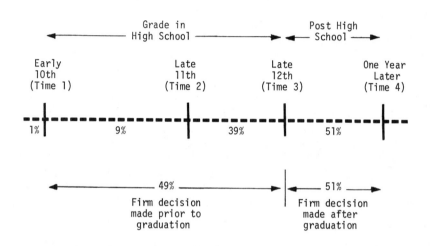

Number of attempted enlistments after high school   N=187.

tary service is made rather late for most of those in these activities. For a very
large proportion, the decision gets made after leaving high school.

Earlier Plans of Those Who Tried to Enlist. Figure 3-1 presents graphi-
cally the data for military service entrants. It considers consistency of plans
as an indicator of the point in time when a choice became firm for an individual. It shows that only 10 percent of the enlistees were committed to this
choice by the end of eleventh grade, and only one-half were committed by the
end of twelfth grade. The other half appear to have become committed at
some point between the end of high school and actually signing up for a tour
of duty. The question now arises: what plans did these enlistees have during
high school which they found more attractive than military service? Table 3-3
presents their 11th and 12th grade plans. Look first at the eleventh grade
plans. Over one-half of the enlistee group thought in eleventh grade that they
would pursue some form of advanced education after high school. Nineteen

percent expected to take a job, and only about one-quarter expressed plans of enlisting (and many of these one-quarter did not plan on military service in twelfth grade). Now look at the twelfth grade plans. One-half of the enlistees anticipated correctly that they would be enlisting after high school. Another one-quarter expected that they would end up in college, while six percent thought they would be getting a job. Fifteen percent had no plans; i.e., they checked the response: "I don't have any definite plans; I'm just going to wait and see what happens." To get some indication of how to classify these boys with no definite twelfth grade plans, a separate analysis was run showing their plans in eleventh grade. The breakdown appears below.

Eleventh grade plans:	job	4
	college	8
	military service	2
	other	1
		15%

It can be noted that one-half of them were anticipating going to college at that time. It is likely that a similar proportion had some thought of college in twelfth grade as well. This would bring up to one-third the proportion of enlistees who had hoped to continue their education instead of enlisting.

TABLE 3-3

Plans in the 11th and 12th Grades
of Those Who Attempted to Enlist
After High School

Plan	11th Grade Plans	12th Grade Plans
1. Work	19%	6%
2. Mil	27	49
3. Education	52	27
4. Other unique plan	2	(Inap)
5. Continue H.S.*	(Inap)	3
6. No plans/undecided*	(Inap)	15
Totals**	100	100

*Categories 5 and 6 were distinguished only in the 12th grade data. In Table 3-1 these were collapsed into the "other" category.

**Attempted to enlist after high school, N=187.

Summary and Conclusions

This chapter has examined the relationship between plans and behavior. The plans refer to plans during high school for an activity after high school (work, enlist, advanced education); the behavior is the major activity pursued during the first year after high school, expressed as one of the same three categories. Looking at the consistency of plans with later behavior revealed the following. Plans in tenth and eleventh grades to work or enter the service were found to be very poor forecasters of later behavior. College plans were much better. Twelfth grade plans for all three activities showed a higher rate of follow-through, with two-thirds to three-quarters of the three plan-groups following through with their stated intentions. These analyses indicated that there is a considerable amount of "slippage" between the declaration of a plan and its implementation.

The relationship of plans to behavior was considered from a different angle by looking at the three post-high school behavior groups and asking how many in each group planned, while still in high school, to pursue that activity. A very small percent of the job or military service groups had expressed earlier plans to follow these pursuits. But the advanced education group had persistently planned to enter advanced education from the tenth grade on. From these data it was concluded that the decision to go to college is made fairly early for most college-goers; however, the decision to get a job or enter the service is typically made very late in high school or even subsequent to graduation. Apparently advanced education is the most popular first choice early in high school. Military service and work often become first choices only after it is realized that continued education is an unsuitable or impossible goal to achieve.

Finally, the group that enlisted after high school was examined in more detail. It was discovered that only one-half of them had expressed the choice of military service as late as the end of twelfth grade. Approximately one-third were still expecting at that time to pursue some form of advanced education. From these data and others it was concluded that the choice of enlisting becomes a firm commitment for 39 percent of the enlistees between the end of eleventh and the end of twelfth grade; for another 51 percent it occurs between the end of high school and the actual time of enlistment. These figures do not imply that young men are not predisposed to an enlistment choice at some earlier point in time; only that the firm commitment does not occur until these times.

---

[1]The judgment of major activity was made by the respondent himself, using the time span of January to June of 1971 for his reference point. This was six to 12 months beyond graduation for most respondents. If a young man enlisted at any time during this period, he was classified as having entered military service. If he attempted to enlist, and was rejected for service, he was placed in the enlist category also, even though his major activity one year after high school was not military service.

[2]It is interesting to note, however, that the particular individuals that comprised, say, the work-plan group in eleventh grade were not the same as those who comprised it in tenth grade. In this case the tenth grade plan-group consisted of 316 respondents. Only one third of these continued to have this plan by the end of eleventh grade. Another one-half of them changed their plans to advanced education and another 10 percent decided they would enter military service. A similar phenomenon occurred between eleventh and twelfth grades.

CHAPTER 4

SOME BASIC MOTIVES FOR ENLISTMENT

Each of the next five chapters examines a domain of variables which is thought to be related to the choice of a post-high school activity—in particular to the choice of enlisting in military service. Chapter 4 considers three basic motives that are thought to operate in the decision-making process. Chapter 5 examines a number of related attitudes and behaviors of the individual. Chapter 6 looks at the influence of school experiences. Chapter 7 investigates the role of a number of factors that may have shaped a decision to enlist, including cultural, family and peer influences, and finally Chapter 8 considers the role of economic factors such as area unemployment and wages.

Each of these chapters presents a number of hypotheses about why young men might enlist. The hypotheses come from occupational-choice theory, from studies made of servicemen, and from popular literature and Pentagon speculation about why young men enlist. In the course of each chapter the hypotheses are evaluated empirically by seeing whether or not the relevant variables can account for variance in the criterion. In all cases the criterion is attempted enlistment at some time during the first year after high school.

The first hypothesis comes from the literature of occupational choice, in particular from the self-concept theory of Donald Super. The essence of this theory is that people seek out jobs that match their personalities, i.e., jobs where there is a good perceived fit between their skills, interests, and life style and the role demands of an occupation. Super explains it in this way:

> . . . in expressing a vocational preference a person puts into occupational terminology his idea of the kind of person he is; . . . in entering an occupation, he seeks to implement a concept of himself; . . . in getting established in an occupation he achieves self-actualization. The occupation thus makes possible the playing of a role appropriate to the self concept. (Super, 1963, p. 1)

Such thinking leads to the hypothesis that some young men choose military service because it represents to them their kind of life. As they see it, the people and tasks in military life complement their own talents and interests. This will be called a "military fit" motivation for enlistment. The concept of fit is further explained and operationalized below.

A second hypothesis has similar roots. Central to self-concept theory is the idea that adolescents go through a period of vocational exploration from about ages 16—23 during which they experiment with various vocational identities. The pace at which individuals progress through this period varies considerably. Some young men at 17 know exactly what they are going to do while others are still unsure at age 23. Accordingly, at ages 17—19, when young men are entering the labor market for the first time, many are still quite undecided. Their orientation to post-high school decisions may be one of vocational exploration. For these persons a logical post-high school choice is an environment which promises exposure to a multitude of career possibilities while not demanding a lifetime commitment to any of them. Military service is uniquely suited to this need.

A final hypothesis is a most obvious one. Some enlistments are motivated in part by the desire to avoid the draft. This seeming contradiction comes from the fact that enlistees have more options available to them, both in branch of service and in specific job assignments. Equally important, enlistees in 1969—1970 were less likely to go to Vietnam. Advantages like these are thought to make the draft a strong determinant of enlistment.

In the paragraphs that follow, each of these hypotheses is considered individually. For each hypothesis the key concepts are defined and operationalized using data from the study. The resulting variables are used to test the strength of the hypothesis. At the end of the chapter, an investigation is made of the interrelationships among the hypotheses.

HYPOTHESIS 1: Young Men Who Perceive a Good Fit Between Themselves And Military-type Jobs Are More Likely To Enlist

The key concept in this hypothesis is that of fit. In this section the concept is defined, and several ways are presented in which it can be operationalized. These are all evaluated and then reduced and combined into a single summary measure of fit with military service.

Job Fit. The basic concept of fit refers to the relationship of a person's needs and the environmental supply of that need (Super, 1963; French, 1962). The degree to which needs and supply match determines the goodness of fit. For this study, needs are defined as aspects of a job that are thought to be salient to a job choice. These appear in Table 4-1. The dimensions fall loosely into three categories. One is the need for advancement and self-utilization (C3, C6, C11), represented by such items as the need to get ahead, to learn new skills, and to use skills already developed. Another category is that of reward (C9, C10, C12), with items which ask for the importance of

TABLE 4-1

Job Items

Section C, Questions 1-13

The next questions are about the kind of job you would like to have. Different people want different things from a job. Some of the things that might be important are listed below. Please read each of the things on the list, then check the box that tells how important this thing would be to you.

Don't just check *Very Important* for everything. Try to think what things really matter to you, and what things really aren't that important.

			Very important (1) (+3)	Pretty important (2) (+2)	A little important (3) (+1)	Not important (4) (0)	Missing Data
H21a*	C1.	A job where there's no one to boss me on the work	12%	40%	34%	12%	2%
H21b	C3.	A job where I can learn new things, learn new skills	51	39	7	1	2
H21d	C4.	A job where I don't have to work too hard	7	24	44	23	2
H21e	C6.	A job with good chances for getting ahead	61	31	4	1	3
H21k	C7.	A job where I don't have to take a lot of responsibility (recode scale reversed)	6	20	40	33	2
H21f	C8.	A job that leaves me a lot of free time to do what I want to do	15	38	36	10	2
H21n	C9.	A job where the pay is good	56	35	5	1	2
H21s	C10.	A job that my friends think a lot of--has class	12	28	38	21	2
H21c	C11.	A job that uses my skill and abilities--lets me do the things I can do best	57	33	7	1	2
H21l	C12.	A job that has nice friendly people to work with	45	43	9	1	2
H21b	C13.	A job that doesn't make me learn a lot of new things (recode scale reversed)	5	12	34	47	2

recode column shown under headers: (+3) (+2) (+1) (0)

How important is this for you?

---

*Matching items from "Mil/Civ Items" in Table 4-2.

money, prestige, and friendly co-workers on the job. The third category might be labelled ease and independence (C1, C4, C7, C8, C13). These items ascertain whether or not the young man is looking for a job that is easy and in which he does not have to take much responsibility.

The other aspect of job-fit is the environmental supply of things to satisfy these needs. More correctly, it is the individual's perception of the environmental supply. In this study, the supply aspect is defined as the individual's perception of the ability of a military job to satisfy each of the "need" dimensions.

TABLE 4-2

Military/Civilian Job Items

Section H, Question 21

Suppose that at the end of your education you are trying to decide between a career in the military and a civilian job. Which would be better for the following things?

			Military much better	Military somewhat better	Both about the same	Civilian job somewhat better	Civilian job much better	Missing Data
		recode:	(+2) (1)	(+1) (2)	(0) (3)	(-1) (4)	(-2) (5)	
C1*	H21a.	Chance to be your own boss . . .	3%	3%	17%	31%	45%	2%
C3, C13	H21b.	Chance to learn new and useful skills	9	18	35	22	15	2
C11	H21c.	Chance to use one's skills and abilities	5	11	33	29	19	3
C4	H21d.	Chance for a job where I don't have to work too hard	3	10	27	39	20	2
C6	H21e.	Chance to get ahead	7	11	31	25	23	3
C8	H21f.	Chance to control your personal life	3	5	16	34	39	2
C7	H21k.	Chance to take a lot of responsibility	16	23	38	11	9	2
C12	H21l.	Type of people you would work with	6	11	45	22	14	2
C9	H21n.	Amount of money you would earn .	2	4	11	35	46	3
C10	H21s.	Prestige--looked up to by others	16	21	40	11	10	2

---

*Matching items from "Job Items" in Table 4-1.

To assess each individual's fit with military service, the following question was used. It was designed to capture in a single question the perception of both individual needs and the perception of a military job's ability to satisfy that need. "Suppose that at the end of your education you are trying to decide between a career in the military and a civilian job. Which would be better for the following things?" Following this question were the eleven job dimensions shown in Table 4-2. Note that each of the items parallels a job attitude item from Table 4-1.

One way to operationalize a person's perceived fit with military service is to take a mean across all of the items in Table 4-2. However, there was some doubt that the lead question was direct enough to insure that all respondents replied with their own needs in mind. Some people could have had in mind the less specific question: Which is better for young men in general for each of these things? To insure that each individual's summary measure of fit with military service reflected his own specific job needs, the job attitude items of Table 4-1 and the military-civilian contrast items of Table 4-2 were combined into an index of fit (called MIL-FIT) in the following manner. First, scores for the dimensions in Table 4-2 were recoded so that the value ranged from +2 for "military much better" to – 2 for "civilian job much better." Likewise, the scale for the "need" dimensions was reversed so that "Very important" had a value of +3 while "Not at all important" was zero. On any one dimension fit is defined as the person's evaluation of military service on that dimension multiplied by the importance to him of that dimension. For example, consider a person who thought the "military somewhat better" (+1) when it comes to a "chance to learn new and useful skills." If it was "pretty important" (+2) for that person to find a job where he could learn new and useful skills, then his fit score on this dimension would be 1 x 2 = +2. Each person's index of MIL-FIT is simply the mean of all such products, as summarized in the following formula.

$$\text{MIL-FIT} = \frac{\sum_{y=1}^{11} \left(\begin{array}{c}\text{Subjective need} \\ \text{for dimension y}\end{array}\right) \left(\begin{array}{c}\text{Evaluation of MS} \\ \text{on dimension y}\end{array}\right)}{11}$$

The resulting index of MIL-FIT was collapsed into five equal-interval categories to facilitate the use of this variable in computer analyses requiring a small number of predictor categories. The distribution of the Youth in Transition (YIT) sample and the percent enlisting from each category are shown in Table 4-3. The relationship of MIL-FIT to enlisting is basically monotonic. The two categories showing the poorest fit had the lowest percentages enlisting—about four percent—and the numbers increase as the fit improves. At the upper levels of MIL-FIT the relationship is fairly dramatic, with 21 and 31 percent enlisting from the two categories of best fit. These

38   YOUTH IN TRANSITION

TABLE 4-3

Relationship of "Military-Fit"
to Enlistment Behavior

Military-Fit Categories		Percent of Total Sample (N=1556)*	Percent of Category That Tried to Enlist
Poor Fit	1	12%	4.4%
	2	25	3.3
	3	35	10.1
	4	22	20.6
Good Fit	5	6	30.7
		100	

Grand Mean= 11.2%
Eta= .253
Eta-square= .064

5310
*
NOTE: The N for tables in this chapter will vary somewhat from
1719 (the number who responded in twelfth-grade on whom there is
information about post-high school enlistment behavior.) This
fluctuation is due to varying amounts of missing data on the predictors. When those in a missing data category show a rate of
enlisting appreciably above or below the Grand Mean, they will
be included in the table. Otherwise it will be assumed that missing
data are distributed randomly in the sample.

percentages are two and three times the average for the entire sample. The
overall relationship is summarized in the eta statistic.[1] The eta of .253 indicates that this variable by itself can account for six percent (eta-square =
.064) of the variance in enlisting behavior.

Those interested in more theoretical aspects of person-environment fit
might be interested in some data which compare the simple mean score of all
items in Table 4-2 with the more complicated measure of MIL-FIT. The two
measures are very highly correlated ($r = .917$) and predict almost equally
well to attempted enlistment. The simple mean score is associated with attempted enlistment as follows: eta = .236, eta-square = .056. The pattern of
association is almost identical to that for MIL-FIT.

Military Service as a Career Choice. A second way in which an individual can indicate an orientation to military life is to express a vocational aspiration of military service. This in itself is an indication of perceived fit. In
one way this is better than MIL-FIT. In making the match between self and

military life that culminated in this job preference, the individual used dimensions with the greatest importance for himself. At the same time the measure is much more restrictive than MIL-FIT. Many young men might see themselves fitting well into the military style of life and even aspire to a term of service after high school, and yet not aspire to a career in the service. So, while choice of military service as a lifetime-job preference should be indicative of an orientation to military life, the reverse is not true: many people may be predisposed to service life without expressing it as a job preference.

In tenth grade, job preferences were ascertained by asking respondents, "What sort of work do you think you might do for a living?" The answers were coded for first and second preferences. From this information it was found that 3.6 percent of the sample indicated military service as either their first or second choice. At the end of eleventh grade, in response to a similar question, 3.1 percent expressed this preference. At the end of twelfth grade the number was 2.7 percent. For convenience, these groups will be referred to as MS=OCC PREF groups. Table 4-4 shows the interrelationships of the preferences over time. The *number* of respondents expressing the preference of military service as a job was fairly constant over time. But the *specific individuals* comprising the groups changed at each grade. There were no more than 19 people who aspired two years in a row to a lifetime job in military service, although almost three times that number aspired to a military job at any one time during high school.

In Table 4-5 this preference is related to actual enlistment. It can be seen that aspiring in any grade to a job in military service is a fairly good predictor of military entrance after high school. Three to four times as many enlisted from the MS=OCC PREF groups as from the groups who never mentioned it as an occupational preference. On the other hand, it is somewhat surprising that more did not enlist from these groups. In an attempt to explain this, it was discovered that a large proportion of these groups went on to college after high school—in most cases the percent going to college was almost as high as the percent enlisting right after high school (see Table 4-6). It may be that most of those who went on to college planned eventually to go into service, entering as officers. Thus, it might be that the MS=OCC PREF variable is more strongly related to enlistment behavior than is apparent when the criterion is restricted to early enlistments.

Several pieces of data confirm this hypothesis. The expectations and behaviors of the entire sample were compared with those of the subgroup defined as having the occupational aspiration of military service at the end of twelfth grade and yet went on to college the following year. In both groups the proportion expecting to serve at some time during the next ten years was the same—about two-thirds. But, when they were asked how they expected to enter, there were large differences. Only 17 percent of the entire sample expected to enter as officers while almost two-thirds of the subgroup expected to enter as officers. One year later, larger proportions of the subgroup were in an ROTC program, or said they would be if it were offered at their school (15 percent in the total sample, 40 percent in the subgroup). Finally, there were

TABLE 4-4

Occupational Aspiration is Military Service

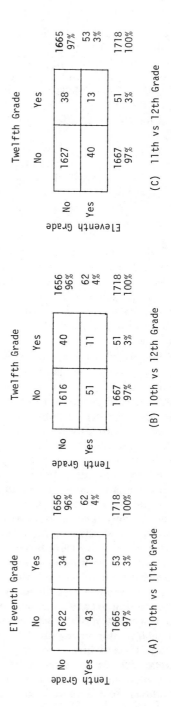

(A) 10th vs 11th Grade

Tenth Grade	Eleventh Grade No	Yes	
No	1622	34	1656 96%
Yes	43	19	62 4%
	1665 97%	53 3%	1718 100%

(B) 10th vs 12th Grade

Tenth Grade	Twelfth Grade No	Yes	
No	1616	40	1656 96%
Yes	51	11	62 4%
	1667 97%	51 3%	1718 100%

(C) 11th vs 12th Grade

Eleventh Grade	Twelfth Grade No	Yes	
No	1627	38	1665 97%
Yes	40	13	53 3%
	1667 97%	51 3%	1718 100%

TABLE 4-5

MS-IS-OCCUPATIONAL-PREFERENCE
Related to Enlistment After High School

Category	Percent of Sample (N=1719)	Percent of Category That Tried to Enlist
10TH GRADE		
MS is occup pref	3% (n=56)	33.9%
MS is not occ pref	97	10.9
		Eta= .128
		Eta-square= .016
11TH GRADE		
MS is occup pref	3 (n=52)	34.6
MS is not occ pref	97	10.8
		Eta= .130
		Eta-square= .017
12TH GRADE		
MS is occup pref	3 (n=45)	44.4
MS is not occ pref	97	10.8
		Eta= .168
		Eta-square= .028

5355

large differences in the proportion who one year after high school expected they would enter military service during the following five years. It was one-quarter in the full sample but one-half in the subgroup.

As originally conceived, the three MS=OCC PREF variables were expected to predict to enlistment better when taken in combination. The hypothesis was that both recency and frequency of mention were important dimensions. If a young man expressed this aspiration at the end of twelfth grade, this was a more valid indicator of his interest in service than a mention at any other time. Additionally, it was hypothesized that mentioning this aspiration for two or three years indicated a deeper abiding interest in the service than a single mention. Accordingly, a variable was built which included all possible combinations of recency and frequency of mention of MS as an occupational aspiration. The result appears in Table 4-7.[2] The first category would seem to offer some support for the recency/frequency idea. This group of 12 people mentioned MS as an occupational preference in both 11th and 12th grades, and one-half of this group enlisted. But the remaining categories do not show an orderly progression. The mean for category four lies between categories two and three. There are two possibilities here: 1) Recency and frequency are not important in the prediction, or 2) the base for the percentage-enlisting figures is so small that error alone accounts for the differences. Regardless of the reason, the multi-category variable did not

TABLE 4-6

MS-IS-OCCUPATIONAL-PREFERENCE
Related to Post-High School Behavior

| Occupational Preference | --- POST-HIGH SCHOOL BEHAVIOR ---- | | | | | Total Percent (*Frequency*) |
	ENL*	DNR**	COLL	WRK	OTHER+	
MS=OCC PREF 10TH GRADE	37%	5	29	25	4	100 (*59*)
MS=OCC PREF 11TH GRADE	34%	2	36	18	10	100 (*51*)
MS=OCC PREF 12TH GRADE	40%	11	24	22	3	100 (*44*)

5281

*ENL: Enlisted in a regular branch of military service, including Coast Guard.

**DNR: R was Drafted, joined the National Guard, enlisted in the Reserves of some branch of MS, or data on his post-high school activity is missing.

+OTHER: Some unique plan, e.g., "go to Greenwich Village"; plans were very unclear; no definite plan offered.

help sufficiently in understanding the way in which MS=OCC PREF was related to enlisting.

Possibly, the only thing that matters is knowing whether or not a person aspired to military service as an occupation at any time during high school. Perhaps vocational development is not orderly enough to produce a monotonic relationship as had been expected. Accordingly, the multi-category variable was collapsed to a dichotomous version which indicated simply whether or not a person had ever thought of entering the service for a career. The relationship of this variable to enlisting is shown in Table 4-8. It can be seen from the eta-square figure that this form of the varible is almost as good as the multi-category version; it accounts for only 0.2 percent less of the variance than the five-category version. For this reason, it was decided that the dichotomous version would be an adequate summary measure.

Combining Two Measures. MS=OCC PREF and MIL-FIT are two different ways in which predisposition to military life can be operationalized. Since they were both proposed as different ways to measure the same dimension, the possibility of combining them was considered.

TABLE 4-7

MS-IS-OCCUPATIONAL-PREFERENCE/CROSS-TIME VERSION
Related to Enlistment After High School

Category	Percent of Sample (N=1644)	Percent That Tried to Enlist
1 MS is occupational preference in both 11th and 12th grades	1% (12)	50.0%
2 MS is occupational preference in 12th grade, but not 11th	2 (32)	40.6
3 MS is occupational preference in 10th and 11th grade, but not 12th	2 (40)	30.0
4 MS is occupational preference in 10th grade only	2 (33)	36.4
5 MS is never occupational preference	93 (1527)	9.6

Grand Mean= 11.6%
Eta= .224
Eta-square= .050

5355
NOTE: Bold-face numbers are percents; italics are frequencies

TABLE 4-8

MS-IS-OCCUPATIONAL-PREFERENCE
Related to Enlisting After High School

Category	Percent of Sample (N=1644)	Percent of Category That Tried to Enlist
Mentioned MS as occ preference some time during high school	7%	36.8%
Never mentioned MS as occ preference during high school	93 100	9.6

Grand Mean= 11.6%
Eta= .218
Eta-square= .048

5355

Conceptually, there is some difficulty in combining them. It seems reasonable that someone who aspires to military service as a career would have a high score on MIL-FIT. But the reverse does not follow; a person could fit well with military life and yet not desire to make a career of the service. This is borne out by the data shown in Table 4-9. Of those who fit best (category 5 on MIL-FIT) only 21 percent aspired to a military service job, while 50 percent of those with aspirations of MS had high scores (4 or 5) on the MIL-FIT measure (65/127). This moderate relationship is summarized in the gamma of .41.[3]

Another criterion which can be used to decide whether they should be combined is to see how well they can predict in combination to enlistment. Separately, MIL-FIT can account for 6.4 percent of the variance in enlist-

TABLE 4-9

Relationship of Military-Fit to
MS-IS-OCCUPATIONAL-PREFERENCE

MS=OCC PREF
Sometime During
High School

		NO	YES	TOTALS
1 Poor Fit		183	8	191
2		391	13	404
3		536	41	577
4		342	44	386
5 Good Fit		79	21	100
		1531	127	1658

Categories for MIL-FIT

Gamma = .41

5302

ment, and MS=OCC PREF 4.8 percent. Entering the two into a MCA[4] produced a Multiple R^2 (unadjusted) of .099; i.e., in an additive combination they can account for 9.9 percent of the variance. This figure is almost as big as the sum of the two taken separately and indicates that the two variables do not overlap much in their prediction. This suggested that the best method for combining them would be one that retained all the distinctions of the two ingredients. Accordingly, a "pattern variable" was constructed which had one category for each possible combination of the two variables; thus 5 x 2 = 10 categories. Three of these were collapsed because of low frequencies. The final version appears in Table 4-10. As demonstrated before, MIL-FIT relates positively to enlisting. However, having expressed a preference for MS as an occupation multiplies this effect. It is as though occupational preference were an important predictor in its own right, but much more important when it is expressed by a young man whose job-needs are congruent with his image of a military-service job.

TABLE 4-10

MIL-FIT/MS=OCC COMBINATION
Related to Enlisting After High School

Category	Percent of Sample (N=1556)	Percent of Category That Tried to Enlist
MS WAS NEVER AN OCCUPATIONAL PREFERENCE		
1. Poor Fit with Military Life	11%	2.3%
2.	25	2.9
3.	33	9.7
4.	20	17.6
5. Good Fit with Military Life	5	23.0
MS WAS AN OCCUPATIONAL PREFERENCE DURING HIGH SCHOOL		
6. Poor Fit with Military Life*	3	21.8
7.	2	44.7
8. Good Fit with Military Life	1	64.7
	100	

Grand Mean = 11.2%
Eta= .323
Eta-square= .105

5319

*This category includes MS=OCC PREF and MIL-FIT=1,2, and 3. The numbers in each of these categories were too small to retain as separate categories.

Consistency of Vocational Choice With Military-type Jobs. A third way to operationalize predisposition to military life was suggested by the work of John Holland, a vocational psychologist. He has hypothesized and tested a theory of vocational choice that has potential relevance for an enlistment decision (Holland, 1966). He postulates that all people can be classified into one of six basic personality orientations or types. The names for the types are Realistic, Investigative, Enterprising, Social, Conventional, and Artistic. Associated with each of these types is a cluster of jobs to which people of that type gravitate. As a result, jobs can be characterized according to the predominant type of person filling the job. A brief description of each of the types and their associated occupations appears below.[5]

REALISTIC. The model type is masculine, physically strong, unsociable, aggressive; has good motor coordination and skill; lacks verbal and interpersonal skills; prefers concrete to abstract problems; conceives of himself as being aggressive and masculine and as having conventional political and economic values. Persons who choose or prefer the following occupations resemble this type: airplane mechanic, construction inspector, electrician, filling station attendant, fish and wildlife specialist, locomotive engineer, master plumber, photoengraver, power shovel operator, power station operator, radio operator, surveyor, tree surgeon, tool designer.

INTELLECTUAL.[6] The model type is task-oriented, intraceptive, asocial; prefers to think through rather than act out problems; needs to understand; enjoys ambiguous work tasks; has unconventional values and attitudes; is anal as opposed to oral. Vocational preferences include aeronautical design engineer, anthropologist, astronomer, biologist, botanist, chemist, editor of a scientific journal, geologist, independent research scientist, meteorologist, physicist, scientific research worker, writer of scientific or technical articles, zoologist.

SOCIAL. The model type is sociable, responsible, feminine, humanistic, religious; needs attention; has verbal and interpersonal skills; avoids intellectual problem solving, physical activity, and highly ordered activities; prefers to solve problems through feelings and interpersonal manipulations of others; is orally dependent. Vocational preferences include assistant city school superintendent, clinical psychologist, director of welfare agency, foreign missionary, high school teacher, juvenile delinquency expert, marriage counselor, personal counselor, physical education teacher, playground director, psychiatric case worker, social science teacher, speech therapist, vocational counselor.

CONVENTIONAL. The model type prefers structured verbal and numerical activities and subordinate roles; is conforming (extraceptive); avoids ambiguous situations and problems involving interpersonal relationships and physical skills; is effective at well-structured tasks; identifies with power; values material possessions and status. Vocational preferences include: bank examiner, bank teller, bookkeeper, budget reviewer, cost estimator, court stenographer, financial analyst, IBM equipment operator, inventory controller, payroll clerk, quality control expert, statistician, tax expert, traffic manager.

ENTERPRISING. The model type has verbal skills for selling, dominating, leading; conceives of himself as a strong, masculine leader; avoids well-defined language or work situations requiring long periods of intellectual effort; is extraceptive; differs from the Conventional type in that he prefers ambiguous social tasks and has a greater concern with power, status, and leadership; is orally aggressive. Vocational preferences include business executive, buyer, hotel manager, industrial relations consultant, manufacturer's representative, master of ceremonies, political campaign manager, real-estate salesman, restaurant worker, speculator, sports promoter, stock and bond salesman, television producer, traveling salesman.

ARTISTIC. The model type is asocial; avoids problems that are highly structured or require gross physical skills; resembles the Intellectual type in being intraceptive and asocial; but differs from that type in that he has a need for individualistic expression, has less ego strength, is more feminine, and suffers more frequently from emotional disturbances; prefers dealing with environmental problems through self-expression in artistic media. Vocational preferences include art dealer, author, cartoonist, commercial artist, composer, concert singer, dramatic coach, free-lance writer, musical arranger, musician, playwright, poet, stage director, symphony conductor.

The essence of Holland's theory concerns the way in which personality types and job types become linked. He posits that individuals seek out job environments where the predominant personality type matches their own personality type. To make this match they utilize stereotypes of people who work in different jobs.

As Holland accrued data on his theory he recognized that the personality types were not all pure—that there was some overlap among characteristics of the types. For example, the Realistic type was somewhat similar to the Investigative and Conventional types but not at all similar to the Social type. Further, he found that these overlaps were very orderly. This is summarized in the circumplex ordering of personality types, and/or job types shown in Figure 4-1 on page 48. The categories that are immediately adjacent to a type are somewhat alike, while those farthest removed are least alike. Thus it would be unusual, but not incompatible, for a Realistic type person to choose a Conventional type of occupation. But it would be very incongruous for this type of choose a Social type of job. If an individual made a choice this far removed from his type, Holland predicts that he would be unstable in his job and soon move to another. This has obvious implications for the distribution of personality types in various jobs. A job classified as Realistic will have mostly Realistic types on the job, but will also have some Investigative and Conventional types as well.

Holland categorizes most types of jobs available to the enlisted man as Realistic, and secondarily Investigative or Conventional.[7] If this is accurate, then another measure of a person's orientation or predispostion to military life is the closeness, measured on the circumplex, of his personality type to Realistic. Thus, a Realistic type person would be assigned the top score of three, indicating that he is most congruent with the type of job available to

FIGURE 4-1

Circumplex of Holland Classifications
Of Personality Types and Job Types

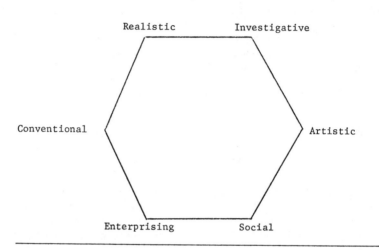

enlistees. A score of two would be assigned to Conventional and Investigative types; a score of one to Enterprising and Artistic types; and a score of zero to Social types. The hypothesis, then, is this: the more congruent a person is with the predominant type of person in military service, the more likely he is to enlist.

Holland has proposed two ways to measure personality type. The first way uses the Vocational Preference Inventory (VPI) which he developed. In this, a person indicates his preferences among 160 occupations. These preferences are scored to indicate the person's type. Unfortunately the VPI was not included as part of the YIT instrumentation. However, Holland has recently found that using a person's statement of his most preferred occupation will classify him as to type at least as accurately as the VPI.[8] Information on vocational preference is available on everyone in the YIT sample.

The distribution of the panel on the Holland typology and the percent that enlisted from each category is shown in Table 4-11. The largest proportion enlisting were of the Realistic type. Next largest were the Investigative and Conventional. The smallest proportion came from the Artistic and Enterprising types. When it comes to the Social type the theory breaks down. The rate of enlisting for this group was as high as for the Investigative and Conventional types. (It should be noted that for an n of 101 the confidence interval $(p < .05)$ for the estimate of 11.1 percent is wide enough to allow the true mean to be as low as 6.5 percent. This is not as low as theory would predict but it is less in conflict with the prediction.)

The Realistic category included 45 respondents whose occupational preference at the end of twelfth grade was that of military service. This is the group that was examined earlier in the chapter and referred to as MS=OCC PREF. In testing the applicability of Holland's theory, this subgroup should be eliminated, because the hypothesis is that people aspiring to jobs that are similar to, but not the same as, military-type jobs are more likely to enlist. Removing this subgroup from the analysis reduced the total number in the Realistic group from 620 down to 575, and the percent enlisting from 18.1 percent down to 16.2 percent. It turns out, then, that the MS=OCC PREF subgroup did not change the shape of the distribution radically. The overall relationship with this group removed is described by an eta-square of .018. This is 0.6 percent lower than for the entire sample, indicating that aspiring to military service as an occupation can account for one-quarter of the variance that appeared attributable just to the Holland classification of occupational aspiration.

More troublesome for the theory is the deviation of the Social group from the expected trend. As the theory suggests, the characteristics of the Social type look very incongruous with jobs available to enlisted men. The Social type ". . . prefers activities involving religious, social, and esthetic expression, including church, student government, community services, music, . . . arranging entertainment . . . and creative hobbies in art, music and lit-

TABLE 4-11

Relationship of Holland Personality
Types to Enlistment Behavior

Holland Personality Type	Congruency With Military Jobs	Percent of Sample (N=1690)	Percent of Category That Tried to Enlist
Realistic	3	36%	18.1%
Investigative	2	20	9.4
Conventional	2	8	8.3
Artistic	1	14	5.9
Enterprising	1	16	7.2
Social	0	6	11.1
		100%	

Grand Mean = 11.7%
Eta = .155
Eta-square = .024

5355   5369

erature." In addition, he is supposed to avoid ". . . masculine roles that require motor skills, use of tools and machines, or physical danger. Such activities include shopwork, horsemanship, racing, auto repair, model building." (Holland, 1966, pp. 25-26)

However, there are some ways in which the Social type can be seen in the military role. The Social type is supposed to select tasks in which ". . . he can use his skills with an interest in other persons in order to train or change their behavior. The Social person is typified by his social skills and his need for social interaction. . . . He is concerned with the welfare of dependent persons: the poor, uneducated, sick, unstable, young, and aged." (Holland, ibid.) This description is not totally incongruous with one reason given by some enlistees to explain their behavior. A Department of Defense Survey in 1964 found that there are some enlistees who explained their behavior by saying they wanted to serve their country—an altruistic society-serving motivation (Wool, 1968, p. 111). A similar finding was reported by Johnston and Bachman (1970, p. 61) in a preliminary report of twelfth grade data from this study.

The Social person also rates himself high on leadership, speaking skills, popularity, drive to achieve, self-control and practical-mindedness. This is congruous with the image of an officer and is reminiscent of the Marine Corps advertising campaign which asked, "Why wait until you're 40 to head your own company?"

The work of Anne Roe provides further evidence for an interpretation of Social that would make it reasonable to expect an average number of enlistments from among this type of individual. In her classification of occupations she places privates and sergeants in the armed forces into a category which she calls "Service Occupations." (Roe, 1956, p. 169) In the same category are such occupations as social workers, religious workers, and policemen. To Roe, such occupations always involve one person doing something for another, even though the services may be minor ones.

While this interpretation does not support Holland's theory to a large extent, it does suggest that the motivations for enlistment after high school are probably very broad and diverse, matching the great variety of jobs available to the enlistee. In the next section the Holland variable will be compared with the two variables already discussed.

Interrelationships Among Military Fit Variables. The three variable sets were intercorrelated to see if there was empirical support for the idea that they were all measuring the same dimension. Since the variables under consideration could at best be called ordinal scales, the statistic chosen to summarize the relationship is the Goodman and Kruskal gamma. (See Chapter 1 for a discussion of this statistic.) Table 4-12 shows the matrix of gammas. MIL-FIT and Holland Congruency both relate moderately well to MS=OCC PREF; but they do not relate strongly to each other. This was one indication that Holland Congruency should not be joined with MIL-FIT.

Multivariate Prediction of the Military Fit Set to Enlistment. An additional criterion for choosing which of the three variables to keep is obtainable from MCA. For a predictor to be worth keeping it should continue to explain

TABLE 4-12

Interrelationships Among Military Fit
Variables

	MIL-FIT	MS=OCC PREF
MS=OCC PREF	.41	
Holland Congruency	.18	.40

NOTE: Table entries are gammas. All are significant beyond the .01 level.

some minimal proportion of unique variance when used in conjunction with other variables in a multivariate prediction.

The three military fit-type variables were entered into an MCA predicting to enlisting. The results are shown in Table 4-13. The first column of figures gives the zero-order relationship of each of the variables in the form of

TABLE 4-13

Multiple Classification Analyses of Three Military Fit
Variables Predicting to Enlisting

Military Fit Predictors	Predicting From Each Characteristic Separately	Predicting From Several Characteristics Simultaneously				Marginal Proportion of the Variance Explained
		Run 1	Run 2	Run 3	Run 4	
	Eta²	Beta²				
MIL-FIT	.064	.043	*	.053	.048	.037
MS=OCC PREF	.050	.030	.040	*	.034	.029
Holland Congruency	.024	.008	.016	.012	*	.004
MULT R (adjusted)		.310	.243	.259	.303	
MULT R² (adjusted)		.096	.059	.067	.092	

5357

* Variable excluded in this MCA analysis run.

eta-square values. The next columns present the results of four MCA runs—
first using all three variables, then using each combination of just two variables. The adjusted R^2 for Run 1 shows that all three of these measures together can account for almost 10 percent of the variance (.096). In Run 2,
dropping MIL-FIT cuts the variance explained by two-fifths—from .096 to
.059. The beta-square figures in Run 2 show that MS=OCC PREF and Holland Congruency each gain in importance in the absence of MIL-FIT; but
the variance they explain does not overlap sufficiently to compensate for its
loss. Run 3 shows similar results when MS=OCC PREF is dropped. Finally,
Run 4 shows that omitting the Holland Congruency score hardly affects the
prediction at all. The Multiple R^2 drops from .096 to .092, indicating that the
Holland score can account marginally for only 0.4 percent of the variance.
The rest of its predictive power (η^2=.024 minus marginal R^2=.004) is apparently shared with the other two predictors. These findings resulted in a decision to eliminate the Holland Congruency score from further consideration.

Discussion and Summary. In sum, analyses of the three predictors in
the military fit set resulted in the retention of two of them, MIL-FIT and
MS=OCC PREFERENCE. Further consideration led to collapsing these two
variables into a single measure of fit with military service, called MIL-FIT/
MS=OCC PREF. The relationship of this variable to enlisting might be interpreted as follows. The more an individual sees a congruency between what
he wants in a job and the characteristics of a military job, the more likely he
is to enlist.

This relationship suggests that there is an element of choice operating in
a young man's selection of a post-high school activity, and that this choice is
based in part on his general attitude towards, and anticipated fit with, military service life. However, this is only one interpretation. Cognitive consistency theory provides good reason to think that people alter their attitudes
toward military service *as a result* of having made their decision about enlisting. Abelson (1959) or Festinger (1957) would contend that if an individual
had decided to enlist he could not hold negative feelings about military service and believe that he would fit poorly with service life. Accordingly he
would "bolster" his decision by changing his attitudes to correspond to his
behavior.

This raises two issues. One, what role does fit play in the decision itself?
Two, if it is to some degree influencing the decision to enlist, how important is
it relative to other less changing dimensions like intelligence, draft status, or
area unemployment? These two issues will be returned to at various times as
the data suggest answers to them.

HYPOTHESIS 2: Young Men Who Are Undecided On Their Vocational Plans Are More Likely To Enlist In Military Service After High School

The hypothesis associated with this predictor set states that an individual who is unsure of what he wants to do is more likely to enlist than someone

whose plans have crystallized and who has clearly in mind where he is going and how he is getting there. For the vocationally unsure, a period of time spent in the military could serve as a moratorium—a time away from home to think things through and gain exposure to a variety of different life styles and occupations. To test the validity of this hypothesis two measures were derived; one looking at the individual's commitment to his long-range vocational preference and the other focusing on commitment to his short-range plans.

Vocational Maturity: Commitment to Long-Range Vocational Plans. Vocational maturity is a concept that has been discussed and researched extensively by Donald Super (1957, 1960, 1963). At the most general level it is a measure of the degree to which an individual engages in vocational planning activities which are thought to be characteristic of his particular stage of vocational development. Super considers the majority of older adolescents to be in what he calls the "Exploratory Stage," right at the point of "specifying" their vocational preference:

> The specification of a vocational preference is . . . the converting of a generalized vocational preference, or a very tentatively formulated specific preference, into a specific preference to which one feels committed with some assurance. Specification also means the filling in of the details concerning one's preference, for example, more specific information and planning, including planning for implementation. It is a process which appears to be characteristic of the middle and later adolescent years. (Super, 1963, pp. 87-88)

Super goes on to list 12 behaviors or attitudes which are appropriate to this stage, and which therefore might be used as measures of whether an individual had reached the "specification" level of the exploratory stage. Specification appears to involve the following attitudes and behavior continua (ibid., p. 88):
  1. Awareness of the need to specify a vocational preference
  2. Use of resources in specification
  3. Awareness of factors to consider
  4. Awareness of contingencies which may affect goals
  5. Differentiation of interests and values
  6. Awareness of present-future relationships
  7. Specification of a vocational preference
  8. Consistency of preference
  9. Possession of information concerning the preferred occupation
  10. Planning for the preferred occupation
  11. Wisdom of the vocational preference
  12. Confidence in a specific preference

Super places special emphasis on the last item—confidence in a specific preference—to differentiate adolescents who have reached the "specification" stage from those who are only at the point of "crystallizing" their ideas of a future occupation. Super suggests that this dimension can be measured from "direct expressions of certainty in self-ratings and in open-ended interviews . . ." (ibid., p. 88).

Four of Super's twelve dimensions—including confidence in a specific preference—can be operationalized with twelfth-grade Youth in Transition data. In the list that follows, the notations in italics are questions from the twelfth-grade questionnaire.

1. Specification of preference (*In the long run, what sort of work do you think you might do for a living?* This question was coded for whether or not the individual expressed a choice.)
2. Confidence in specified preference (*How likely is it that things will actually work out this way?*)
3. Wisdom of preference (*How certain are you that this is a good choice for you?*)
4. Expected satisfaction from choice (*How satisfying do you think you will find this kind of work?*)

The question covering the first dimension was asked of everybody and then coded for whether or not the respondent mentioned a specific occupation. For those who did mention a specific occupation (around 85 percent at Time 3), the questons covering the last three dimensions were asked. The questions and the distribution of responses appear in Table 4-14. On the face of it these questions are tapping the extent to which an individual has thought through and committed himself to his occupational preference. The second column of figures in Table 4-14—the percent of each category that enlisted—makes it quite clear that there is little relationship between any of the items and enlistment behavior. Either the hypothesis does not hold up or the method of operationalizing the concepts is inadequate. As would be expected, combining these into a single index of Vocational Maturity[9] does nothing to improve the relationship. Table 4-15 shows the percent enlisting from each category of the combination variable. As the eta of .023 indicates, there is virtually no association between enlistment behavior and Vocational Maturity as defined in this study.

Commitment to Post-High School Plans. One possible explanation for the lack of association noted above is that vocational indecision is not a motive for choices at this age. It could be that at age 18 a young man is not concerned if his long-range occupational plans have not yet crystallized. His vocational behavior (i.e., his post-high school choices) may be motivated by nothing more far-sighted than resolving each choice at the point in time when it presents itself. If this is the case, then the concept of vocational maturity can be translated into a concept of commitment to immediate post-high school plans, and the hypothesis becomes: the less committed a young man is to his immediate post-high school plans, the more likely he is to enlist. The rationale is the same as for Vocational Maturity: the undecided individual seeks a moratorium—a chance to think through what it is that he wants to do in the immediate future. A term in the service offers such an opportunity, coupled with exposure to a large variety of alternatives. To test this hypothesis a measure was constructed of twelfth-grade indecision over post-high

TABLE 4-14

Ingredients of Vocational Maturity
Measure Related to Enlisting

In the question immediately preceding the ones below the respondents
were asked: "In the long run, what sort of work do you think you
might do for a living?"

Questionnaire Item	Response Category	Percent of Sample (N=1602)*	Percent of Category That Tried to Enlist
3MA2 How likely is it that things will actually work out this way? -- how certain is it that you will do this sort of work?	1 Certain	12%	11.2%
	2 Very likely	45	10.9
	3 Fairly likely	30	11.7
	4 Somewhat likely	10	9.1
	5 Not very likely	3	18.2
		100	
			Eta= .048 Eta-square= .002
3MA4 How certain are you that the sort of work you mentioned above is a good choice for you?	1 Completely certain	21%	13.5%
	2 Very certain	44	10.8
	3 Fairly certain	26	9.7
	4 Somewhat certain	5	13.3
	5 Not at all certain	4	6.1
		100	
			Eta= .055 Eta-square= .003
3MA5 How satisfying do you think you will find this kind of work?	1 Not very satisfying	3%	9%
	2 Somewhat satisfying	12	12
	3 Quite satisfying	21	9
	4 Very satisfying	37	12
	5 Extremely satisfying	27	11
		100	
			Eta= .035 Eta-square= .001

5287

* The reduced N results from approximately 13% expressing no occupational preference.

school plans. The following method was used. In the twelfth-grade questionnaire (Spring 1969) everyone was asked what he planned to do the following
fall.

What about your plans for this coming fall (1969)? Pick out the one plan
that will most likely work out for you, and fill out only the section that applies to that plan.

THIS FALL I PLAN TO:

1. Continue my present full-time job
2. Work full time at a new job and/or receive on-the-job training
3. Work full-time on my present part-time job
4. Be in Military Service
5. Go to technical or vocational school
6. Go to college
7. Continue high school
8. I don't have any definite plans; I'm just going to wait and see what happens

In the section appropriate to each plan there appeared the question: "How likely is it that you will actually be (in college, on a job, etc.) this coming fall?" The responses ranged from "certain" to "very unlikely." This resulted in a measure of commitment of each person to his own particular plan.

Two groups were not asked this question and their position on the scale had to be inferred. Those who were planning to continue their present full-time jobs were not asked about the certainty of their plan. They were assigned a score of "certain," since there was no reason to assume that they were going to be changing jobs. The other exception is for those who indicated that they had no definite plans. They were not asked about the uncertainty of their plans, and instead were assumed to be the most undecided of all.

The hypothesis states that those uncertain about what they wanted to do

TABLE 4-15

Relationship of Vocational Maturity
to Enlistment Behavior

Vocational Maturity Categories		Percent of Sample (N=1717)	Percent of Category That Tried to Enlist
Vocationally Immature	1 no occupational plans	13%	10.7%
	2 has occupational plans; but not committed to them	5%	9.4
	3	27%	12.4
	4	42%	11.7
Vocationally Mature	5 has occupational plans; and very committed to them	13% / 100%	11.2

Grand Mean = 11.6%
Eta = .023
Eta-square = .000

5355

would be more likely to enlist after high school. However, some people at the end of twelfth grade were already planning to enlist, and it cannot be ascertained whether they were making a positive choice for military service or had been so undecided over other plans that they were already indicating an intention to enlist. To resolve this problem, those who stated a plan to enlist were separated from the others, their scale of indecision was reversed, and these additional categories were included to make a new continuum that appears in Figure 4-2 below. The scale is anchored at one end by a firm

FIGURE 4-2

Commitment to Post-High School Plans

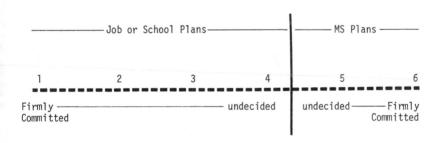

commitment to plans other than military service and at the other by a firm commitment to military service. In between are various degrees of indecision over the plans one is considering. If this is a continuum, then the proportion enlisting from each point on the scale should increase the closer one gets to the right hand end of the scale. The results can be seen in Table 4-16 showing the distribution of the sample on the variable and the percent enlisting from each category. As noted in Chapter 3, the vast majority of respondents were not planning to enlist (89 percent at the end of twelfth grade). Furthermore this table shows that the majority of them were cetain of their non-military plans. As individuals became less sure of their plans (categories 2—4) they became increasingly likely to enlist, with the highest proportion enlisting coming from those with no plans at all. Category 5 can be thought of as comprised of individuals who have already made a tentative commitment to enlisting but still were considering alternate plans. The very fact that they already mentioned military service plans at the end of senior year gave them a much higher likelihood of enlisting than those who simply did not know what they wanted to do. At the end of the scale are those who were very sure that they would enlist. The highest percentage enlisting came from this group.

TABLE 4-16

Commitment to Post-High School Plans
Related to Enlistment

Categories	Percent of Sample (N=1680)	Percent of Category That Tried to Enlist
POST-HIGH SCHOOL PLANS ARE NOT TO ENLIST		
1. Completely sure of plans	65%	4.5%
2. Very sure of plans	9	8.5
3. Somewhat to not at all sure of plans	4	11.5
4. No plans	12	15.2
POST-HIGH SCHOOL PLANS ARE TO ENLIST		
5. Less than completely sure of plans to enlist (corresponds to category 2-3)	3	44.9
6. Completely sure of plans to enlist (corresponds to category 1)	7	67.6
TOTAL	100	

FOR THOSE NOT PLANNING TO ENLIST   Eta = .152
    (Categories 1-4: 89% of sample)   Eta-square = .023

FOR THOSE WITH PLANS TO ENLIST   Eta = .214
    (Categories 5-6: 11% of sample)   Eta-square = .046

FOR ENTIRE SAMPLE (Categories 1-6)   Eta = .517
                                           Eta-square =.267

FOR ENTIRE SAMPLE (Dichotomized: Eta = .495
    (Categories 1-4=1, 5-6=2)   Eta-square = .245

5355

To summarize the relationship of this variable to enlistment behavior the eta-statistic is presented four different ways. The first summarizes the relationship of only the first four categories to enlistment—i.e., those who were not planning to enlist at the end of senior year. The eta of .14 is statistically significant but shows only a moderate degree of association. One reason for this is that a very large number declared themselves to be firmly committed to their plans. As measured, commitment to plans did not spread out the sample sufficiently to account for more than two percent of the variance (eta-square = .023). But the trend over categories 1—4 suggests that uncertainty does relate to choosing military service after high school.

Looking at those already planning to enlist, categories 5 and 6, the relationship is much stronger (eta=.214). Indecision among those with MS plans is very important in explaining whether or not they will follow through on their plans, again supporting the importance of uncertainty.

Combining the two groups produces a very potent variable. The eta-square of .267 indicates that the combination variable can account for more than one-quarter of the variance in the criterion of enlistment. However, nearly all of the relationship is due to plans, not indecision. If the variable is dichotomized into MS PLANS/OTHER PLANS (categories 1—4 collapsed, 5—6 collapsed), one can account for 24.5 percent of the variance just knowing whether or not a young man is planning to enlist and only an additional two percent knowing how committed he is to his plans. While the figure for indecision is small relative to that for plans, it is large enough in comparison with predictors that will be discussed in later chapters to warrant retaining it. To capture this two-fold relationship, the variable will henceforth be referred to as MS PLANS/INDECISION, connoting that it is most important to know whether or not an individual has post-high school plans to enlist, but it is also helpful to know how committed he is to his plans, no matter what the plans are.

Discussion and Summary. The findings for Vocational Maturity lead to the rejection of the hypothesis that young men undecided about their long-range vocational future are more likely to enlist. However, looking at commitment to short-range vocational plans (post-high school work or education), there is some support for the hypothesis that indecision over more immediate plans is associated with higher enlistment rates.[10] Apparently some young men enlist because they are not decided on or committed to any of the civilian alternatives. As stated earlier, one explanation for this finding is that such individuals are seeking a moratorium on decision-making and thus want to delay for a few years committing themselves to a particular civilian activity. Military service provides a chance for an individual to think things through at the same time he is gaining exposure to a variety of alternative choices. However, this cannot be taken as unequivocal evidence for the moratorium theory. An alternative explanation is that the undecided were in the process of changing their plans and military service was simply a second choice for them, not a moratorium.

HYPOTHESIS 3: Young Men Who Face a High Likelihood of Being Drafted Are More Likely To Enlist

Measuring the impact of the draft is of special importance in most studies of enlistment behavior. Typically, the question being asked is how many recruits enlist in order to avoid serving as draftees. The objective is to discover the number which might be expected to enlist in the absence of a draft. The present study is not optimally suited to provide accurate answers to this question. There are two reasons for this. The first is related to the nature of the sample. When this study was initiated, the Youth in Transition panel of young men was thought to be a good choice for the very reason that they were then of an age that enlistees from the sample would be minimally draft-motivated.[11] In spring of 1969—graduation time for most of the YIT sample—the minimum age at which men were being inducted was 19½. At that time the average age of the panel was 18, old enough to enlist but too young to be drafted. By one year later—the last data collection and the point at which enlistment behavior was determined—the panel was closer to the age at which they could be drafted, but not old enough for all panel members to have been exposed equally to this possibility.

A second reason this study is not ideal for assessing draft motivation concerns a change in Selective Service policy. The first draft lottery was inaugurated in December of 1969; it altered completely the way in which a young man calculated the likelihood of his being drafted. Only one-quarter of the YIT panel was old enough to receive numbers in this lottery. Certainly, few of the remaining three-quarters would have enlisted to avoid the draft until after the next lottery. This second lottery (July 1970) occurred after most of the YIT interviews had been completed and consequently was too late to have had an impact on their enlistment behavior.

The above argument does not negate the possibility of the draft influencing the enlistment behavior of the sample. To the contrary, some of the older respondents would have been very close to being drafted even prior to the first lottery. While the average age in spring of 1969 was 18, a small group (10 percent) were 19 or older, and accordingly would have been very vulnerable during their first summer out of high school. Others, prior to the first lottery, might well have perceived the draft as an all-encompassing net that catches nearly everyone at some time and therefore would eventually catch up to them. For these, enlisting to "get it over with" would be a reasonable course of action.

Some support for this reasoning comes from the twelfth-grade data. Those planning on enlisting were asked the reasons for their choice. Their responses were summarized in an earlier report on these data:

> When asked to respond to a list of potential reasons they might have for enlisting, they placed great stress on learning a trade or skill valuable in civilian life, obtaining advanced education, and becoming more mature and self-reliant. Equally prominent were two reasons that reveal the importance of the draft in a choice to enlist; about one-half of our respondents

gave a "very important" rating to "Fulfill my military obligation at a time of my choice" and "Want my choice of service rather than be drafted." Another 30 percent gave a "very important" rating to one of the two. Of course, many of these young men might enlist even if there were no draft; nevertheless, it seems clear that as many as 80 percent may lean toward enlistment as an alternative to being drafted. (Johnston and Bachman, 1970, p. 22)

One year later those who had actually enlisted were asked, "How likely is it that you would have enlisted if you were sure you would not have been drafted?" Forty-one percent of the enlistees thought they probably or surely would *not* have enlisted without the draft. Both of these findings support the idea that a large portion of those who enlisted or planned to enlist *thought* that they did so as an alternative to being drafted. But there are good reasons for an individual to say this, even if it is not a central motivation. The individual who is at the stage of stating a preference for enlisting after high school may be contending with a group of peers who do not think highly of enlisting. Data presented in Chapter 7 suggest that enlistees received more discouragement for their plan than any other group (work, college, tech/voc). For his own peace of mind, the person planning to enlist may rationalize his behavior by, in essence, saying he has no choice in the matter. For the individual who has already enlisted a similar phenomenon can occur if he is not completely happy with his experience in the service, a likely situation for the new recruit who may still be in the midst of basic training—typically an unpleasant experience for even the most enthusiastic of military-service types. So one must discount somewhat an individual's own assessment that he was draft-motivated.

What kind of measure is appropriate then? It should have three characteristics. (1) It should assess the likelihood that an individual assigns to being drafted in the near future. (2) It should array all individuals—enlistees and non-enlistees alike—on the same scale, and (3) it should be assessed prior to enlistment. This study has three measures which, in combination, can be used to infer how threatened by the draft an individual would have been during his first year out of high school. These include (1) whether or not he had a "semi-permanent" deferment; (2) whether or not he planned to enter a temporarily deferrable activity after high school; and (3) his age. These variables and their distributions in the sample are displayed in Table 4-17.

The following deferments are included under the heading of "semi-permanent."

I-A-O; I-O Conscientious objector

I-Y Registrant qualified for military service only in the event of war or national emergency

III-A Registrant with a child or children; or deferred by reason of extreme hardship to dependents

IV-A Sole surviving son

IV-F Registrant not qualified for any military service

IV-D Divinity student

TABLE 4-17

Ingredients of Draft Status
Related Separately to Enlisting

Category	Percent in Sample (N=1556)	Percent of Category That Tried to Enlist
SEMI-PERMANENT DEFERMENT		
0 No	86%	13.4%
1 Yes, including I-Y, III-A, IV-A, IV-F, and I-0	14	5.5*
	100	

Grand Mean = 11.6%
Eta = .084
Eta-square = .007

POST-HIGH SCHOOL PLANS		
0 No (non-education plans)	38 %	22.7 %
1 Yes (education plans)	62	5.0
	100	

Grand Mean = 11.6%
Eta = .269
Eta-square = .072

AGE (October, 1969)		
1 less than 18	9 %	6.9 %
2 18 - 18 1/2	37	6.7
3 18 1/2 - 19	33	11.3
4 19 - 19 1/2	11	24.7
5 older than 19 1/2	9	21.7
	100	

Grand Mean = 11.6%
Eta = .197
Eta-square = .039

5309

* 5.5% tried to enlist and received their semi-permanent deferments when they could not meet the requirements.

These classifications were chosen for this category because they all, in effect, take a young man out of the draft eligible category and, in most cases, make him ineligible to enlist as well.[12]

For all those who have not been classified in one of these categories the immediacy of being drafted depends on whether the individual can secure a temporary deferment (I-S, II-A, II-S) for educational purposes. Those expecting to pursue any of the following activities are almost assured of receiving at least a one-year deferment: college, junior college, technical or vocational school, or an additional year of high school if necessary to graduate. With the exception of a few defense-related jobs, no other activities can be included. Accordingly, those planning draft-deferrable activities should be less threatened by the draft than those who are not. The data in Table 4-17 would seem to confirm this. Only five percent of those with education plans tried to enlist while 22.7 percent of the others did. The eta of .269 is quite high for a single predictor.

Age is the third ingredient. It was hypothesized to be important because Selective Service, prior to the lottery system, operated on a policy of not drafting men until they were at least 19½. As Table 4-17 shows, age is related to enlisting, with a sharp increase in the percent enlising occuring at age 18½ and reaching a peak at 19½. The peak corresponds to the youngest age young men were being drafted in 1969. The slight drop in enlistments for those over 19½ is related to the fact that the YIT sample is a grade cohort; those who were older than 19½ and just completing high school were less likely to meet the standards for enlisting. When those with semi-permanent deferments were eliminated from the age groupings the curve flattened out with an equal percent enlisting from both categories 4 and 5.

In this study the effect of age is somewhat exaggerated because the sample is a grade cohort. In such a design, the older boys are those who were held back a grade at some point in their schooling and are therefore less likely to get into college or even have aspirations of going to college. This makes them particularly vulnerable to being drafted: they are not as likely to be in a draft-deferrable activity and they are in a prime age group for induction. In a later chapter on school experiences it will be seen that several predictors, like being held back in school, are related strongly to enlisting. At that time it will be noted again that these variables are confounded with age and that draft vulnerability is a more parsimonious explanation of their relationship to enlisting.

Combining Ingredients of Draft Status. It was hypothesized, and confirmed by the data, that there would be interactions among these variables. For example, if a person has a semi-permanent deferment none of the other factors should matter. Among those who do not have these deferments, age should be a critical factor, but much more among those with no deferments than those with educational deferments. Accordingly a variable was built which captured these interactions. It is called DRAFT STATUS and appears in Table 4-18.

Category one—semi-permanent deferment—had only one enlistee, a boy

TABLE 4-18

DRAFT STATUS Combination Variable
Related to Enlisting

	Percent in Sample (N=1556)	Percent of Category That Tried to Enlist
1. Semi-permanent deferment	12%	5.5%*
2. PHS** Plans provide temporary deferment, age: <18 1/2	32	2.4
3. PHS Plans provide temporary deferment, age: 18 1/2 - 19	21	4.3
4. PHS Plans provide temporary deferment, age: >19	6	16.8
5. PHS Plans not draft-deferrable, age: <18 1/2	13	17.4
6. PHS Plans not draft-deferrable, age: 18 1/2 - 19	8	31.3
7. PHS Plans not draft-deferrable, age: >19	8	39.8
	100	

Grand Mean = 11.2%
Eta = .377
Eta-square = .142

₅₃₁₉
* 5.5% tried to enlist and received their semi-permanent deferment when they could not meet the requirements.

** PHS = Post-High School

whose I-Y was changed to I-A. With this one exception, the figure of 5.5 percent is attributable entirely to young men who tried to enlist but were rejected when they were tested. Categories two to four contain those who planned to enter draft-deferrable activities. As hypothesized, a very small proportion of categories two and three enlisted. But those in category four enlisted at a rate four times that of their younger college-bound classmates (16.8 percent). This is not surprising. As noted earlier, young men of this age in the YIT panel had been held back at least one grade during their earlier schooling. Thus, they were less likely to have been able to get into or persist at further education. Further evidence for this explanation comes from noting that classroom grades in senior year averaged C for this group, compared to B+ for Categories two and three.

Within the non-deferrable-plan group, categories 5—7, age shows a much more striking relationship. The youngest in this group enlisted as frequently (17.4 percent) as the oldest in the group with educational plans, and the oldest enlisted at a rate more than twice as frequent (39.8 percent). The overall relationship of DRAFT STATUS to attempted enlistment is summarized in the eta of .377: this measure can account for 14.2 percent of the variance in enlistment attempts. This is the strongest effect of any of the motive predictors.

Discussion and Summary. Using three variables from which one could infer a young man's threat of being drafted, it is possible to account for considerable variance in enlistment attempts. Even though most of the respondents were not old enough to be drafted immediately after high school, many of them responded to what they must have deemed the inevitable—that they might be drafted. Instead of waiting to be inducted, they chose to enlist, presumably to have greater choice in branch of service and type of duty. Among those who did not have draft-deferrable plans, this response was particularly strong.

Multivariate Prediction

In this chapter three variables have shown a reasonably strong relationship to the criterion of attempted enlistment after high school: MIL-FIT, MS-PLANS/INDECISION, and DRAFT STATUS. In this section, all three are related to the criterion in a series of Multiple Classification Analyses (MCA). This form of analysis serves two purposes. First, it indicates the power of these measures taken in combination to predict to a choice of enlistment. Second, it provides a useful approximation of the *unique* effects of these predictors, as though they were uncorrelated with one another.

Summary statistics from various MCA's are presented in Table 4-19. In

TABLE 4-19

Multiple Classification Analyses of Motive
Variables Predicting to Attempted Enlistment

Motive Predictors	Predicting From Each Characteristic Separately	Predicting From Several Characteristics Simultaneously				Marginal Proportion of the Variance Explained
		Run 1	Run 2	Run 3	Run 4	
	Eta^2	Beta^2				Proportion
MIL-FIT/MS=OCC PREFERENCE	.105	.031	.063	*	.036	.025
MS-PLANS/INDEC-ISION	.274	.190	*	.217	.222	.129
DRAFT STATUS	.142	.025	.102	.036	*	.020
MULT R (adjusted)		.567	.438	.544	.549	
MULT R^2 (adjusted)		.321	.192	.296	.301	

5319

*Indicates that this variable was not included in this run.

combination the three variables can account for 32 percent of the variance in attempted enlistment. The beta-square figures under Run 1 indicate the relative contribution of each variable to the prediction. MIL-FIT and DRAFT STATUS appear to be about equal in their predictive power; the beta-square for MIL-FIT is .031 while that for DRAFT STATUS is .025. MS-PLANS/ INDECISION is the variable that accounts for the most variance; the most important single piece of information in predicting eventual behavior is knowing whether or not at the end of senior year a young man planned to enlist. (Recall that indecision is only a small part of this measure.) However, this is not very helpful to understanding the underlying reasons for enlisting.

Another MCA was run dropping MS-PLANS/INDECISION from the prediction to see how the other two variables would behave in the absence of this information. The results appear under Run 2 in Table 4-19. The Multiple R^2 dropped from .321 to .192, showing that the unique variance accounted for by MS-PLANS/INDECISION is 12.9 percent. This still leaves 19 percent of the variance which can be accounted for by MIL-FIT and DRAFT STATUS. (Some of this 19 percent overlaps with MS-PLANS—5.3 percent— but is not unique to it.) The beta-squares for Run 2 show that each of these variables is important to explaining this variance, although DRAFT STATUS is somewhat stronger. Figure 4-3 illustrates this with a Venn diagram. It can be seen that DRAFT STATUS accounts for 8.7 percent of the variance uniquely and MIL-FIT/MS=OCC PREF accounts for 5.0 percent uniquely. The shared variance amounts to 5.5 percent; i.e., this much of the variance can be explained by either one of the predictors.

It was noted earlier that it was not clear what role MIL-FIT/MS=OCC PREF plays in the enlistment decision. It could serve as a motive, causing people to be more or less disposed to enlisting; or it could serve to "bolster" a decision already made on other grounds. Since shared variance results when two predictors are correlated, one might conclude that the correlation between DRAFT STATUS and MIL-FIT/MS=OCC PREF indicates that the former is causing the latter, thus supporting the cognitive consistency theory. A problem with the definition of DRAFT STATUS does not permit interpreting the correlation in this way.[13] However, some other data suggest that the fit measure is serving at least partly as a motive for later behavior. The data come from the joint relationship of MIL-FIT and MS-PLANS/INDECISION to attempted enlistments; this is shown in Table 4-20. The rows and columns are bracketed versions of the two predictor variables. The percent enlisting is the top number in each cell. Note that the effect of fit is consistent across each row. A higher score on MIL-FIT results in a greater likelihood of trying to enlist at some time during the year *after* fit was measured. This is true even in row one, which contains only those who did not plan to enlist at the time fit was measured. Thus the attitude toward military service preceded even the declaration of behavioral intent.

Interaction Among the Predictors—a Note. The MCA model assumes additive relationships among predictors; this assumption is appropriate in the present case since there are no significant interactions among the three vari-

FIGURE 4-3

Venn Diagram of Variance in Attempted Enlistments
Accounted for by MIL-FIT and DRAFT STATUS

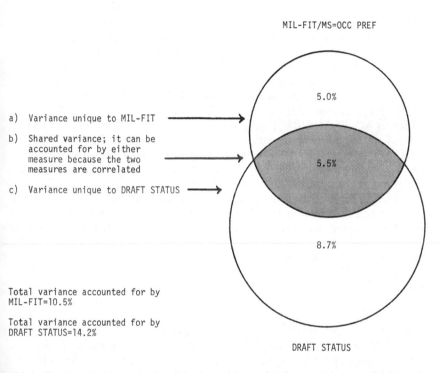

MIL-FIT/MS=OCC PREF

5.0%

a) Variance unique to MIL-FIT ⟶

b) Shared variance; it can be
   accounted for by either
   measure because the two
   measures are correlated ⟶

5.5%

c) Variance unique to DRAFT STATUS ⟶

8.7%

Total variance accounted for by
MIL-FIT=10.5%

Total variance accounted for by
DRAFT STATUS=14.2%

DRAFT STATUS

ables. To measure its contribution, a single variable was created which contained a category for each possible combination of the three variables. This was then collapsed to 22 categories so that there would be enough respondents in each category to have confidence in the estimate of the enlistment rate. This variable contained all of the main additive effects as well as any interaction. A one-way analysis of variance was performed on this variable predicting to attempted enlistment. From this analysis came an eta-square measure which indicated the amount of variance that could be accounted for by both the main and interaction effects. This figure was then compared with the Multiple R^2 from an MCA which used the three variables separately. Such an analysis identifies only the main effects. The difference between the eta-square and the R^2 figures is the effect that is attributable to interaction. The eta-square from the analysis of variance was .314, while the unadjusted R^2 from the MCA was .297. Thus, a maximum of 1.7 percent more variance can be accounted for by knowing the interactions among the three variables.

TABLE 4-20

MS-PLANS and MIL-FIT Related Jointly
to Attempted Enlistment

		MIL-FIT/MS=OCC PREF		
		Low Fit*	High Fit*	
	Does not plan to enlist	2.4% *910*	10.7% *325*	4.6% *1235*
MS PLANS/ INDECISION	Has no post-high school plans	9.0% *99*	21.3% *75*	14.3% *174*
	Plans to enlist	50.8% *97*	66.6% *90*	58.4% *187*
		7.5% *1066*	22.6% *490*	
		67	*33*	11.9% *1596*

Italic: frequencies

BOLD: percent of frequency that attempted to enlist

*MIL-FIT/MS=OCC PREF: Low = 1-3, High = 4-6

This was not considered large enough to negate using the MCA technique as an analysis strategy.[14]

Chapter Summary and Conclusions

Three different motives that come to bear on a young man's decision to enlist in military service after high school have been evaluated in this chapter. The motives were presented as a series of propositions to be tested; they are summarized here. A person enlists for one or a combination of the following reasons: (1) he feels that he "fits well" into a military-type job; (2) he is undecided about what else he might do; (3) he wants to beat the draft, i.e., he wants to avoid having to serve in the military as a draftee. For each of these hypotheses a summary variable was derived which operationalized the key concept in the hypothesis. The first was fit with military service (MIL-FIT). The measure was constructed by comparing responses to two different sets of questions. In the first set, a respondent was presented with a list of job dimensions and asked for each one whether it was important to him in choosing a job. Examples of some of the job dimensions are these: a job where you don't have to work too hard, where there is a good chance for getting ahead, where there are ample opportunities for training, where the pay is good. In the second set, a respondent was asked to rate a job in military service on the same dimensions. A person was considered to fit well if the job dimensions he rated as typical of military service were the same dimensions he had rated as important to himself in a job.

The second motive variable was indecision over post-high school plans. This variable measured both whether or not a person had a plan of enlisting while he was still in twelfth grade, as well as how committed he was to his plans, regardless of what the plan was.

The third motive variable was draft threat. The relevant concept was an individual's draft status. The variable, DRAFT STATUS, arrayed everyone according to how likely it was that he would be drafted during the year after high school. This status was inferred from a combination of an individual's age and deferment status.

The most important predictor of attempted enlistment in military service after high school[15] is knowing whether or not a young man planned to enlist when he was *still in* high school. This statement should not be taken as a restatement of the obvious; only one-half of those who planned to enlist at the end of twelfth grade actually followed through with their plans. The question remains, then: what factors are important in explaining the actual behavior of enlisting? After plans, the most important motive derives from draft-threat factors. If a young man is not college-bound, and therefore is not eligible for a temporary deferment, he is much more likely to enlist. Within this class of individuals, age is a critical factor. If a boy is older than his grade cohort and therefore more vulnerable to being drafted, he is more than twice as likely to enlist than his younger classmates. This effect of age applies to the college-bound as well. If a young man is much older than his classmates and expects in twelfth grade to go on to college, he is much less likely than the younger twelfth grader to make it into college; when this plan fails, enlisting is a frequent alternative. The most parsimonious explanation for this effect of age is that the older boys are most vulnerable to being drafted.

Almost as important as the draft factor was a young man's perception of how well his personal job needs fit with his perception of what jobs were like in the service. The better the perceived fit between these job needs and the service, the more likely a young man was to enlist. Data supported an interpretation which saw fit as a motive for enlisting in military service after high school.

The least important factor was vocational indecision. It was hypothesized that young men unsure about what they wanted to do in the future would turn to military service for a chance to think things through and gain exposure to a variety of jobs and life styles. Long-range vocational indecision was found to be unrelated to enlistment behavior. However, short-range indecision was found to relate moderately. There was a tendency for undecided individuals to seek out military service more frequently than those who were sure of their immediate plans after high school.

---

[1] As explained earlier, eta is the correlation ratio. It indicates the ability of the predictor—in this case MIL-FIT—to explain variation in the dependent variable. Unlike a Pearson product-moment correlation, eta takes into account both linear and curvilinear relationships. Eta-square indicates the amount of variance in the dependent variable that can be explained by the independent variable.

[2] "All possible combinations" would result in an 8-category variable. Three of these categories had very low frequencies and were collapsed with adjacent categories.

[3] Looking only at those who aspired to MS in senior year, the relationship is much stronger—gamma=.72. See Chapter 1 for a discussion of the gamma statistic.

[4] The technique of Multiple Classification Analysis (MCA) is described in Chapter 1.

[5] From Holland, 1966, pp. 16-17. Reprinted by permission of the author.

[6] Holland has recently changed this name to "investigative" to broaden the connotation to include the many non-academic types that are included in this cateogry; e.g., millwright, tool and die maker, and other technical occupations where the worker is involved in creative solutions to technical problems.

[7] Holland, personal communication (1971). Based on unpublished data.

[8] Holland, personal communication (1971).

[9] This was done by taking a mean of items 3MA2, 3MA4, and 3MA5. The scales for the first two items were reversed first so that "certain" had a high score and "not at all certain" a low score.

[10] To further investigate this hypothesis, future research should try to collect measures of indecision prior to an individual's expressing the twelfth grade *plan* of enlisting.

[11] At the time the study was negotiated a major objective was to project enlistments in an all-volunteer armed force. It was assumed at the time (late 1968) that such a force would not be phased in, but rather inaugurated at one definite point in time after the war was completed and the draft terminated.

[12] Strictly speaking, a conscientious objector is eligible to be drafted, being second in order of consideration only to those with a I-A classification. However, it is almost inconceivable that a CO would enlist in active military service as an alternative to performing the appropriate CO activities.

[13] If DRAFT STATUS could have been operationalized by lottery numbers, then it would be possible to say that draft status largely determined the way that a person felt about his fit with military service. However, as it has been defined for this study (done in the pre-lottery days), one of the components of DRAFT STATUS is choice of a post-high school plan. Not to have chosen college automatically places an individual in a more vulnerable category on the DRAFT

STATUS measure. Thus, a person could have perceived in senior year that military service was a good match for his needs and expressed the plan of enlisting. This would result in a higher score on DRAFT STATUS. It is equally possible that an individual could have felt highly threatened by the draft, decided to enlist, and then began perceiving himself as a type of person who would fit well into military life.

[14]Note that the purpose here is not to identify all of the effects that can be attributed to interaction, but rather to establish whether or not it is reasonable to use an additive model like MCA for analyses.

[15]The criterion was restricted to enlistments during the first year after high school. In addition to actual enlistments, those who tried to enlist but were turned down by the military were also included.

CHAPTER 5

ATTITUDES ABOUT WORK
AND VIETNAM

The last chapter focused on several motives that were thought to be particularly salient to an enlistment decision. This chapter considers two potential conditioning factors which were hypothesized to be important, but less central to a decision to enlist. These include attitudes about work and Vietnam.

Attitudes About Work

It has been suggested by some that enlisting is a "copout" by the unambitious who want to avoid the insecurity of a job in the civilian sector. Janowitz and Little summarized this thesis as follows:

> In a society in which individualism and personal gain are paramount virtues, it is understandable that some elements in the civilian population view the military career as an effort to "sell out" cheaply for economic security, despite low pay and limited prestige. In this view the free enterprise system is real and hard, so that the persons who are unable to withstand the rigors of competition seek escape into the military. Enlisted men especially are viewed as placing individual security ahead of competitive achievement. (Janowitz and Little, 1965, p. 52)

The fact that some may view enlistees in this light does not establish lack of ambition as a motive for enlistment. It may be that some unambitious men in need of job security do enlist, but it is not clear that the unambitious are attracted to military service in unusually large proportions.

A series of questions in both the tenth and twelfth grade interviews can be used to characterize the ambitiousness of a young man's attitude toward working. These can be used to test the "unambitiousness hypothesis" in the Youth in Transition sample. The items are the same ones used in making the MIL-FIT measure described in the last chapter. However, here they are used in an attitude index, while in MIL-FIT they served as weights in the construc-

73

tion of a measure of fit with military service.
The appropriate items appear in Table 5-1. A respondent was asked to
consider the kind of job he would like to have. He was then presented with

TABLE 5-1

Job Attitudes Related to Attempted
Enlistment for Total Sample
(Twelfth Grade Measures)

Questionnaire Item	Very Important	Pretty Important	A Little Important	Not Important	Total	Eta
PREFERENCE FOR "A JOB THAT DOESN'T BUG ME"						
C1. A job where there's no one to boss me on the work	8.8 *194*	10.1 *695*	12.3 *593*	16.0 *206*	11.4 *1688*	.066
C4. A job where I don't have to work too hard	15.7 *115*	7.5 *411*	10.5 *759*	15.7 *400*	11.4 *1685*	.098
C7. A job where I don't have to take a lot of responsibility	13.8 *94*	8.5 *328*	11.8 *692*	12.0 *573*	11.4 *1687*	.046
C8. A job that leaves me a lot of free time to do what I want to do	11.3 *266*	9.1 *640*	11.1 *613*	21.3 *169*	11.4 *1688*	.109
C10. A job that my friends think a lot of -- has class	7.5 *199*	10.4 *479*	12.6 *651*	13.0 *355*	11.5 *1684*	.055
C13. A job that doesn't make me learn a lot of new things	9.4 *85*	9.1 *186*	10.7 *589*	12.7 *829*	11.4 *1689*	.041
PREFERENCE FOR "A JOB THAT PAYS OFF"						
C3. A job where I can learn new things, learn new skills	12.9 *855*	10.0 *692*	11.7 *120*	0.0 *14*	11.5 *1681*	.054
C6. A job with good chances for getting ahead	11.4 *1036*	11.8 *535*	15.7 *70*	4.0 *25*	11.6 *1666*	.040
C9. A job where the pay is good	13.2 *958*	8.9 *609*	12.1 *99*	6.7 *15*	11.5 *1681*	.065
C11. A job that uses my skill and abilities -- lets me do the things I can do best	12.1 *976*	10.6 *578*	10.2 *118*	9.1 *11*	11.4 *1683*	.026
C12. A job that has nice friendly people to work with	10.8 *779*	11.9 *740*	8.3 *145*	33.3 *21*	11.3 *1685*	.084

5377

NOTE: Percent attempting to enlist from each category in bold face type;
percentage base in italics.

the list of job traits shown in the table and asked to indicate for each one its importance to him in the choice of a job. Using Cluster Analysis, two sub-scales were identified.[1] These were given names which connoted the apparent meaning of each cluster. Preference for a "job that doesn't bug me" applies to those items in which respondents could indicate the importance of finding an easy job that did not demand too much. Preference for a "job that pays off" summarizes items in which respondents could indicate the importance of having a job where they could get ahead, earn good money, and learn a lot of new things.

Table 5-1 shows for each scale category the number who endorsed it and the percent of that number who tried to enlist. The last column contains the eta statistic summarizing the relationship of responses on that particular item to attempted enlistment. The items under a "job that pays off" show little or no association with enlistment. The etas are not significant, and the enlistment rates across categories show no interpretable patterning. The items under preference for a "job that doesn't bug me" show a slightly stronger association; the pattern for enlistments is more interpretable in that it is closer to being monotonic. The more concerned a young man is to find a job that is easy, the *less* likely he is to enlist.

These relationships can be seen more clearly using the indexes shown in Table 5-2. Included in this table are identical measures from both the tenth and twelfth grade interviews. Consider first the analyses based on the total sample. As seen in the case of the individual items, there is little association between the Payoff index and enlistment. This is true for both tenth and twelfth grade measures. For the Bug-me index there is little or no association in tenth grade (eta = .040); but by twelfth grade this dimension acquires some importance.

Eliminating the college-goers from the analyses unmasks some relation-ships. The Payoff indexes continue to be less important, but the Bug-me in-dexes discriminate more sharply between those enlisting and those taking civilian jobs. This is true for the attitude measures collected as early as tenth grade. Those who were desirous of jobs that were easy and undemanding en-listed much less frequently. The trend is heightened in twelfth grade where those scoring high in need for an easy job enlisted only one-third as fre-quently. The consistency of the tenth and twelfth grade data support the in-terpretation that an individual's attitude about easy *vs.* demanding jobs is established by early adolescence and is not subject to extensive change over the high school years. This job orientation serves to a small extent as a motive for one kind of post-high school job choice, namely the choice of military ser-vice.

What are the implications of these findings for the "unambitiousness" thesis described by Janowitz? The unambitious are attracted to military ser-vice, but so are the ambitious. For the Payoff index the distribution of enlist-ments across the measure is very flat. But, while the rate may be the same for those who are low and high in ambitiousness, there are many more respon-dents at the high-ambitiousness end of the scale. A look at Table 5-2 shows

TABLE 5-2

Job Attitude Indexes Related to Enlistment

Index	Unimportant (1)	(2)	(3)	(4)	Important (5)	Total	Eta
TOTAL SAMPLE							
1. Job That Pays Off (Tenth grade measure)	19.7 *147*	11.6 *232*	*	10.8 *701*	10.6 *639*	11.6 *1719*	.078
2. Job That Pays Off (Twelfth grade measure)	10.8 *158*	9.8 *295*	*	10.9 *761*	13.7 *468*	11.5 *1682*	.045
3. Job That Does Not Bug Me (Tenth grade measure)	13.8 *58*	12.6 *294*	12.3 *588*	9.7 *497*	12.1 *282*	11.6 *1719*	.040
4. Job That Does Not Bug Me (Twelfth grade measure)	24.5 *94*	13.2 *462*	9.8 *655*	9.1 *364*	10.5 *114*	11.4 *1689*	.112
NON-COLLEGE ONLY							
5. Job That Pays Off (Tenth grade measure)	26.7 *101*	21.5 *121*	*	23.1 *308*	22.3 *283*	23.0 *813*	.036
6. Job That Pays Off (Twelfth grade measure)	19.0 *84*	21.0 *138*	*	22.2 *342*	26.0 *227*	22.8 *791*	.054
7. Job That Does Not Bug Me (Tenth grade measure)	29.6 *27*	32.4 *105*	26.5 *253*	18.1 *254*	18.4 *174*	23.0 *813*	.127
8. Job That Does Not Bug Me (Twelfth grade measure)	45.8 *48*	26.9 *208*	23.0 *265*	15.0 *206*	14.5 *69*	22.6 *796*	.182

5377

NOTE: Each index is a mean of the appropriate items, bracketed for display purposes. The Bug-me indexes have four brackets and the payoff five due only to a different bracketing procedure. Percent attempting to enlist from each category in bold face type; percentage base in italics.

that about three-quarters of the sample are in the top two categories of the Payoff index (lines 2, 6). Thus, a very high proportion of those who enlist are looking ultimately for a good job that will have a high personal payoff.

A similar generalization can be made based on the Bug-me indexes. Some of those looking for an easy job do enlist; but only 23 percent of the total group who enlisted were in the top two categories of the Bug-me index (lines 4, 8 in Table 5-2). Thus, those most likely to want to avoid the rigors of competition comprised less than one-quarter of the group who enlisted.

In sum, it appears that the unambitious do enlist, but that their numbers are small in comparison with those who, in the long run, are seeking a good job that has a high payoff and which provides a challenge to work hard, take responsibility and acquire and use new skills.

Vietnam Attitudes

One of the measures of interest in the previous chapter was an individual's perceived fit with a military type of job, where the job was defined in very general terms. A related dimension is the individual's attitude toward the specific object of that military job. In 1969 the armed forces were engaged in a variety of activities around the globe, but the central military activity in the minds of the public was armed combat in Vietnam. It seems likely that attitudes about this specific conflict would have influenced a young man's enlistment decision.

The first attempt to assess the Vietnam attitudes of the Youth in Transition sample was in 1969 when the typical panel member was a high-school senior. The six questions that were used appear in Table 5-3. The first two items asked respondents to assess the War in terms of this country's national interests. The third item asked them about the importance of the War to fight communism. The last two items asked them to assess the War's importance to America in terms of maintaining our international integrity. With appropriate reversals these six items were combined into a single index which is displayed in Figure 5-1. The bar in the center is made up of a group that can perhaps best be described as neutral on the issue, since their responses indicated a mixture of support and disagreement. The bars on the left represent those who tended to support U.S. policy in Vietnam; in spring of 1969 they totalled 40 percent. The bars to the right of center represent respondents who disagreed with basic U.S. policy, and these numbered 20 percent. In the spring of 1969 these high school seniors seemed to be more in support of the War than opposed to it, although a large group was centered in the neutral category.

The relationship of Vietnam attitudes to enlistment is displayed in Table 5-4. The association in the total sample is close to monotonic, with those supporting Vietnam policy being much more likely to enlist, and those holding views antithetical to the cause for which they might have to fight being less inclined to enlist. The eta-value is not very high (.133), so these attitudes cannot be interpreted as a very strong factor in the enlistment decision.

When those who went on to college were eliminated from the analysis (see the right-hand two columns of Table 5-4), the shape of the distribution remained the same, and the strength of association increased slightly. This last point raises some interesting questions. Are not the college-goers more strongly opposed to the War than the non-college group? If so, shouldn't the relationship of the Vietnam Dissent Index to enlisting be weaker within the non-college group? There are two answers to the first question. At the end of senior year of high school there was little difference in Vietnam dissent scores between those who later went on to college and those who did not. One year later this was not the case; those who did not continue their education beyond

TABLE 5-3

Items Comprising the
Vietnam Dissent Index
(Spring-Summer 1969)

Do you agree or disagree with each of the following statements?

		Percentage Frequencies				
N=1799		Strongly Agree (1)	Agree (2)	Disagree (3)	Strongly Disagree (4)	Missing Data (9)
a.*	Fighting the war in Vietnam is damaging to our national honor or pride	10	37	43	8	2
b.*	Fighting the war in Vietnam is really not in the national interest	9	35	46	8	2
c.	Fighting the war in Vietnam is important to fight the spread of Communism	20	54	21	4	2
d.*	Fighting the war in Vietnam is bringing us closer to world war	14	51	31	2	2
e.	Fighting the war in Vietnam is important to protect friendly countries	12	55	27	3	3
f.	Fighting the war in Vietnam is important to show other nations that we keep our promises	14	53	26	5	3

NOTE: Cell entries are the response distribution for each item.
*These items were reversed in the construction of the index.

high school held about the same attitudes on the Vietnam issue, but the college-goers shifted to an appreciably more dissenting stance. Thus, the anti-War position so often associated with college-goers is something that developed largely during the first year of college. The lack of difference in senior year of high school explains why the association of Vietnam dissent to enlisting did not become weaker when the college-goers were eliminated from the analysis. The fact that Vietnam attitudes did relate to enlistment and that college-goers became more dissenting suggests that later enlistment decisions of those who pursued any form of post-high school education will be affected by events in Vietnam; decisions like whether to join ROTC, enter OCS, or simply enlist as a regular in one of the several branches of service.[2]

Another issue that was explored was the potential interaction of

FIGURE 5-1
Distribution of Scores on the
Vietnam Dissent Index

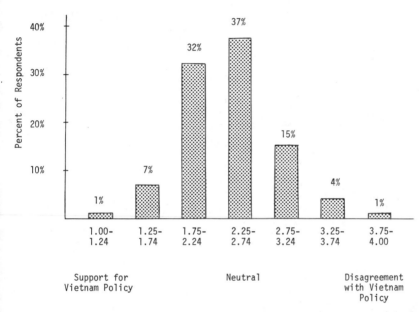

Support for   Neutral   Disagreement
Vietnam Policy   with Vietnam
                                                          Policy

Vietnam attitudes with the MIL-FIT measure examined in the previous
chapter. The reasoning was this. It was possible that the way in which Vietnam attitudes have their effect is to negate the impact of perceived fit with
military service among those who are strongly against the War. Thus, among
the Vietnam dissenters, enlistments would be flat across the various levels of
MIL-FIT; but among those who supported the War, MIL-FIT would show
the same monotonic relationship seen for the total sample. This turned out
not to be the case. Of the total variance for which these two variables could
account, only six percent could be attributed to interaction. It was concluded,
then, that their effect is basically additive.

Entering the two measures into an MCA analysis shows the relative
strength of the two measures, ignoring the small amount of interaction. The
diagram in Figure 5-2 presents the findings. Most of the variance in enlistment behavior is attributable to the unique effects of MIL-FIT; i.e., to how
an individual feels about his fit with a military service type of job. The impact
of Vietnam attitudes is only a small fraction of this, and most of this is variance that is shared with the MIL-FIT measure.

TABLE 5-4

Vietnam Dissent Index (12th Grade)
Related to Attempted Enlistment

Category	--------Total Sample--------		------Non-College Only------	
	Percent of Sample (N=1678)	Percent of Category That Tried to Enlist	Percent of Sample (N=790)	Percent of Category That Tried to Enlist
1 Support Vietnam Policy	5%	22.2%	5%	44.4%
2	8	14.4	9	27.5
3	27	14.4	27	28.8
4 Neutral	29	12.0	33	21.3
5	17	5.6	15	12.6
6	8	8.6	7	17.5
7 Disagree with Vietnam Policy	6 —— 100	4.3	4 —— 100	11.8
	Grand Mean = 11.6% Eta = .133 Eta-square = .018		Grand Mean = 22.9% Eta = .179 Eta-square = .032	

5376

Multivariate Prediction

Neither of the two predictors in this chapter is strongly related to attempted enlistment. In terms of variance accounted for, "job that doesn't bug me" accounted for 1.4 percent and Vietnam attitudes 1.7 percent. Recall from the previous chapter that each of the three motives by itself was able to account for at least 10 percent of the variance.

Table 5-5 shows the results of several Multiple Classification Analyses. The first run included only the job attitudes and Vietnam attitudes. Comparing the eta-square and beta-square figures for each predictor, it can be seen that MCA made only minor adjustments when using them in a joint prediction to the criterion. This indicates that they are mostly orthogonal, and that they overlap very little in their prediction of attempted enlistment.

Run 3 shows the result of adding these two variables on top of the three motives. Overall they improve the prediction by less than one percentage point (.329—.321). A comparison of the beta-squares for Run 1 and Run 3 shows that it is the impact of Vietnam Dissent that is most reduced in the joint prediction. A separate correlational analysis indicated that the reason

FIGURE 5-2

Venn Diagram of Variance in Attempted Enlistments
Accounted for by MIL-FIT and Vietnam Dissent Index

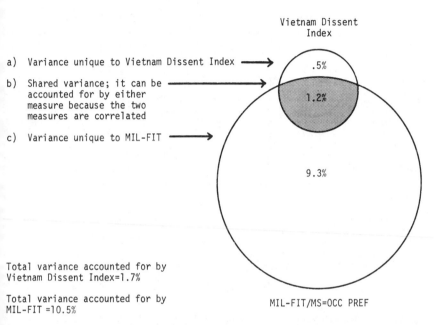

Vietnam Dissent
Index

a) Variance unique to Vietnam Dissent Index ⟶   .5%

b) Shared variance; it can be ⟶
   accounted for by either
   measure because the two
   measures are correlated   1.2%

c) Variance unique to MIL-FIT ⟶

9.3%

Total variance accounted for by
Vietnam Dissent Index=1.7%

Total variance accounted for by
MIL-FIT =10.5%   MIL-FIT/MS=OCC PREF

for this is a moderate correlation of Vietnam Dissent with MIL-FIT
($r = -.23$).

When the MCAs were repeated for the non-college subsample (the data
are not shown), there was a sizeable increase in prediction to five percent
(Mult. R^2) overall for the two predictors in combination. Adding the motives,
however, produced the same results as in the total sample. For the non-
college group, these two attitude dimensions accounted for only one percent
additional variance beyond what the three motives could account for.

Summary and Conclusions

In this chapter two potential conditioning factors were examined. One is
attitude toward jobs and the other is feeling about U.S. policy on the War in
Vietnam. Two measures were used to describe job ambition: desire for a job
that pays off and desire for a job that is easy and undemanding. Job payoff was
found to be unrelated to enlistment. But those looking for an easy job were
much less likely to enlist than those who were unconcerned about this aspect of
a job. This was especially true in the non-college subsample. Apparently a

TABLE 5-5

Multiple Classification Analyses of
Motive and Attitude Variables
Predicting to Attempted Enlistment

Motive Predictors	Predicting From Each Characteristic Separately		Predicting From Several Characteristics Simultaneously		
	Eta^2		Run 1	Run 2	Run 3
				$Beta^2$	
MIL-FIT/MS=OCC PREFERENCE	.105		*	.031	.029
MS-PLANS/INDECISION	.274		*	.190	.185
DRAFT STATUS	.142		*	.025	.025
JOB THAT DOESN'T BUG ME	.014		.013	*	.011
VIETNAM DISSENT	.017		.016	*	.003
MULT R (adjusted)			.154	.567	.574
MULT R^2 (adjusted)			.024	.321	.329

5395

*Indicates that this variable was not included in this run.

tolerance for hard work is a predisposing factor for enlistment.

Attitude toward the War showed a weak association with the enlistment decision but in the expected direction. Those opposed to the War were less likely to enlist. These attitudes were found to shift considerably during the year following high school for those who entered post-high school educational environments. This suggests that attitudes about Vietnam might become a more important factor in enlistment decisions in later years, especially among those who went to college.

The lack of a stronger association for these two measures is supportive of the notion that military service is attractive to a broad spectrum of youth with varying outlooks on work and the War.

---

[1]See Bachman, 1970, for details on the items and their interrelationships.

[2]A more detailed discussion of Vietnam attitudes and the shifts that occurred between the end of senior year and one year later can be found in Chapter 12.

CHAPTER 6

SCHOLASTIC ABILITY AND SCHOOL EXPERIENCES

How do a young man's abilities and behaviors in school relate to his disposition for enlistment? Bachman et al., (1971) found that aptitude, academic performance, and school experiences are related to whether or not a young man goes to college. And, of course, those who enter college directly after high school do not at the same time enlist for active duty. Therefore, one would expect that enlistment soon after high school would occur least often among high ability and scholastically successful young men—the very ones who are most likely to go on to college. In short, anything strongly related to college entrance is likely to show an inverse relationship to attempted enlistment.

But what about those who do not go on to college? If the analyses are limited to non-college-goers, do school-related abilities and behaviors help in the prediction of enlistment? Are enlistees any more or less intelligent than their job-bound classmates? Is their experience in high school any more or less successful or happy? To answer these questions this chapter will focus on six dimensions: scholastic aptitude (intelligence), classroom grades, school failure (being held back a grade), school curriculum, delinquency in school and attitudes toward school.

In previous chapters the focus has been on vocational choices during the year after the date when the majority of the sample graduated from high school (June 1969). Excluded from analyses have been all high school dropouts who enlisted (N=56) or attempted to enlist (N=24) prior to this time. The reasoning for this is that this study is mainly concerned with the relationship of measures collected in twelfth grade to later enlistment behavior. However, in this chapter there are several predictors which were measured earlier, such as intelligence and junior high grades. When examining the relationship of such measures to enlistment it will occasionally be useful to show a parallel prediction to a different criterion: "enlisted or attempted to enlist at any time after the beginning of tenth grade."

Scholastic Aptitude

General Aptitude Test Battery—Part J: Vocabulary (GATB-J). This test is part of the well standardized multi-factor test battery developed by the U.S. Employment Service for vocational counseling (Super, 1957). The entire test and the vocabulary subscale in particular are significantly related to other measures of intelligence, including the Otis, California (CTMM), and Army General Classification Test (AGCT).[1] The vocabulary subscale measures verbal aptitude as well as intelligence. This test was administered in the tenth grade to the entire sample. Their average age at this time was 15. Because of the presumed stability of intelligence scores, the test was not repeated in later data collections.

As usual, to facilitate data presentation, scores were bracketed into five categories. Since many readers may be more familiar with the Armed Forces Qualification Test (AFQT) than with the GATB test, the figures in Table 6-1 may prove helpful. This table shows the distribution of the Youth in Transition sample of males on the GATB compared with the distribution of all males aged 19-21 on the AFQT. (The AFQT is a successor to the AGCT with which the GATB-J correlates highly.[2]) "Mental Groups" is the term associated with bracketed scores on the AFQT. The purpose of this comparison is to show that the GATB-J bracketing results in a very similar distribution.

TABLE 6-1

Comparison of GATB-J Scores with Army
"Mental Group" Scores

| GATB-J Bracket | ----------Youth in Transition Sample----------| | ----DoD Sample[+]--- | |
	Tenth Grade Total Sample (N=2213)	Twelfth Grade Respondents** (N=1799)	Mental Group	Males 19-21
1 Low	9%	8%	V Low	8%
2	25	23	IV*	20
3	31	30	III	37
4	25	28	II⎱ High	35
5 High	10	11	I⎰	
	100	100		100

5376

[+]"Normal Male Population, Ages 19-21." Department of Defense (1966), p. 12.d.5.

*This is the lowest acceptable mental category for military service.

**This is the distribution of tenth-grade scores on the GATB-J for those participating in the study at the end of twelfth grade.

This does not make the two classifications fully comparable, since the YIT sample is not as comprehensive as the one used to establish the mental groups. YIT includes only boys who got as far in their education as the tenth grade, and thus fails to represent some proportion of the male population which dropped out of school prior to this grade. The lowest ability group on the GATB probably included some in the bottom of Mental Group IV as well as a majority who are actually Mental Group V. Otherwise, the groupings are fairly equivalent.

The relationship of the GATB-J to enlisting is shown in Table 6-2. The two left-hand columns show the relationship in the total sample at the end of twelfth grade. The overall strength of association is moderate to weak (eta = .123) but the trend is clear. For the higher levels of intelligence, enlistments are much less frequent.

The enlistment rate for category one—the lowest intelligence group—is much lower than the trend line would suggest. The explanation for this derives from the particular criterion being used. Dropouts who enlisted or attempted to enlist while their former classmates were still in high school are not included in this criterion. Table 6-3 shows the result of using the expanded criterion of attempted enlistment any time after the beginning of tenth grade. The column showing total attempted enlistments displays the monotonic relationship that was expected, with those lowest in intelligence attempting to enlist more frequently. The table also shows the rate of enlist-

TABLE 6-2

GATB-J Test of Intelligence Related to
Attempted Enlistment After High School

Category	--------Total Sample-------- Percent of Sample (N=1717)	Percent of Category That Tried to Enlist	------Non-College Only------ Percent of Sample (N=812)	Percent of Category That Tried to Enlist
1 Low	8%	14.2%	14%	15.9%
2	23	16.3	33	23.9
3	30	13.3	32	25.4
4	28	7.9	18	22.1
5 High	11	4.7	3	26.9
	100		100	

Grand Mean = 11.6%   Grand Mean = 23.0
Eta = .123   Eta = .074
Eta-square = .015   Eta-square = .005

5376

TABLE 6-3

GATB-J Test of Intelligence Related to
Both Actual and Attempted Enlistments
at Any Time After the Beginning of Tenth Grade

| Category | Percent of Sample (N=1923)* | --------------Percent of Category-------------- | | |
		Actual Enlistments	Attempted (but rejected) Enlistments	Total Enlistments (Actual + Attempted)
1 Low	8%	13.6%	8.7%	22.3%
2	25	17.5	2.8	20.3
3	31	13.7	1.6	15.3
4	26	8.8	0.6	9.4
5 High	10	3.0	2.0	5.0
	100			

5407

NOTE: This is the only table that distinguishes between successful and unsuccessful enlistment attempts. In all other tables, the column title, "Percent of Category That Tried to Enlist" includes both types and is thus equivalent to the right hand column.

*Excluded from this table are (1) those who were drafted, joined the National Guard or Reserves, or entered a military academy; (2) those for whom no information was available on their status as of the summer of 1970.

ment rejections. As could be forecast, the lowest group on the GATB-J had the highest rejection rate by a factor of at least three.

Return now to the data in Table 6-2. The right-hand two columns display the results of repeating the analysis for those who did not go on to advanced education. The strength of association is reduced to a non-significant level (eta = .074) and the distribution of enlistment attempts is quite flat, if Category One is ignored. The rates of enlistment are all within three percentage points of 24 percent and the distribution shows no interpretable pattern. The analyses were repeated, changing the criterion to enlistment at any time after the beginning of tenth grade, and the results were almost identical. Our conclusion from these findings is that aptitude predicts to whether or not individuals will choose to enter college, but it says very little about whether non-college types will enter a job or enlist in the service. We prefer to interpret this as indicating that high intelligence predisposes young men to further education rather than saying that it leads to a distaste for military service. This interpretation is based not on this analysis alone, but on the fact that a number of measures which are highly correlated with intelligence, such as classroom grades and socioeconomic status, predict to college entrance in the same way. These will be discussed later.

The nature of the draft laws in 1969 might qualify this interpretation somewhat. At that time a young man could avoid (or at least postpone) being drafted by pursuing almost any form of post-high school education. Consequently, many young men may have chosen college in order to avoid the draft. It is certainly difficult to discern the motives for college attendance. However, this much is known; when asked a year after high school why they went to college, twenty percent of the college group identified avoiding the draft among the three most important reasons.[3] Whether these individuals would have gone on to further schooling had there been no draft is impossible to determine with the data in this study.

The variables examined in the remainder of this chapter all have to do with school success and failure. They include such measures as school failure prior to high school, dropping out during high school, classroom grades, delinquency in school, and attitudes toward school. These variables were selected for examination because they were thought to encompass the major dimensions of what might be called school fit. Underlying their selection was the hypothesis that failure in school or a feeling of alienation toward scholastic activities would make young men more receptive to severing ties with their home environment and making a fresh start. True, simply entering a job is a large step towards independence; it offers a chance to prove oneself in an environment where success is more within reach of the less intelligent, and the reward (money) may be more satisfying than high grades and praise. Nonetheless, military service offers a more dramatic chance to start fresh in an activity that in past decades has been widely respected and held somewhat in awe by adults and peers alike. It is as though taking a job is an easy way out for the school misfit, while military service provides another chance to prove one's worth despite a drab performance in school. The measures examined in the next sections of this chapter will be used to evaluate the thesis that poor performance or "fit" with school serves as a motive for choosing to enlist in the service after high school.

Average Classroom Grades

Classroom grades are the best indicators available of academic achievement during high school. Information on grades was gathered in a questionnaire using the following question: "What is the average grade you have been getting in your classes this year? Putting them all together, how do your grades average out?"[4] The relationship of grades to enlistment is summarized in Table 6-4. Within the total sample (left-hand two columns) the shape of the distribution is very similar to that for intelligence. Seniors with the lowest average grades enlisted most frequently. The rate remains high up through the grade of C+, then drops precipitously for the 49 percent of the sample with grades of B− or better. Those not in school at the end of twelfth grade ended up enlisting at a rate slightly higher than the average. These dropouts will be examined in more detail shortly.

Again, the findings can be explained most parsimoniously by noting the

TABLE 6-4

Average Grades in Twelfth Grade
Related to Attempted Enlistment

Category	-------Total Sample------ Percent of Sample (N=1649)	Percent of Category That Tried to Enlist	------Non-College Only------ Percent of Sample (N=762)	Percent of Category That Tried to Enlist
1 E to D	2%	20.5%	5%	22.2%
2 D+ to C-	10	17.8	16	22.2
3 C to C+	32	17.0	37	30.0
4 B- to B	29	7.3	20	19.4
5 B+ to A+	20	5.0	8	25.4
6 Not in school at the end of twelfth grade	7	13.2	14	13.9
	100		100	

Grand Mean = 11.6%   Grand Mean = 23.6
Eta = .169   Eta = .135
Eta-square = .029   Eta-square = .018

5376

relationship of grades to college entrance. Less than one percent of the D average students went on to college while 81 percent of those with an A average did. College is simply the first preference of the high academic performers. When the college-goers are eliminated from the analysis, the curve flattens out; enlistments came as frequently from those with grades above C+ as it did from those with grades below C. The only rate that is appreciably higher is the one for boys in the very middle of the range, C to C+. The eta-value of .135 is largely due to the deviance of the dropout category and not to the differences among the first five categories.

These analyses were repeated for average grades in ninth grade predicting to enlistment at any time after the beginning of tenth grade. The same pattern emerged, both for the total sample and for the non-college subsample.

One other hypothesis was considered. This concerned the interaction of ninth and twelfth grade performance. It was thought that young men whose grades dropped appreciably between these two years would be especially prone to enlist. This group would be the ones most likely to have aspired to college while in ninth grade, but who would have discovered in the later years of high school that they could not do the calibre of work necessary for admission. The choice of military service as an alternative to college would be prompted by the desire to avoid admitting to family and friends that they simply could not "make the grade" for college and the types of jobs that college opens up. A period of time in the service would allow them to think things over. At the same time they could be doing something that would have general community approval; thus they could avoid the embarrassment that would accompany a college-prep student choosing a menial job immediately after high school.

The data are shown in Table 6-5. It was expected that some of the highest enlistment rates would be in the four cells in the lower left corner of the table. These represent those whose grades fell from the A-B range down to the C-E range. It was assumed that this would correspond to dropping from acceptable to unacceptable for admission to most colleges. The N in two of these cells is too small to place much confidence in the estimate of the enlistment rate; but in the other two the rate is very close to the mean, 12.1 percent and 14.2 percent.

In the summary statistics the table is collapsed into 3 groups, depending on whether grades went up, down, or remained the same over the three years. The rate of enlistment was higher for those whose grades went up than down. In sum, there seems little support for the hypothesis. The relationship of grades to enlistment is moderate, and important only in their ability to predict to college entrance. The even distribution across grades when the college-goers are eliminated suggests that there is a very broad range of ability among enlistees.

Failing a Grade Prior to High School

A clear indication of school failure is being held back a grade. Much more dramatic than a poor report card, it separates a young man from the rest of his classmates and labels him clearly as a failure. Such an experience might be a motive for enlistment because such an individual is likely to desire some of the success experiences he has missed in school. Military service could provide a chance to prove oneself in non-academic areas.

In the Youth in Transition sample, 24 percent of the boys had been held back at least one grade by the time they started tenth grade in 1966. The relationship to attempted enlistment is shown in Table 6-6. Those who were held back enlisted three times as frequently as their classmates. The strength of association is high, eta=.205 in the total sample. The relationship is almost as strong within the non-college subsample, suggesting that this measure discriminates between those who choose a job and those who enlist.

However, there is a more compelling explanation for this finding than the failure syndrome. It is hard to imagine that failure in elementary or junior high school could have quite this strong an influence on this particular choice. A more parsimonious explanation derives from earlier findings on draft status (Chapter 4). Recall that those who were old for their grade level were much more likely to enlist (Table 4-17). In fact, the rate for those older than 19 was very close to the rate for those who failed a grade. To have failed one or more grades, then, meant in 1969 that a young man was much more

TABLE 6-5

Interaction of Classroom Grades from
Ninth and Twelfth Grades
Predicting to Attempted Enlistment
After High School

		Twelfth Grade			
		E to C-	C to C+	B- to B	B+ to A+
Ninth Grade	E to C-	25.5 *51*	28.3 *53*	(4.7) *21*	(0.0) *12*	27.7 *137*
	C to C+	10.2 *108*	14.4 *270*	11.6 *147*	17.0 *41*	13.1 *566*
	B- to B	(28.6) *21*	14.2 *162*	5.3 *227*	5.3 *94*	9.1 *504*
	B+ to A+	(25.0) *4*	12.1 *33*	5.1 *79*	2.6 *191*	4.6 *307*
		16.8 *184*	15.6 *518*	7.17 *474*	5.0 *338*	

10.7%

Missing Data: N = 204, Rate = 10.6%

SUMMARY STATISTICS

	N	%	%-Enlisting			
Grades up:	368	24	14.7			Variance Accounted for*
Grades static:	739	49	9.3		Main effects + interaction	.040
Grades down:	407	27	12.1		Main effects only	.030

5395

*NOTE: "Main effects + interaction" derived from a 17-category pattern variable
predicting to attempted enlistment; "main effects only" derived from an MCA
using two grades measures separately. Both estimates were adjusted for degrees
of freedom.

likely to be drafted by virtue of his being a year or more older than his classmates. In the absence of any other evidence, draft vulnerability, rather than
compensation for failure, seems the most parsimonious explanation for the
observed relationship.

Dropping Out of High School

Yet another indication of failure, even more pronounced and apparent,

TABLE 6-6

School Failure Prior to Tenth Grade
Related to Attempted Enlistment
After High School

Category	--------Total Sample--------		------Non-College Only------	
	Percent of Sample (N=1718)	Percent of Category That Tried to Enlist	Percent of Sample (N=812)	Percent of Category That Tried to Enlist
1. Never held back, grades 1-9.	82%	8.5%	70%	18.7%
2. Held back one or more times, grades 1-9.	18	25.4	30	32.8
	100		100	

Grand Mean = 11.6%   Grand Mean = 22.9%
Eta = .205   Eta = .152
Eta-square = .042   Eta-square = .023

5378

is dropping out of school. To drop out is to admit to an inability to derive a meaningful experience from the school environment. Assuming that some sense of shame derives from the act of dropping out, such an individual would have good reason to want to get away from the community in which his failure occurred and at the same time find an environment in which he could both be secure and make a new start. Again, military service would seem to offer this opportunity.

To look at the effect of dropping out it is necessary to use the criterion of enlisting any time after the beginning of tenth grade, since many dropouts who enlisted did so shortly after leaving school. Table 6-7 presents the data. Dropouts did attempt to enlist at a rate that is higher than "stayins" who graduated from high school but did not go on to further education. This does provide some support for the alienation hypothesis, but it is a relationship that is important only with the expanded criterion. Two-thirds of the dropouts who enlisted by the end of this study had already done so by the time the Class of 1969 graduated. Thus, using the criterion of enlistment after high school, a *smaller* proportion of dropouts enlisted than did stayins. (The dropouts who enlisted are the subject of Appendix C.)

Rebellious Behavior in School

In tenth grade a questionnaire segment consisting of 13 items asked respondents to report how frequently they engaged in disruptive behavior in

TABLE 6-7

Educational Attainment Related to
Enlistment at Any Time After the
Beginning of Tenth Grade

Category	--------Total Sample-------		------Non-College Only-----	
	Percent of Sample (N=1918)	Percent of Category That Tried to Enlist[†]	Percent of Sample (N=1016)	Percent of Category That Tried to Enlist
1. High School Dropout	14%	31.2%	26%	31.2%
2. High School Stayin/no further education	39	22.7	74	22.7
3. High School Stayin/entered post high school educa- tion**	47	2.1	*	*
	100		100	
	Grand Mean = 14.2 Eta = .336 Eta-square = .112		Grand Mean = 24.9 Eta = .086 Eta-square = .007	

5407

**Includes all respondents who entered any form of post high school education. Some of these completed their program or dropped out of college by the summer of 1970.

†The percent of the Dropout group who were rejected for enlistment was 5.6 percent; for stayins it was 2.8 percent; and for the college group it was 1.0.

school, broke the rules, or did poor school work. The items covered such topics as fighting and arguing with other students, goofing off in class so others couldn't work, coming late to school or class, skipping class, coming unprepared, copying assignments, and cheating on tests. Each item asked the respondent to indicate how often he did each thing, using a scale ranging from "almost always" to "never." (These questions were not asked in the twelfth grade interview.)

Items such as these were thought to be indicators of the extent to which a person feels he fits the academic environment. Certainly some variability in these behaviors depends on whether one's peers are approving or disapproving of them; but to a large extent, variation should correspond to one's reactions to the whole school environment. When an index of these items was used to predict to enlistment any time after tenth grade there was virtually no association. The small hint of a pattern showed that in the total sample enlistees came more frequently from among the rebellious; but in the non-college subsample they came more frequently from among the conforming students.

(While not elaborated on here, it should be noted that none of the other measures of delinquency available in the Youth in Transition data bank related to enlistment in any strong or interpretable fashion. These measures include "frequency of delinquent behavior," "seriousness of delinquent behavior," and "interpersonal aggression" [see Bachman, 1970, for a description of the measures]. On the average they predict to attempted enlistment after high school with a strength of association of about eta=.10 in the total sample and eta=.11 in the non-college subsample. The relationships are non-linear but show a slight tendency for greater enlistments to come from those more frequently delinquent but involved in less serious delinquent behaviors. When the college-goers [the least delinquent of all] are eliminated from the analyses, there is a very slight downward shift, with attempted enlistment being more frequently among the less delinquent. The one exception to this is for dropouts who enlist. Compared with other dropouts, dropout enlistees were more delinquent, both inside and outside of school. This is detailed more in Appendix C.)

Attitudes Toward School

Another measure of a young man's response to school is the attitude he expresses toward school activities. A number of items were asked which were later combined into two summary measures of school attitudes. These were described in Volume II of the Youth in Transition Series.

The first index, which we have termed positive school attitudes, contains items that stress the intrinsic value of education; for example, 'I think school is important, not only for the practical value, but because learning itself is very worthwhile.' . . . Every one of the items is endorsed by at least three-quarters of the respondents, who say they feel this way either 'pretty much' or 'very much.' It should be noted that the items possess a great deal of social acceptability—they sound like the right thing to say, and it may be that some of our respondents are inclined to tell us what they think we want to hear. . . .

The second index, termed negative school attitudes, consists of eight items ranging from general dissatisfaction ('School is very boring for me, and I'm not learning what I feel is important') to a devaluation of school in comparison to other sources of experience ('A real education comes from your own experience and not from the things you learn in school'). The items indicating general dissatisfaction received little endorsement, on the whole, while the items stressing the relative superiority of experience outside school were endorsed more often. . . .

The two scales are, of course, inversely related; the product-moment correlation between them is −.51. (Bachman, 1970, pp. 106-108)

TABLE 6-8

Positive School Attitudes in Twelfth
Grade Related to Attempted Enlistment
After High School

| Category | ---------Total Sample--------- | | -------Non-College Only------- | |
	Percent of Sample (N=1512)*	Percent of Category That Tried to Enlist	Percent of Sample (N=643)*	Percent of Category That Tried to Enlist
1 Low	28%	14.0%	38%	22.3
2	24	8.4	22	20.3
3	20	8.4	15	24.7
4	14	13.5	11	36.6
5 High	14	13.5	13	30.6
	100		100	

Grand Mean = 11.4%   Grand Mean = 24.9%
Eta = .084   Eta = .120
Eta-square = .007   Eta-square = .014

5388

*NOTE: School dropouts were not asked these questions.

The relationship of Positive School Attitudes in twelfth grade to attempted enlistment after high school is shown in Table 6-8. For the total sample there is virtually no association, and the pattern of relationships is uninterpretable. However, within the non-college subsample the association is larger and the pattern suggests that a greater percentage of enlistments come from those who have positive feelings about their school experiences. Unlike the findings for intelligence and grades, the strength of association is stronger within the non-college subsample than for the whole sample. This indicates that the strength of the predictor lies in its ability to discriminate enlistees from other non-college types.

The Negative School Attitudes measure shows a weak association with enlistment (Table 6-9). In addition there is no clear pattern of enlistment across the categories. Those with little negative feeling about school are as likely to enlist as those with strong negative feeling. There is a *slight* tendency for the least negative to enlist more frequently.

School Curriculum

One other school-related variable was examined. This is the curriculum in senior year of high school. In this study five curricula were distinguished: vocational, college prep, business, general and agricultural. One of the hypotheses about curriculum was that boys in the general curriculum would be most likely to enlist. The rationale was that these boys were not aiming for any specific goal like college or a technical job, so they would be most open to considering the service for purposes of vocational exploration. The data, however, do not support this theory. As Table 6-10 shows, it is the vocational curriculum that is associated with the highest rate of enlistment. This suggests that military service is viewed quite positively by those with a leaning toward vocational skills such as mechanics, etc. The next highest rate is associated with the general curriculum; but the rate is only a few percentage points higher than for business and agriculture. This certainly does not support an indecision theory.

Eliminating the college-goers from the analysis flattens out the distribution, except for the vocational types whose rate remains higher than the rest. Surprisingly, the college prep boys who do not go to college do not enlist any more frequently than any other group.

In the course of this chapter eight school-related measures have been examined and found to relate only moderately to enlistment after high school. Even this moderate association is reduced sharply when college-goers are eliminated from the analyses. In other words, most of these variables predict to enlistment *only* because they predict to college entrance.

TABLE 6-9

Negative School Attitudes in Twelfth Grade
Related to Attempted Enlistment
After High School

Category	---------Total Sample---------		-------Non-College Only-------	
	Percent of Sample (N=1511)*	Percent of Category That Tried to Enlist	Percent of Sample (N=642)*	Percent of Category That Tried to Enlist
1 Low	21%	11.3%	15%	34.3
2	28	6.8	19	23.3
3	24	12.6	27	23.6
4	15	13.8	19	22.8
5	8	17.2	14	24.4
6 High	4	16.1	6	20.0
	100		100	

	Grand Mean = 11.4	Grand Mean = 24.9
	Eta = .103	Eta = .096
	Eta-square = .011	Eta-square = .009

5388

*NOTE: School dropouts were not asked these questions.

TABLE 6-10

High School Curriculum (Twelfth Grade)
Related to Attempted Enlistment
After High School

Category	--------Total Sample--------- Percent of Sample (N=1600)*	Percent of Category That Tried to Enlist	-------Non-College Only------- Percent of Sample (N=721)*	Percent of Category That Tried to Enlist
Vocational	12%	21.5%	19%	29.1%
College Prep	46	5.0	20	20.8
Business	7	14.4	10	20.3
General	32	16.3	48	23.5
Agricultural	2	13.3	2	23.5
Other	1	(23.5)	1	(33.3)
	100		100	

Grand Mean = 11.6
Eta = .200
Eta-square = .040

Grand Mean = 23.9
Eta = .073
Eta-square = .005

5392

*NOTE: Dropouts not included in this measure.

Multivariate Prediction

Do these variables predict more powerfully to attempted enlistment when taken in combination? Considered as a set of measures, do they add explanatory power beyond what is already explainable by the three motive measures discussed in Chapter 4? These questions will be addressed in the following paragraphs.

For a number of reasons it was desirable to exclude some of the predictors from the multivariate analyses. One reason was that several of the measures reflect little more than the college/non-college distinction, so they shed very little light on the relationship of the high school experience to enlistment. For example, curriculum predicts to enlistment almost entirely because of its strong correlation with college plans. The aim, then, was to enter into an MCA the minimum number of measures that could adequately represent an individual's ability, school performance, and attitudes toward school with measures that did not correlate strongly with college entrance. The following list shows which ones were chosen.

RETAINED
1. GATB measure of intelligence

2. Average classroom grades, twelfth grade
3. Positive school attitudes

DROPPED
4. Negative school attitudes
5. Rebellious school behavior
6. Educational attainment (dropping out)
7. Failing a grade prior to high school
8. Curriculum

(4.) Negative school attitudes were dropped because the measure related so highly to Positive school attitudes ($r = -.51$). MCA can handle correlated predictors—indeed, this is one of its advantages as an analysis technique—but it has difficulty solving the underlying equations if measures are too highly correlated. (5.) Rebellious school behavior was not associated with enlisting in a bivariate prediction, and so could offer little in a multivariate equation. The last three measures on the list were eliminated because they were largely measures of the college/non-college distinction which was represented already in the DRAFT STATUS variable. (Recall that DRAFT STATUS is a combination of whether or not a person is permanently deferred, whether or not he has college plans, and his age.) (6.) Educational attainment was a trichotomy, one category of which was for college attainment; the other two categories distinguished between high school dropouts and high school stayins. When the college group was eliminated the association of the remaining dichotomy with enlistment was only .057 (eta). (7.) Failing a grade prior to high school was a measure which was captured in the age component of DRAFT STATUS—to be old for your grade was to have been held back a grade at some point. Finally, (8.) the curriculum measure was very highly correlated with college plans, since most of the effect was due to the distinction between college preparatory and all other curricula.

As expected, the three retained variables do not account for an impressive amount of variance. The data appear in Table 6-11. Run 1 shows that, in combination, these three measures account for three percent of the variance in attempted enlistments after high school. The fact that each of the beta-square figures is almost one-half of the corresponding eta-square figure indicates that the three variables are highly related to one another. When these measures are added to a run with the three motives (Run 3), the beta-squares drop even more, showing that most of the variance that the school variables explain can also be explained by the motives. The difference between the Multiple R^2 for Runs 2 and 3 summarizes this. The school variables can explain uniquely only four-tenths of one percent of the variance. Throughout this chapter each of the moderate bivariate relationships has been reduced when the college-goers were eliminated from the analysis. MCA did something similar in Run 3. The college/non-college distinction is already contained in MS-PLANS/INDECISION and DRAFT STATUS. Accordingly, the three school variables are not able to add much when this distinction is

TABLE 6-11

Multiple Classification Analyses of Motives and
School-Related Experiences Predicting to Attempted
Enlistment After High School

Motive Predictors	Predicting From Each Characteristic Separately	Predicting From Several Characteristics Simultaneously			Marginal Contribution to the Variance Explained
		Run 1	Run 2	Run 3	
	Eta^2		$Beta^2$		Proportion
MIL-FIT/MS=OCC PREFERENCE	.105	*	.031	.031	
MS-PLANS/ INDECISION	.274	*	.190	.192	
DRAFT STATUS	.142	*	.025	.024	
GATB-J	.017	.008	*	.005	
AVE GRADE/ SENIOR YEAR	.029	.020	*	.005	.004
POS SCHL ATT	.009	.007	*	.005	
MULT R (adjusted)		.176	.567	.570	
MULT R^2 (adjusted)		.031	.321	.325	

5397

*Indicates that this variable was not included in this run.

NOTE: N=1566.   This reduced N comes from eliminating cases with missing data
on the motive variables.   As a result, the eta-square figures are slightly
different from those reported in the bivariate analysis section of this chapter.

already contained in the data.

From these findings it can only be concluded that school experiences
contribute to a motive to enlist only in that they influence intentions to go to
college, and therefore *not* to enlist. A similar finding was reported in another
volume in the Youth in Transition series (Bachman, et al., 1971). The authors
noted that college attendance is largely predictable from factors evident in a
young man at the time he enters high school. The findings in this chapter not
only confirm this finding, but also indicate that among non-college youth
school factors are unable to account for why some will choose military service
and others a civilian job.

Summary

The underlying thesis of this chapter has been that school failure should serve as a motive for enlistment. This thesis has found only limited support in the data. True, those with failing grades, and negative attitudes about school do enlist, but no more frequently than any other group. In fact, what trends exist suggest the opposite. Enlistment follows more frequently from a school experience that is average or above average as defined by grades, feelings about the value of education, and conformity to school behavior norms. The "above average" characteristics are more strongly related to enlistment when college-goers are eliminated from the analysis and the comparison is between enlistees and those who choose jobs after high school. Putting these findings together with those of the last chapter on job attitudes, the following composite emerges. Among the competing alternatives available to the high school graduate, college is the most valued. Among young men who do not go on to college, the attraction of military service is somewhat greater among young men with average job ambitions, who are not afraid of hard work, and who have had a reasonably successful and happy high school experience.

---

[1]See Bachman, et al., 1967, pp. 68-71 or the GATB Manual (1962), Sec. III, Ch. 14 for further details.

[2]$r=.70$. For additional information see the GATB Manual, Sec. III, 1962, Ch. 14.

[3]The reasons were ascertained using an open-ended interview question. There were no probes for particular responses.

[4]There is evidence that self-reported grades are fairly valid and reliable. Part of the evidence comes from the expected relationships with background measures and intelligence (Bachman, 1970, pp. 168-171). The other evidence comes from an attempt to confirm average grades by an independent report from school officials. Based on 920 cases for which there were both principal and student reports, the product-moment correlation between the two measures was .71. What bias there was tended to be in the direction of over-rating average grades by one point. Thus, a boy might report an average grade of B − while school officials would indicate a C+.

CHAPTER 7

CULTURAL, FAMILY, AND PEER INFLUENCES

This chapter focuses on a wide variety of potential conditioning factors. These include cultural, family, and peer influences. Each of these defines in some way the context in which a young man finds himself at the time of making his decision regarding a post-high school activity.

The cultural and family background factors represent the forces which have the earliest impact on a young man's vocational dispositions. The analyses in this area will deal with nine dimensions, each measured when the respondents were starting tenth grade. The three cultural dimensions are race, region, and urbanicity. The family background factors are socioeconomic status and quality of home environment, family size (number of siblings), broken home, family relations, and father's and brother's military experience.

A third group of factors is called influence sending measures. These were administered at the end of high school and consisted of an individual's perception of what parents and friends want him to do regarding a decision to enlist.

As in the previous chapter, a number of the variables being examined were measured, and had their initial impact, prior to twelfth grade. While the criterion of central interest to this study continues to be attempted enlistment after high school, it will occasionally be useful to look also at the relationship of these factors to another criterion, attempted enlistment any time after the beginning of tenth grade.

Escape and Opportunity. An underlying theme which guided the selection of several clusters of variables for this study is that of escape and opportunity: i.e., to what extent does enlistment represent a choice by a young man to select himself *out* of his present environment and into another one that offers either an escape from distasteful elements of his old environment or the opportunity to better himself in the new environment? In this chapter there is an attempt to see whether the poor, the blacks, or those who experienced home lives that might be termed undesirable are any more likely to enlist than those not disadvantaged in these ways. The rationale for this orientation is well summarized by Janowitz:

> For the potential recruit, especially the volunteer, a positive attitude [toward military service] is based not only on the task of the armed forces but also on the fact that the military offers an adequate and respectable level of personal security. For the enlisted man seeking a professional career, it offers relatively promising possibilities. The strong regulations requiring nondiscriminatory practices—whether they be regional, or racial-ethnic, or social class—have had the consequence of attracting the socially disadvantaged, especially lower-class persons with rural backgrounds, and Negroes who develop strong career commitments to the services. (Janowitz and Little, 1965, pp. 51-52)

Janowitz asserts, and few would deny, that many among the disadvantaged have enlisted in military service. But it is not clear that such individuals are more strongly attracted to military service because of their condition. If it is simply a matter that the disadvantaged can be found in the service in about the same proportion as they are distributed throughout the society, then one can conclude only that the military has very broad appeal. If, on the other hand, the disadvantaged enlist at a much higher rate, several things are possible. It may be that the disadvantaged find service life more attractive or that other opportunities, for example college, are less available to them.

Cultural Factors

Race. In American society one can be disadvantaged by virtue of his race. In the past two decades special prominence has been given to the problems of mobility and advancement associated with being black. Accordingly, one can ask: Do blacks try to enlist at a higher rate than whites?

Before answering this question, it is necessary to extend a precaution with regard to racial data in this study. While the percentages of blacks in the Youth in Transition sample (11 percent) approximates the national average, the ability to generalize about racial differences is somewhat restricted by the sampling design. This problem was discussed in Volume II (Bachman, 1970). Because of the current interest in·racial differences, it is important for the reader to appreciate the limitations of the racial data. Accordingly, Bachman's discussion of the problem is reproduced here.

> It would be tempting to make rather broad generalizations from some of our findings concerning racial differences. However, our sample was not designed primarily for this purpose, and the number and distribution of black respondents is not adequate for it. Our overall sampling plan clustered respondents in 87 schools, thus facilitating the study of school effects and providing a reasonably accurate description of the total population of boys in tenth grade. The sample design is less well suited, however, to the description and comparison of small subsets of the population, particularly when the subset is located in a small number of schools. Only 256 of our

2213 respondents are black; more serious from a sampling standpoint is the fact that over two-thirds of them are concentrated in only nine of our sampled schools (with the remaining third scattered in 25 other schools). In short, our ability to generalize accurately from the black subsample is severely limited, and this argued against a strong concentration on racial differences.

Another possibility, therefore, would have been to limit our analysis and discussion to the 87 percent of respondents who are white. Such a solution is safe–it avoids one large complication in an already complex analysis and eliminates the risk of reporting findings that can be misunderstood or distorted—by ourselves or by others. An all-white analysis would, however, be a less than complete picture of tenth-grade boys and, even less acceptable, it would withhold information that is important, if not precise.

The remaining possibility was to examine racial differences in our sample with a clear understanding of their limitations. In adopting this approach we did not discard useful information, but bore in mind the limits of its usefulness. At the very least, our findings in this area may provide the basis for new hypotheses which can be tested more thoroughly with samples designed for that task. (Bachman, 1970, p. 25)

The relationship of race to attempted enlistment after high school is shown in the top of Table 7-1. It appears that the rate for blacks is considerably lower than for whites,[1] however, this is only an artifact of the way the criterion is defined. The period "after high school" was determined by the time when most of the panel graduated from high school. This was June, 1969. Included among those who "enlisted after high school" were some of the high school dropouts. It is the dropout-enlistee group which caused the apparent difference in enlistment rates. Note the figures in the bottom part of Table 7-1. When the criterion is changed to attempted enlistment any time after the beginning of tenth grade, the rates are virtually identical, indicating no racial differences in preferences for military service. Additional analyses (detailed in Table 7-1X in Appendix G) indicated that the apparent discrepancy in rates has to do with the time when dropouts attempted to enter the service. Most frequently, the black dropouts tried to enlist very soon after dropping out, while the white dropouts more often waited around, many of them not going to the recruiter until after the time when their classmates graduated from high school.

In sum, preferences for military service were not tied to racial differences. If one assumes that blacks are among the disadvantaged in this society, this finding provides little support for the escape and opportunity hypothesis.

Region. There are several popular notions about the effects of geographical location on enlisting. One of these is that serving in the military is more popular among southerners. This expectation seems to be based on the assumption that serving in the military is a proud tradition in the culture of

TABLE 7-1

Race Related to Attempted Enlistment
(A) After High School (B) Any Time
After the Beginning of Tenth Grade

Category	Percent of Sample (N=1719)*	Percent of Category That Tried to Enlist After High School
1 White[+]	88%	12.2%
2 Black	12	7.5
	100	

Grand Mean = 11.6%
Eta = .047
Eta-square = .002

Category	Percent of Sample (N=1925)**	Percent of Category That Tried to Enlist at Any Time After The Beginning of Tenth Grade
1 White[+]	89%	14.5%
2 Black	11	14.4
	100	

Grand Mean = 14.5%
Eta = .013
Eta-square = .000

5412   5368

*This sample includes all YIT panel members who responded at the third data collection (end of senior year of high school), including dropouts. Excluded from the table are all respondents who were drafted, entered the National Guard or the Reserves.

**This sample includes all YIT panel members, except (a) those about whom no followup information could be obtained (N=209) and (b) those who were drafted, entered the National Guard or the Reserves.

[+]Minority groups other than Negro are included in this category. They are not distinguished in this table because their numbers are too small.

the southern states. The Gates Commission was influenced enough by this thinking to include a measure of region in several of their regression equations predicting to enlistment (U. S. President's Commission, 1970B, II-2-5). However, after looking at the results they concluded that "the Southern dummy[2] appears to have virtually no effect on the combined total military equations, therefore the evidence does not support the hypothesis that there are regional differences in 'tastes' toward the military in general (Ibid., II-2-20)."

The data from the Youth in Transition study confirm the Commission's finding: there was no tendency for southerners to enlist more frequently than young men from other regions. Table 7-2 shows the data. Young men from the South enlisted at a rate slightly (but non-significantly) lower than those from other regions. The region from which enlistments appear to be higher is the West. However, the overall effect is small (eta=.064) and statistically non-significant.

While serving in the enlisted ranks is not unusually popular among Southerners, serving as an officer may be. Appendix A on ROTC entrants indicates that those voluntarily enrolled in ROTC programs were much more likely to come from the South than any other part of the country. It may be that the "proud tradition" exists, but that it is associated only with serving as an officer.

Urbanicity. Another popular notion about enlisting is that boys from small towns and rural areas enlist more frequently than boys from large metropolitan areas. A number of reasons are offered for rural youth finding military service more attractive. These range from fewer job opportunities be-

TABLE 7-2

Region Related to
Attempted Enlistment After High School

Region	Percent of Sample. (N=1719)	Percent of Category That Tried to Enlist
1 West	16%	16.8%
2 N. Central	32	11.5
3 N. East	23	11.5
4 South	29	9.1
	100%	

Grand Mean = 11.6%
Eta = .064
Eta-square = .004

ing available to the notion that "small-town America" is more supportive of American institutions such as the Armed Forces. To assess this hypothesis, the urbanicity of a boy's place of residence was run against enlistment. The findings appear in Table 7-3. While the overall

TABLE 7-3

Urbanicity Related to Attempted
Enlistment After High School

Urbanicity	Percent of Sample (N=1719)	Percent of Category That Tried to Enlist
1 Rural	20%	9.9%
2 Small town under 15,000	20	14.2
3 City (15,000-50,000) not a suburb	14	16.2
4 Suburb (Residential or Industrial)	21	10.8
5 City over 50,000	25	8.9
	100%	

Grand Mean = 11.6%
Eta = .081
Eta-square = .007

5322

relationship is weak (eta=.081) there are some interesting trends. It appears that there is a small tendency for boys from small towns and small cities to enlist more frequently, while those from farming areas and large metropolitan areas are among the least likely to enlist.

A number of other analyses added support to these findings. College-goers were eliminated from the analysis, and this did not alter the shape of the distribution. The criterion was changed to attempted enlistment at any time after the beginning of tenth grade, and again the profile was similar, although the eta was somewhat smaller (.070). One other comparison used a different predictor: the urbanicity of the area where the respondent was raised as a child. It was thought that childhood experiences might have had a greater impact on response to the service. This was not the case; the strength of association with attempted enlistment after high school was considerably weaker (eta=.024) than for the urbanicity of his present location.

The findings for these two measures do not provide much support for the escape and opportunity theme. While there is some evidence that small-town and small-city youth enlist more frequently, boys from the farm areas where the job opportunities should be among the worst are least attracted to the service.

107

Family Background Factors

Socioeconomic Level and Quality of Home Environment. Do young men from poor families enlist more frequently than those from more well-to-do families? To answer this question a measure of socioeconomic status (S.E.S.) was run against enlistment behavior to see if there were differential rates for low and high levels of S.E.S. Initially, the measure used was Duncan's S.E.S. rating of father's occupation. This status ranking of occupations was developed combining three pieces of information about each of the major job categories used by the Census Bureau. These include the NORC prestige ratings, average education required for the job, and the average income received. Details on the construction of the measure are available in Reiss (1961); examples of occupations and their ratings can be found in Appendix G, Table 7-4X.

A six-category version of this variable was related to enlistment behavior. The data appear in Table 7-4. The overall relationship is weak (eta=.125), but the trend is quite clear: enlisting is most frequent among boys in the lower classes. As father's occupational status increases, there is a steady decrease in the percent enlisting, with no one enlisting from the highest category. This latter class of occupations includes most of the professions

TABLE 7-4

Socioeconomic Status (Duncan) of
Father's Occupation Related to
Attempted Enlistment After High School

Category	Percent of Sample (N=1568)*	Percent of Category That Tried to Enlist
1 Low	8%	15.7%
2	35	15.8
3	24	11.0
4	18	8.2
5	13	6.0
6 High	2	0.0
	100	

Grand Mean = 11.6%
Eta = .125
Eta-square = .016

5368

*There were 151 respondents for whom information on father's occupation was inadequate to perform a Duncan status recode.

like lawyer and doctor as well as other high-status jobs such as bank manager and federal official.

The quotation from Janowitz at the beginning of this chapter suggests that it is the "socially disadvantaged" who are more likely to enlist. Socioeconomic status captures much of what is implied by this term. However, there is a more comprehensive measure which has been used in other phases of the Youth in Transition study. It is derived from a combination of the S.E.S. measure and other factors which might be thought of as indicative of social advantage and disadvantage. The measure is called Socioeconomic Level (SEL), although it might more accurately be called a "quality of home environment" scale. It consists of six equally-weighted ingredients: father's occupational status (Duncan Scale), father's educational attainment, mother's educational attainment, number of rooms per person in the home, number of books in the home, and a checklist of other possessions in the home. Bachman describes the measure in this way:

> In summary, the measure consists of one "part" father's occupational status, two "parts" parents' education, and three "parts" having to do with family possessions. While most or all of these ingredients undoubtedly have a bearing upon a family's status in the eyes of the community, they have perhaps even more to do with the quality of home environment available to children. To the extent that this is true, the SEL index is particularly well suited as a measure of one class of family background influences in our study of adolescent boys. (Bachman, 1970, p. 14)

The relationship of SEL to enlistment behavior is shown in Table 7-5. The strength of association is slightly larger (eta=.152) than for S.E.S. alone. But, with one exception, the shape of the distribution is much the same: those at the lower levels of SEL enlisted much more frequently than those at the upper levels. The exception is for the lowest category, where the enlistment rate was lower than for the next highest category.

The departure of the bottom category from the trend is of some interest. Is the estimate to be believed, with the implication that the lowest SEL group is for some reason less attracted to military service? To investigate this, additional analyses were carried out. These are described in Appendix G. The results of these analyses suggest that the lower rate of enlistment for the bottom SEL category is no more than an artifact, and that the relationship of this measure in the real population is a linear one, with almost 25 percent enlisting from the lowest level of SEL.

Now consider the more general question: what is the meaning of the inverse relationship of SEL with enlistment? The phenomenon appears to be the result of class preferences for, and expectations of attaining, a college education. Upper class youth are more likely to choose to enter college right after high school than enlist in military service. Bachman found that, "just over 10 percent of the young men in the bottom SEL category were primarily students (post-high school) in spring of 1970, compared with about three-quarters of those in the top SEL category" (Bachman, et al., 1971, p. 27).

TABLE 7-5

Socioeconomic Level (Quality of Home Environment)
Related to Attempted Enlistment After High School
in the Total Sample

Category	Percent of Sample (N=1667)	Percent of Category That Tried to Enlist
1 Low	5%	(11.2%)*
2	14	19.7
3	27	15.4
4	28	9.9
5	17	6.2
6 High	9	4.1
	100%	

Grand Mean = 11.8%
Eta = .152
Eta-square = .023

5322

*These percentages represent a systematic underestimate of actual attempted enlistments. See text.

This is illustrated in Figure 7-1. The relationship of SEL to college entrance is strongly linear and opposite to its relationship with enlistment.

Recall from Chapter 3 that three-quarters of those who entered college had plans to do so when they were in tenth grade, while 89 percent of those who tried to enlist did not develop this plan until twelfth grade or later. At the time of graduation one-third of the enlistees still thought they would be going on to college. The different timing for the two decisions indicates that, for most young men, college is higher than military service in the hierarchy of choices. Military service is chosen most frequently when it is clear that college cannot be attained. Given the strong positive association of SEL with intelligence scores and classroom grades, it is not surprising to find that lower-class youth are less likely to attain college, and, as a result, turn to military service.

As further confirmation for this explanation, SEL was run against attempted enlistment for the subgroup that did not go on to college. The findings appear in the two right-hand columns of Table 7-6. The relationship is considerably attenuated; the eta drops from .152 to .079. Most important, there is little interpretable difference in the rate of enlisting among the top five SEL groups. They cluster within three percentage points of the grand mean. Taken together, these findings can be interpreted in this way: upper-class youth choose college over any other post-high school activity. However,

FIGURE 7-1

Socioeconomic Level
Related to Post-High School Education

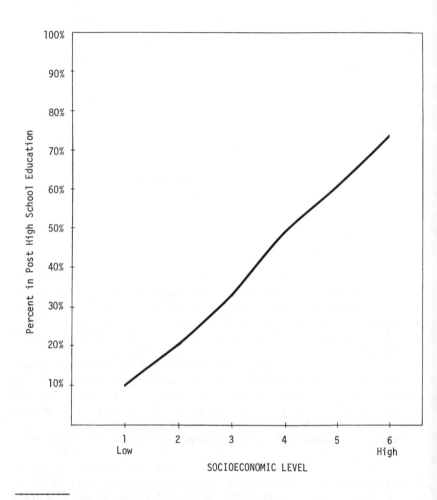

Adapted from Bachman, et al., 1971, Table 3-2

among those who do not go on to college, military service is chosen over a
job as frequently among upper class youth as it is among the lower class.
These results, coupled with similar ones from the previous chapter on

TABLE 7-6

Socioeconomic Level (Quality of Home Environment)
Related to Attempted Enlistment After High School
in the Non-College Subsample

Category	Percent of Sample (N=767)	Percent of Category That Tried to Enlist
1 Low	9%	(14.5%)*
2	22	27.1
3	34	26.0
4	23	24.7
5	9	22.4
6 High	3	24.0
	100%	

Grand Mean = 24.5%
Eta = .079
Eta-square = .006

5356

*These percentages represent a systematic underestimate of actual attempted enlistments. See text.

school factors, indicate that there are a number of measures that predict to military service solely because they predict inversely to college entrance (see introduction to Chapter 6). These data suggest that college is simply more attractive to certain types of individuals than is military service; for these individuals the military is simply not competitive with the offerings of educational institutions.

Such an interpretation rests heavily on the assumption that the choice of college is a positive preference for additional schooling and the rewards it opens up, and not simply a means of avoiding the draft. (These data were collected at a time when it was still possible for a student in good standing to secure up to a four-year II-S deferment almost automatically.) The data at hand do not permit an evaluation of the subtleties of motivation behind a college choice. However, this much is known: when asked at Time 4 why they chose the environment they did, 20 percent of the college youth mentioned avoiding the draft among their three most important reasons for entering college. There is no way of telling whether, in the absence of a draft, the sum of forces for these individuals would still result in the choice of college or not. But, in the absence of more convincing evidence, the college choice will be interpreted as an essentially positive one, where college is seen by certain groups of individuals (those with high intelligence, high SEL, etc.) as more attractive than military service.

Family Size. This refers to the number of siblings that a boy has. The importance of this variable in the larger study has been summarized by Bachman et al.:

> The young men in our sample who came from small families were higher in self-concepts of school ability, academic achievement (grades), college plans, and occupational aspirations. Negative school attitudes were more prominent among boys from larger families. Part of these relationships can be attributed to difference in socioeconomic level, but a portion of the effect remains in each case after controlling for SEL. (Bachman, et al., 1971, p. 29)

The same authors also note that boys from large families are almost three times more likely to drop out of school than those from small families; and that this effect remains, although reduced somewhat, when SEL is controlled.

The relationship of this variable to attempted enlistment after high school is relatively weak, eta=.107 and the pattern is difficult to interpret. Changing the criterion to enlistment any time after the beginning of tenth grade results in a much clearer pattern, although the eta is still the same. Boys with only one or two sibs enlist least frequently (eight to nine percent). The rate increases linearly with larger families reaching 20 percent when a boy has six or more brothers and sisters. An exception to this linear relationship is the group with no siblings; they enlist at a rate equal to those with four siblings.

Again, college-attendance explains even this small relationship. Repeating the analysis for the non-college sample, the curve flattens out, except for the only-child category. While the average rate of enlistment among all non-college youth is about 25 percent, the rate for the only-child group is 37 percent. No explanation for this deviation has been found.

Broken Home. This variable is a measure of whether or not a boy comes from a home where both his mother and father reside. Eighty-one percent of the sample come from such a home. The remainder come from homes broken either by death or divorce. Overall, this variable barely relates to enlistment behavior (eta=.038). But there is a tendency for the small number who come from homes broken by divorce (N=190) to enlist more frequently (14.9%) than those from either homes broken by death (10.3%) or intact homes (11.3%). But, as with SEL, even this relationship disappears when the analysis is repeated for only non-college respondents. In this case the enlistment rates are exactly the same for all three groups. Being from a home broken by divorce predicts somewhat to a boy not choosing college, but otherwise it does not predict at all to the choice of a military vs. civilian job.

Family Relations: Parental Punitiveness. It was hypothesized that boys coming from homes characterized by poor relations with their parents might be more inclined to enlist to get away from what they consider to be an undesirable situation. In the Youth in Transition study a single, general-purpose measure of family relations (or parent-son relations) was developed, comprised of 10 items dealing with parental punitiveness and 11 items dealing with closeness to parents and the feeling that parents are reasonable. The measure, based on tenth-grade data, shows a strong positive relationship with dropping out of high school. As Bachman et al. noted,

> ... A substantial correlation does indeed exist between family relations dropout/college entrances: the better a boy reported getting along with his parents at the start of tenth grade, the less likely he was to drop out of high school and the more likely he was to enter college. (Bachman et al., 1971, p. 33)

Further analysis indicated that this relationship is due almost entirely to the 10 items dealing with parental punitiveness. In fact, the index of parental punitiveness items alone shows a slightly stronger association with dropout/college-entrance than does the total family relations scale. Accordingly, this index was used in the enlistment analyses. The ingredients for the parental punitiveness measure are presented in Table 7-7, and the relationship of the summary measure to enlistment is shown in Table 7-8. The pattern for enlisting is fairly flat for the first four categories. In categories five through eight (high punitiveness) the rate of enlisting increases, although the pattern is not easily interpretable. Similarly, the relationship within the non-college subsample defies easy interpretation.

TABLE 7-7

Items Comprising the Parental Punitiveness Index

1. How often do your parents completely ignore you after you've done something wrong?

2. How often do your parents act as if they don't care about you any more?

3. How often do your parents disagree with each other when it comes to raising you?

4. How often do your parents actually slap you?

5. How often do your parents take away your privileges (TV, movies, dates)?

6. How often do your parents blame you or criticize you when you don't deserve it?

7. How often do your parents threaten to slap you?

8. How often do your parents yell, shout, or scream at you?

9. How often do your parents disagree about punishing you?

10. How often do your parents nag at you?

TABLE 7-8

Parental Punitiveness (Tenth Grade Measure)
Related to Attempted Enlistment After High School

Category	------- Total Sample --------		----- Non-College Only ------	
	Percent of Sample (N=1684)	Percent of Category That Tried to Enlist	Percent of Sample (N=756)	Percent of Category That Tried to Enlist
1 Low	6%	10.8%	6%	18.2%
2	15	9.9	13	27.3
3	25	9.0	21	24.3
4	22	10.3	21	21.7
5	15	15.1	16	27.9
6	10	17.5	14	27.9
7 High	6	14.5	9	19.8
	100		100	

Grand Mean = 11.6%   Grand Mean = 24.5%
Eta = .102   Eta = .099
Eta-square = .010   Eta-square = .010

The analyses were repeated for enlistment at any time after the beginning of tenth grade. The strength of association was about the same (eta=
.109 in the total sample, .085 in the non-college subsample), but the curves
were smoother and more suggestive of a mild monotonic relationship. High
parental punitiveness is weakly associated with a greater tendency to trying
to enlist, even among the non-college subsample. But, considering the
weakness of the association, and the lack of interpretable patterning for attempted enlistment after high school, it was concluded that parental punitiveness is not an important factor predicting to enlistment—especially enlistment after high school. Since neither broken home nor parental punitiveness are important predictors, there is little support in this study for an
interpretation of enlisting that views this behavior as more common among
those living in an undesirable family situation. Likewise, given the weak relationships for race and socioeconomic level, the whole theme of escape and
opportunity has to be rejected as an explanation of enlistment behavior.

Father's and Brother's Military Service Experience. Inasmuch as enlisting after high school is an occupational choice, it was thought that the
extent of a father's or brother's experience in military service should influence in some way a young man's choice to enlist or not. Without elaborating

on the mechanism by which it might influence the decision, it seemed reasonable to hypothesize that a "military family" would provide more modeling and support for an enlistment decision than families where male members had not served. The relationship of a father's military experience to a son's attempted enlistment after high school is shown in Table 7-9. For the various categories there are very few differences in the percentage enlisting.

TABLE 7-9

Father's Military Experience Related to
Attempted Enlistment After High School

Length of Father's Service	Percent of Sample (N=1596)	Percent of Category That Tried to Enlist
0 = Never Served	34%	9.3%
1 = < 2 years	10	7.1
2 = 2-4 years	43	11.4
3 = 4-8 years	9	13.8
4 = > 8 years	4	12.1
	100%	

Grand Mean = 11.7%
Eta = .060
Eta-square = .004

5322

It was somewhat surprising to find that a greater percentage did not enlist from Category Four. This category contains boys whose fathers are, or were, career men. In a separate analysis it was discovered that one-half of the sons in this group went on to college. Perhaps after college they will enter the service as officers. At any rate, the length of a father's military experience is not an important predictor of a son's entry into the service immediately after high school. (See Appendix A for a discussion of the relationship of father's experience to entry into ROTC.)

The results of a study by Tiedeman (1963, p. 70) suggest that the influence of the father in occupational choices is mediated by the degree of identification with the father. The Youth in Transition study has such a measure, called Closeness to Father. It is an index of four items: the amount of affection received from the father, frequency of doing things with the father, feelings of closeness with the father, and desire to be like the father as an adult. (For a detailed description, see Bachman, 1970, p. 19.) To test the applicability of Tiedeman's finding, the analysis comparing father's military experience with attempted enlistment was repeated three more times, once each for low, medium, and high levels of closeness to father. There were virtually no differences in the distributions and strength of association. The relationship of a brother's military experience to enlisting is shown in Table 7-10. A young man whose brother has served is more likely to enlist than one whose brother has not served. The difference of six percentage points is statistically very trustworthy, given the frequency on which the two estimates are based. It seems safe to assume that a brother's serving in the military is somewhat more important to a young man's decision to enlist after high school than his father's military experience. Having said this, it must be noted that neither of the eta-square figures are very large. One cannot account for a great amount of the variance in enlistment attempts knowing the military experience of the male members of a young man's family.

TABLE 7-10

Brother's Military Experience Related to
Attempted Enlistment After High School

		Percent of Sample (N=1701)	Percent of Category That Tried to Enlist
	Category		
0	Brother(s) never served or has no brothers	75%	10.2%
1	Brother(s) served	25	16.1

Grand Mean = 11.6%
Eta = .079
Eta-square = .006)

5366

Influence Sending

One way of conceptualizing the decision point at the end of high school is to consider an individual to be enmeshed in a type of Lewinian force-field regarding any particular choice he might make. In this force-field there are a number of forces which push him toward making a choice such as enlisting, while at the same time there are other forces which push him away from such a choice. Among these forces are the opinions, responses, or wishes of those people who are held in high esteem by the individual. In this study these opinions are called "influence sending" from significant others.

There are a number of issues regarding the role of influence sending in post-high school decisions. Two that are focused upon here are these: considering the total amount of influence sending that an individual receives regarding a post-high school choice such as enlisting, what is the importance of this dimension relative to other forces such as family background, draft status, etc.? Second, which people have the greatest impact on the decision? Of particular interest is discovering whether parents or peers are more central to the decision. In the literature on adolescent development much has been made of how ". . . the peer group increases and the family wanes in emotional significance . . ." during this period (Douvan, 1966, p. 84). While this may be accurate in matters of taste for music and clothes, it has not been shown to be the case for decisions that are more fundamental to the very definition of self. Selection of a post-high school activity is a choice of this type.

Influence sending regarding enlisting was first assessed at the end of twelfth grade, just prior to the implementation of post-high school choices. All respondents were asked how their parents, sibs, and best friends would respond if they were to enlist. One of the questions and the response scale appear below.

> How would your parents or guardians feel if you enlisted in the military in the next twelve months?
>
> ☐ (1) They would feel happy about it; they would like it
>
> ☐ (2) They wouldn't care
>
> ☐ (3) They would feel unhappy about it; they wouldn't like it.

On the surface, such a question is assessing the expected response of parents to a situation which may or may not become a reality for the individual. A young man's response to this question, however, is subject to the same types of distortion that were described for Vietnam attitudes (Chapter 5). This is especially true for the young man who expects to enlist. Consider these two examples. One youth might think that his parents want him to enlist and, *as a result,* be more inclined to actually enter the service. His response to the above question can be considered an accurate reporting of his own influence receiving. Another youth intending to enlist might have decided to do so for reasons other than parental wishes, but claim to have their support and encouragement in order to reduce in his own mind any dissonance he might otherwise have over such a weighty decision. This youth's response is not a statement of the message actually being sent, rather it is the message he would like to receive. For a large number of those planning to enlist the truth may be somewhere between these two extremes; for this reason any relationship of influence sending measures to a decision to enlist will be difficult to interpret.

The relationship of the three influence sending measures to attempted enlistment after high school is shown in Table 7-11. If a boy thought at the end of twelfth grade that his parents would be happy over such a course of action, he was much more likely to enlist later on. Thirty percent of those who thought their parents would be happy over such a choice later enlisted, while only seven percent tried to enlist among those who thought their parents would be unhappy about this course of action. The strength of association is sizeable (eta=.250) compared with other bivariate relationships in

YOUTH IN TRANSITION

TABLE 7-11

Reactions of Parents, Sibs, and Peers to
Enlistment After High School Related to Attempted Enlistments

How would your _____ feel if you enlisted in the military in the
next twelve months

Category	Percent of Sample (N=1691)*	Percent of Category That Tried to Enlist
PARENTS		
1. Happy	15%	29.7%
2. Wouldn't care	13	14.6
3. Unhappy	72	7.3
	100	
Grand Mean = 11.6	Eta = .250	Eta-square = .063
BROTHERS AND SISTERS		
1. Happy	13%	27.3%
2. Wouldn't care	24	12.9
3. Unhappy	63	7.2
	100	
Grand Mean = 11.1	Eta = .212	Eta-square = .045
BEST FRIENDS		
1. Happy	9%	24.2%
2. Wouldn't care	47	13.0
3. Unhappy	44	7.9
	100	
Grand Mean = 11.8	Eta = .143	Eta-square = .020

5402

*For "BROTHERS AND SISTERS," N=1589. The remaining 102 cases were the only child
in their family.

this chapter. A similar relationship holds for brothers' and sisters' feelings:
their approval of enlisting was strongly associated with actual behavior
(eta=.212). The opinion of best friends seems less important (eta=.143).

Parents appear to be the most important influence senders for two
reasons. They are least often seen as neutral ("wouldn't care") on the issue,
and the overall strength of association is strongest between expected parent
response and later behavior. Using similar reasoning, sibs are the next most
important and peers the least important influence senders.

For purposes of this study it was desirable to have a single measure of
influence sending which could be used to characterize the entire set of
forces represented by the three groups of people. To achieve this, the three
measures were converted into a single index of military service influence

sending by taking a mean of the items. The index and its relationship to attempted enlistment after high school are shown in Table 7-12. This measure of total influence sending shows a strong monotonic relationship to attempted enlistment after high school. The separate analysis for the noncollege group shows no attenuation of effect, suggesting that the association of this predictor is unrelated to college attendance factors.

TABLE 7-12

Total Influence Sending for Enlistment
Related to Attempted Enlistment After High School

Category	--------Total Sample--------		-------Non-College Only-------	
	Percent of Sample (N=1694)	Percent of Category That Tried to Enlist	Percent of Sample (N=793)	Percent of Category That Tried to Enlist
1. Happy	9%	31.2%	15%	40.5%
2. Happy to Neutral	17	19.4	22	31.0
3. Neutral to Unhappy	15	12.3	16	22.2
4. Unhappy	59	6.2	47	14.2
	100		100	

Grand Mean = 11.6%   Grand Mean = 23.2
Eta = .247   Eta = .233
Eta-square = .061   Eta-square = .054

5366   5417

However, the problem of interpretation still remains: is enlistment more likely if "important others" approve of the decision, or is a supportive response imputed by the individual who wants to enlist for reasons other than pressure from others? A separate analysis provided some evidence supporting an interpretation of influence sending as a cause of later enlistments. For this analysis the sample was divided into four groups, based on a combination of twelfth grade plans and post-high school behavior. Plans and behavior were each dichotomized; plans into planned-to-enlist or not, and behavior into tried-to-enlist or not. Using the 2 x 2 table below, each re-

Post-High School Behavior

		Attempted to Enlist	Did Not Attempt to Enlist
Twelfth Grade Plans	Enlist	1	2
	Not Enlist	3	4

spondent was located uniquely in one of four categories. A one-way analysis of variance was then performed on these groups, with total influence sending to enlist as the dependent variable. The results are shown in Table 7-13. The right-hand column shows the mean influence sending score for each of the four groups. The important comparisons are between the mean scores for Categories One and Two, and then Three and Four. Categories One and Two contain all of the young men who planned at the end of twelfth grade to enlist during the following year. Group One followed through on these plans while Group Two did not. Note that Group One's score on influence sending is one-third of a standard deviation higher than Group Two's, suggesting that those who did not follow through on their enlistment plans were also the ones who were under less "pressure" to enlist from "important others" in their lives. A similar finding applies to Categories Three and Four. While the plans of both groups were alike in not including military service, the boys who later enlisted despite plans to the contrary were clearly different in the amount of influence sending they received in support of an enlistment choice. The mean scores are over one-half a standard deviation apart, with those who enlisted having a mean score close to a "neutral" response from important others, while those who did not enlist had a mean

TABLE 7-13

Relationship of Influence Sending
for Enlistment to Military Plans and Behavior

12th Grade Plans	Post-High School Behavior	Percent in Category (N=1423)**	Mean Score on Influence Sending to Enlist*
1. Enlist	Enlisted	7%	194
2. Enlist	Did not enlist	5	212
3. Not Enlist	Enlisted	4	224
4. Not Enlist	Didn't enlist	84	256
		100	

Grand Mean = 249   S.D. = 56
Eta = .326
Eta-square = .106
$F_{(3, 1419)}$ = 56.3   p<.01

5416

*SCALE: 100 = Parents, sibs, and peers would be happy if I enlisted.
          300 = Parents, sibs, and peers would be unhappy if I enlisted.

**Eliminated from this table are those who: (1) had no plans in twelfth grade, (2) planned to continue high school, (3) were drafted, (4) joined the National Guard or Reserves.

score close to the "unhappy" end of the continuum. Since the report of influence sending clearly preceded the actual decision to enlist, it seems safe to assume that influence sending from significant others does serve as a motive for later enlistment, whether or not it serves dissonance reduction purposes as well.

Influence Sending Seen Retrospectively. Another series of questions from the Time 4 interview (one year after high school) provides some interesting additional insight into the way in which influence sending operates differentially depending on the particular choice. To introduce the questions, the interviewer read the following paragraph.

> People we know can encourage or discourage us from doing things that we want to do. Some of them do this by telling us what they think. Others say nothing, but still we know how they feel. You might call this "silent encouragement." As I read through this list of people, tell me what each of them thought about what you have been doing this past year. Did they encourage you to do what you have been doing or did they think you should do something different?

The list of people included five groups: parents, girlfriend, close friends other than girlfriend, brothers and sisters, and teachers and counselors.[4] Each of the open-ended responses was coded into one of three categories: encouraged, neutral, or discouraged.

The interesting findings concern the difference in the "message" received by those who went on to college (or any form of post-high school education), those who took a job, and those who entered the service. The data are presented in Figure 7-2. There are five small figures, one for each of the "sender" groups. Each of the small figures contains three bars, one for each of the environmental status groups. The bars are divided into three parts, showing the percent who perceived the particular influence sender as having encouraged, discouraged, or been indifferent to the choice he made. The space between the top of the bar and the top of the box corresponds to missing data on the item. The missing data category is important only in the interpretation of the influence sending from "girlfriend," since this category of sender was inappropriate for a large number of respondents.

Consider first the influence sending for a college choice. This choice received the most universal support from the various senders. The percent of boys who were encouraged to continue their education ranges from a low of 59 percent receiving encouragement from sibs, to 91 percent being encouraged by their parents. Less than five percent were discouraged from going to college by anybody. The neutral category can be interpreted as a measure of the importance of a particular group to a decision. This interpretation is based on the types of responses that were categorized as neutral when the interview responses were coded. These include, "they don't question it," "don't care," "don't have too much to do with it," and "indifferent." Using this interpretation, siblings, teachers and counselors, and close friends were most frequently seen as unimportant to a decision about college.

FIGURE 7-2

Perceived Encouragement for Post-High School
Activity: College, Work, Military Service
(Retrospective, 1 Year After High School)

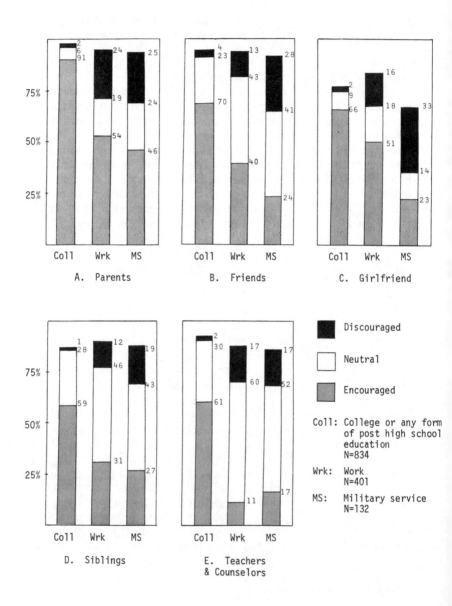

Of those who took a job after high school, only about 50 percent received encouragement for their choice from parents or girlfriends. Even fewer were encouraged by their close friends or siblings. Surprisingly enough, only 11 percent saw their teachers or counselors as supportive of their choice. Sixty percent saw teachers and counselors as neutral or unimportant in their decision to get a job, compared with only 30 percent of the college youth. Others who were frequently seen as unimportant in a decision to get a job were close friends and siblings. Those who were actually discouraged from this route were very few (less than 25 percent for any sender), although it is a larger percent than for college. Parents were most often the ones who discouraged this choice. Fifty-four percent had parents who encouraged them, 24 percent had parents who discouraged them, and another 19 percent had parents who were apparently indifferent to their son's choice of a post-high school activity.

Compare the patterns of support for those who took a job with those who enlisted. The pattern of parent responses is almost identical. About one-half had parents who supported them in their decision, one-quarter had parents who discouraged them, and the remaining one-quarter had parents who were indifferent to the decision. Teachers and counselors were seen as encouraging or discouraging the choice by equal numbers of boys, 17 percent. But, as with the work choice, over one-half saw school personnel as indifferent or unimportant to the choice. These findings suggest that school personnel are identified only with educational alternatives, and that for the non-college-bound, these people are not central to the choice of a post-high school environment.

Like the group who chose a job, a large percentage considered their close friends and girlfriends to be a neutral force in their decision. However, among those who *were* influenced by them, fewer boys received encouragement for their choice and more were discouraged from enlisting from these same senders. It would be reasonable to assume that, compared to parents, friends and girlfriends would be most concerned about the immediate loss of a good friend than the longer range developmental needs of the person.

Summary of Findings on Influence Sending. In summary, practically all of the boys who planned to continue their education after high school were the object of some influence sending, and the message was almost always one of encouragement, especially from parents. Many of the boys who chose to take a job perceived more indifference to their choice, especially from friends and school personnel; only one-half of the work group were encouraged by their parents and girlfriends to take a job. Those who chose to enlist were as frequently the objects of some influence sending as the work group; however, the message was more frequently one of discouragement for the choice. Parents were most frequently mentioned as encouraging enlistment.

The Expected Enlistment Behavior of Friends

The previous section described the influence sending of friends; i.e., the message that friends "sent," either by their expected emotional reaction or by their actual encouragement or discouragement of a behavior. Another way in which friends can influence a decision is through modeling; i.e., by themselves enlisting or planning to enlist. To test the importance of this dimension, respondents were asked the following question at the end of twelfth grade. "Now we'd like to ask about your friends; about how many will volunteer for military service?" The relationship of this measure to attempted enlistment is shown in Table 7-14.

TABLE 7-14

The Relationship to Attempted Enlistment
After High School of the Number of
Friends Expected to Enlist

| | --------Total Sample-------- | | ------Non-College Only------ | |
Category	Percent of Sample (N=1700)	Percent of Category That Tried to Enlist	Percent of Sample (N=799)	Percent of Category That Tried to Enlist
1. All or many	11%	24.0%	15%	32.5%
2. Some	43	13.8	44	27.4
3. Few or none	46	7.1	46	15.7
	100		100	
	Grand Mean = 11.8% Eta = .164 Eta-square = .027		Grand Mean = 23.4% Eta = .156 Eta-square = .024	

5366   5402

The strength of association is moderate (eta=.164) and the shape of the relationship is monotonic. If an individual reported that a number of friends were going to enlist, he was more likely to enlist himself. As with influence sending, there is some question about the meaning of this relationship. Is there any distortion operating in the reporting of the number of friends who are enlisting? Again, there is always the possibility that an individual decides to enlist for a set of reasons independent of his friends' behavior, but he reports that a number of them are going to enlist (regardless of what they are actually going to do) as a way of supporting in his own mind the decision he has made.

There is some evidence that distortion such as this was minimal. The evidence comes from the independence of this measure from influence sending. The correlation between the two (Product Moment Correlation) is only $r = .20$. This indicates that young men were at least discriminating between the influence sending message and the behavior of their friends. If there was consistent biasing of the perception in order to support a particular decision it would be expected that the bias would show up in the responses to both of these questions, and thus that the correlation between the two measures would be fairly high.

Multivariate Prediction

A large number of bivariate relationships have been examined in this chapter. For the most part, the cultural and family background measures showed uniformly weak association with attempted enlistment, while the influence sending measures displayed a moderate association. Two questions now arise: as a set, how much can these variables contribute to explaining the variance in enlistment behavior? Second, how much variance can they explain that is unique of the motives described in Chapter 4? Conversely, how much of their effect operates *through* their impact on the motives? To answer these questions the variables were entered into a number of Multiple Classification Analyses.

Again the question of possible interaction among the predictors was raised prior to entering them into MCA. A search was made for interactions among three groups of variables where it seemed reasonable to expect interaction. These groups were family military experience, influence sending, and stated importance to an enlistment decision of "significant others." No interactions of any size were found. Among the family background and cultural measures there was little reason to suspect interaction, especially among the particular four measures from these two groups which were retained for multivariate analyses (see below).

As in the previous chapter, a number of variables were not carried into the multivariate phase of analysis. The criterion for retention was two-fold. (1) The bivariate relationship had to show an eta-value of at least .070. An eta of this size is required for statistical significance at the level of $p \leqslant .05$.[5] (2) In addition, the measure had to display an interpretable pattern of association with the criterion, attempted enlistment after high school. The results are summarized in Table 7-15.

To measure the effect of eliminating five variables, two MCAs were run, one with all eleven variables, and the other with only the six retained variables. This is shown in Runs 1 and 4, Table 7-16. The Multiple R^2 (adjusted for degrees of freedom) are identical, indicating that the variance accounted for by the five dropped measures overlapped completely with those that were retained. Thus, nothing was lost by eliminating these variables.

The cultural and family variables (the background measures) can account for 3.8 percent of the variance (Run 3). The two influence sending measures are considerably more important; together they can account for 7.8 percent of the variance (Run 2). It's hard to know exactly what to make of the difference in relative importance of these two sets of variables. On the one hand the greater importance of influence sending could indicate that such events are more important to a decision to enlist than those forces that derive from an individual's background. On the other hand, such a finding could be simply an artifact, reflecting the inability of this type of research to capture completely the impact of complex events that occur early in an individual's life.

If the background and influence sending measures are taken together (Run 4), they can account for 10.1 percent of the variance. Comparing the Multiple R^2 for Runs 2-4 reveals that there is some overlap between the two sets, but that it is not very large.

2.3% Unique to background
6.3% Unique to influence sending
1.5% Overlap or shared variance
10.1 Total variance explained

TABLE 7-15

Summary Table of Relationship of Chapter
Predictors to Criterion of Attempted
Enlistment After High School

	Test 1 Minimum Eta*	Test 2 Interpretable pattern
RETAINED		
1. Urbanicity	.081	Yes
2. Socioeconomic level (SEL)	.152	Yes
3. Family Size	.107	Yes
4. Brothers' military experience	.079	Yes
5. Total influence sending to enlist	.247	Yes
6. Enlistment plans of friends	.164	Yes
DROPPED		
7. Race	.047	--
8. Region	.064	--
9. Broken home	.038	--
10. Parental punitiveness	.102	No**
11. Father's military experience	.060	--

*Eta = .070 is the minimum for retention

**While the pattern was somewhat interpretable within the total sample, the lack of patterning in the non-college subsample led to the rejection of this measure.

TABLE 7-16

Multiple Classification Analyses of Cultural,
Family Background, and Influence Sending
Measures Predicting to Attempted Enlistment
After High School

Predictors	Eta/Eta^2	Predicting from Several Characteristics Simultaneously				Non-Coll
		------------Total Sample----------				
		Run 1	Run 2	Run 3	Run 4	Run 5
		$Beta^2$				
CULTURAL						
Race	.043/.002	.003	*	*	*	*
Region	.080/.006	.003	*	*	*	*
Urbanicity	.094/.009	.009	*	.014	.011	.022
FAMILY BKGD						
SEL	.152/.023	.017	*	.022	.015	.006
Family Size	.118/.014	.008	*	.009	.007	.014
Broken Home	.067/.005	.002	*	*	*	*
Parental Punitiveness	.081/.007	.003	*	*	*	*
Father's MS Experience	.050/.003	.002	*	*	*	*
Brother's MS Experience	.097/.010	.004	*	.005	.003	.003
INFL SENDING						
MS Infl Sending	.262/.069	.047	.059	*	.051	.055
Friends Enlisting	.160/.026	.011	.015	*	.012	.021
MULT R (adjusted)		.318	.279	.196	.318	.300
MULT R^2 (adjusted)		.101	.078	.038	.101	.090

5420

*Indicates that this variable was not included in this run

NOTE: N=1556 for Runs 1-4. This reduced N comes from eliminating cases with missing data on the motives set examined in Chapter 4. As a result, the eta figures are slightly different from those reported in the bivariate section of this chapter. N=707 for Run 5, the non-college subsample.

Now look at the beta-square adjustments made by MCA; especially the one for SEL when the influence sending measures were added. Apparently part of the overlap is due to an association of social class with influence sending to enlist. This could reflect either a positive preference for military service on the part of some levels of social class or, what is more likely, a positive message concerning enlisting from those, regardless of their social class, who do not see the individual as "college material." This latter interpretation was supported in a separate analysis of variance, predicting from SEL to mean influence sending. Within the total sample there is a monotonic relationship between SEL and positive influence sending to enlist (eta=.147); the higher the SEL, the lower the encouragement for enlistment. However, when this analysis was repeated in the non-college subgroup, the relationship was very flat (eta=.045) with no class differences associated with influence sending.

Run 4, using both background and influence sending, was repeated for the non-college subsample with some interesting results. This is shown as Run 5 in Table 7-16. Overall, the strength of association is similar, Multiple $R^2 = .090$, but the pattern of the beta-square values is very different. Socio-economic level decreased in importance. This was expected, given the strong association of SEL with the choice of post-high school education. Three other measures increased in importance: urbanicity, family size, and expectation of friends enlisting. Family size did not show an interpretable pattern of relationship with enlistment, but the other two variables showed the same pattern seen earlier: boys from small cities (15,000 - 50,000 population)[6] and boys with a number of friends enlisting were more likely than average to enlist after high school. Influence sending retained the same relative importance in this subgroup analysis: it is the most important single predictor.

Background, Influence Sending and Motives. With each new set of measures the question arises: how much additional explanation do they provide over and above the basic set of motives described in Chapter 4? Table 7-17 summarizes the MCAs that were used to answer this question. The reduced set of cultural, family, and influence sending measures were included in every run. In Runs 1 through 3 each of the motives was added to this set of measures one at a time. In Run 4 all three of the motives were added; Run 5 repeats Run 4 for the non-college subsample only.

Look at Runs 1-4. For each run the question to ask is how much can the cultural, family, and influence sending measures add over and above what the motives by itself can explain? This is derived from the difference between the Multiple R^2 for the entire run and the eta-square value for the motive by itself. This information has been extracted from the table and appears in Table 7-18. Run 4 indicates that the measures in this chapter can explain only an additional 1.1 percent of the variance over and above the motives taken as a set. In other words, background and influence sending have practically all of their impact *through* the motives. Expressed yet another way, the measures in this chapter are important primarily because of their impact on the formation of the motives.

But this is potentially deceptive. One of the so-called motives, MS-

TABLE 7-17

Multiple Classification Analyses of Cultural, Family
Background, Influence Sending, and Motives Predicting
to Attempted Enlistment After High School

Predictors	Eta/Eta^2	Predicting from Several Characteristics Simultaneously				
		--------Total Sample--------				Non-Coll
		Run 1	Run 2	Run 3	Run 4	Run 5
		$Beta^2$				
CULTURAL AND FAMILY BACKGROUND						
Urbanicity	.094/.009	.013	.006	.009	.006	.010
SEL	.152/.023	.011	.006	.007	.005	.003
Family Size	.118/.014	.005	.005	.004	.003	.006
Bros MS Experience	.097/.010	.003	.001	.001	.001	.000
INFL SENDING						
MS Infl Sending	.262/.069	.031	.013	.027	.008	.010
Friends Enlisting	.160/.026	.006	.003	.007	.002	.005
MOTIVES						
MIL-FIT	.323/.105	.066	*	*	.025	.029
MS-PLANS/INDEC	.525/.274	*	.220	*	.172	.196
DRAFT STATUS	.377/.142	*	*	.096	.020	.051
MULT R (adjusted)		.395	.543	.425	.576	.583
MULT R^2 (adjusted)		.156	.295	.181	.332	.340

5420

*Indicates that this variable was not included in this run

NOTE: N=1556 for Runs 1-4. This reduced N comes from eliminating cases with missing data on the motives set. As a result, the eta figures are slightly different from those reported in the bivariate section of this chapter. N=707 for Run 5, the non-college subsample.

PLANS/INDECISION, is little more than a distinction between those who planned to enlist at the end of high school and those who did not. Planning to enlist is bound to capture a good deal of the variance in enlistment behavior. The variables from this chapter that predict well to actual enlistment attempts also predict to having plans to enlist while still in twelfth grade. Consequently, this motive-variable captures much of the variance that the background and influence variables would explain in the absence of knowing an

TABLE 7-18

Summary of Effects of Cultural, Family,
and Influence Sending Measures
Unique of the Motives Set

Run #	Motive	(a) Relationship of motive(s) to enlistment	(b) Relationship of motive + background + influence sending to enlistment	(c) b minus a: the unique effect of background and infl. send.
1	MIL-FIT	$eta^2 = .105$	$R^2 = .156$	.051
2	MS-PLANS/ INDECISION	$eta^2 = .274$	$R^2 = .295$	.021
3	DRAFT STATUS	$eta^2 = .142$	$R^2 = .181$	.039
4	All 3 of the above	$R^2 = .321$	$R^2 = .332$	.011

5420

individual's plans. Knowing that a person plans to enlist is a much more pre-cise (though less informative) indicator of later behavior than characteristics of the person or even influence sending from others.

Eliminating MS-PLANS/INDECISION from the MCA changes the outcome. Look at Runs 1 and 3 in Table 7-18. The measures from this chapter still overlap somewhat with the two remaining motives, but they can account for five percent of the variance that is not shared with MIL-FIT and four percent that is not shared with DRAFT STATUS. This indicates that a person's background, and the influence sending he receives to enlist, affect enlistment behavior both directly and also through their impact on the formation of attitudes about how well one fits into a military type of job and how likely he is to be drafted.

Summary

This chapter has examined a great variety of factors which were thought to be potential correlates of a decision to enlist after high school. These include three sets of measures: cultural, family background, and influence sending. Among the cultural measures, race and region of the country were found to be unrelated to a decision to enlist. Urbanicity, on the other hand, was weakly associated with this outcome, with boys from small towns and small cities being somewhat more likely to enlist than those from farm areas, suburbs, or big cities.

The most important family background factor was a measure of socio-economic level (SEL) or quality of home environment. It was found to relate moderately to enlistment. The dynamics of SEL's effect are important. SEL apparently affects the hierarchy of an individual's preferences for post-high school activities: higher SEL youth choose college over any other alternative.

For these youth, military service can be viewed as competing with college and coming off second best.

Other family background measures were examined to test the hypothesis that a disadvantaged home life (broken home, punitive parents, a large number of siblings) would motivate individuals to seek an escape from home in the form of enlisting in the service. This hypothesis was not supported.

The most powerful predictors in this chapter were the influence sending measures. These were defined as a young man's perception of what others in his life think he should do. These "others" include parents, sibs, close friends, teachers and counselors. The findings indicate that the encouragement from other people—especially parents—for a decision to enlist is an important factor in whether or not the individual does so. So also is his perception of how many of his friends will be enlisting. These findings indicate that vocational decisions are made in a social context, with the individual responding in part to the opinions and pressures exerted by people whom he respects. For this reason, it should be expected that rates of enlistment will be affected by the degree to which there is popular support for youth serving in the military.

---

[1]Other racial subgroups such as Chicano and Puerto Rican total only 1.6 percent of the sample and are too small for separate treatment. They are included with the whites in Table 7-1.

[2]This refers to a dummy variable used in multiple regression. In the individual data records, being from the South is coded 1, while being from any other region is coded zero.

[3]Note that in Table 7-4 there were 151 respondents without information on father's occupation. Using several variables in an index allowed estimating a score for these cases using the remaining four ingredients. See Bachman (1970), especially Appendix B, for a detailed description of the summary measure of SEL.

SEL is very similar to Project TALENT's measure of "socioeconomic environment." See Flanagan and Cooley, 1966, Appendix E.

[4]Information was collected from both teachers and counselors, but the reports were so nearly the same for both groups that they were collapsed into a single category.

[5]This assumes a design effect of approximately 2.0 to 2.4 and a sample size of 1799. See Appendix F.

[6]Why this should be so is unclear. There are no differences in the average amount of influence sending for each level of urbanicity. The unemployment rate is not different enough across degrees of urbanicity to explain the difference either.

CHAPTER 8

UNEMPLOYMENT AND WAGES IN THE CIVILIAN JOB MARKET

In the last few years a number of studies of enlistment behavior have been published which use the perspective and methodology of the labor economist (Altman, 1969; Gray, 1970; Cook, 1970; Fechter, 1968, to mention a few). Two variables which are prominent in their analyses are expected earnings and rates of unemployment in the civilian job market. While the present study does not approach the enlistment problem with the perspective of the economic statistician (supply curves, elasticity, etc.), it does have available some unique data on unemployment and wages which will permit some estimates of the strength of these economic factors in comparison with psychological and other factors.

Unemployment

Early studies for the Department of Defense concluded that the civilian unemployment rate was an important factor in the decision to enlist. This point of view was expressed by Harold Wool in his review of one such study.

> Studies of enlistment trends have shown, as might be expected, that enlistment rates in Services such as the Army, where an "open" market for enlistments existed, have been positively correlated with fluctuations in youth unemployment. One such analysis, part of the Department of Defense Study of the Draft, correlated Army quarterly enlistment trends with changes in the size of the eighteen-to-nineteen-year-old male population and with unemployment rates for the same age group in the period July, 1957, to June, 1965, after eliminating seasonal variation. The regression equation derived indicated that—except for periods of major changes in the military situation or draft outlook—a given percentage change in the unemployment rate for male youth was associated with a similar percentage change in the Army enlistment rate.
>
> (Wool, 1968, pp. 99-100)

The reasoning why higher enlistments would be associated with an increase in the rate of civilian unemployment is fairly obvious: an individual who is unable to find a job in the civilian economy turns to military service as the only alternative for earning a living. However, while this makes intuitive sense, recent studies done for the Gates Commission (Gray, Fechter, and Cook) have not supported the hypothesis. The studies were uniform in reporting that, in the regression equations, the unemployment variable failed to reach significance; so it was dismissed as being unimportant to the enlistment decision.

Studies using time-series econometric methods have an advantage in studying the effects of unemployment. They can use national or regional estimates of the unemployment rate, and these data are readily available from the Census Bureau's monthly surveys. However, surveys of individuals, such as the present one, must utilize a different kind of unemployment data. In a psychological study of enlistment behavior it is necessary to pair individual behavior with unemployment in the small area in which the individual could be expected to search for a job. Thus, even regional data cover too wide an area to be useful. Estimates of county and metropolitan unemployment would be much more appropriate, but the sampling procedures used by Census do not provide reliable estimates for geographic divisions this small.

A solution to this problem for the present study is contained in data recently made available by James Morgan of the Survey Research Center. A panel study of family income dynamics, done for the Office of Economic Opportunity (Morgan, 1969, 1970), has included county-level information on unemployment and average wages. The counties used in the Youth in Transition study overlap completely the counties used in the Morgan study. The unemployment and wage data were collected for the years 1968-1971. The method of gathering them involved contact with each state unemployment security commission. The O.E.O. study was explained briefly, and the state office was asked to help out by supplying some information on each of the areas listed. The list included from five to twenty different counties or metropolitan areas. The contact was made in spring-summer, requesting information for the previous fiscal year. For each area there was a questionnaire with six items to be filled in. Two of the questions which are analyzed in this chapter are presented below in Table 8-1. These represent two different ways to assess the unemployment rate. The first asks for a subjective assessment while the second requests the more traditional statistics used to describe the unemployment situation. One weakness of these questions is that they ask for estimates for either "unskilled male labor" or a referent that is less well defined. For example, "What is the unemployment rate in the area listed above?" Ideally, one would like estimates that refer only to the unskilled male laborer in the age bracket 18-19, but such estimates are not available.

The data on unemployment were available for both FY 1969 and FY 1970. The 1969 data were chosen as the most appropriate. These data described the situation through the end of June, 1969, and most of the enlistments in the Youth in Transition study occurred prior to October of 1969.

TABLE 8-1

County Unemployment Data (FY 1969)[*]
Related to Attempted Enlistment (FY 1970)

Category	Percent of Sample (N=1799)	Percent of Category That Tried to Enlist
1. What is the market for unskilled labor in your county?		
1. Many more jobs than there are applicants	4%	8.3%
2. More jobs than there are applicants	13	10.4
3. Most people are able to find jobs	39	10.6
4. A number of unskilled workers are unable to find jobs	32	12.0
5. Many unskilled workers are unable to find jobs	12 / 100%	17.7

Grand Mean = 11.8%   Eta = .073   Eta-square = .005

Category	Percent of Sample (N=1799)	Percent of Category That Tried to Enlist
2. What is the unemployment rate in your area?		
1. Under 2%	5%	13.2%
2. 2 - 3.9%	67	10.9
3. 4 - 5.9%	22	10.6
4. 6 - 10%	6 / 100%	24.5

Grand Mean = 11.8%   Eta = .103   Eta-square = .011

5335
*Questions answered by state unemployment security commission for specified counties and metropolitan areas.

It can be seen from the data in Table 8-1 that unemployment is not strongly associated with enlistments, although the unemployment rate question (#2) shows a somewhat stronger association than the subjective assessment (#1). The enlistment rate is essentially flat for all levels of unemployment until the rate reaches the critical level of six percent. At that level of unemployment the enlistment rate is double the average rate. It appears, then, that this factor affects choice behavior only under very special circumstances.

This finding is consistent with the results of studies done for the Gates Commission. But it provides a useful qualifier. While area unemployment does not seem to be an important factor in most enlistment decisions, there are certain conditions under which it can play a part. It appears that enlistment becomes a more prominent alternative for a young man only if he is faced with very severe difficulties in finding a job in the civilian work force.

Expected Civilian Earnings

Another variable frequently used by the economists is the individual's expected earnings if he were to choose a civilian job instead of a military one. For this, the economists use estimates of current wages being earned by a group of like age and sex to the one under study. The Morgan O.E.O. data provide an estimate of the wages that "an unskilled male worker might receive" in a job in the county where he resides. Again it would have been desirable to have wage information on only the 18-19 year-old males. But it can be argued that Morgan's less-restricted estimate reflects the relative wage level from county-to-county for 18-19 year-olds, even if it is not a good measure of actual wages for that age bracket.

The data appear in Table 8-2. The trend is in the expected direction, with lower than average wages being associated with higher rates of enlistment. But the overall strength of association (eta=.020) is definitely non-

TABLE 8-2

County Wage Data (FY 1969)[*]
Related to Attempted Enlistment (FY 1970)

Category	Percent of Sample (N=1799)	Percent of Category That Tried to Enlist
What is the typical wage that an unskilled male worker might receive?		
1. Under $1.50	2%	14.3%
2. $1.50 - $1.99	55	11.7
3. $2.00 - $2.49	35	12.1
4. $2.50 - $2.99	8 / 100%	9.9
Grand Mean = 11.8%	Eta = .020	Eta-square = .000

5335

[*]Questions answered by state unemployment security commission for specified counties and metropolitan areas.

significant, indicating that, as measured, the expected wage level is not very important to an initial decision to enlist. This is contrary to findings of the Gates Commission studies, which concluded that relative military pay was an important determinant of enlistment behavior.

One possible explanation for this discrepancy is found in a study by Fechter (1970). He reports that, looking at enlistment rates over time, the fluctuations were somewhat sensitive to the number of casualties in Southeast Asia: "the coefficient of the interaction term implied that enlistments become less sensitive to relative pay changes as casualties rise" (Fechter, 1970, p. II-3-22). The Youth in Transition data were collected in Summer of 1969 when anti-Vietnam sentiment was widespread and casualty rates in Southeast Asia were at a high level. The studies for the Gates Commission were based on data collected, for the most part, during the early and mid 1960s. Thus, it is possible to conclude that the non-finding in the present study is the result of "unusual market conditions," and that wages would play a larger role in the decision to enlist at a time when the enlistment alternative was not fraught with so much personal danger.

Similar reasoning would modify somewhat our earlier conclusion about the relationship of unemployment to enlistment behavior. It is possible that under more favorable conditions of service—either peacetime or a time when this country is engaged in a more popularly supported conflict—the association between enlistment and civilian unemployment would be stronger and more linear.

Multivariate Prediction

The data were checked for possible interactions between unemployment and wages, on the assumption that the effect of unemployment would be heightened in areas where the average wages were low. Some interaction was found to exist, but the pattern was uninterpretable. Because some interaction did exist, a single pattern variable was used in the multivariate prediction instead of the two measures taken independently. The joint effect was not strong enough to bear detailed reporting.

Summary

Early studies done for the Defense Department reported that increased unemployment in the civilian labor market is related to higher rates of enlistment. More recent studies done for the Gates Commission have not supported this finding. Similarly, the present study found that there is very little association between rates of unemployment among unskilled males in a county-wide area and rates of enlistment in the same area. An exception to this occurred when the unemployment rate exceeded six percent: the enlistment rate was double that for areas with lower rates of unemployment.

Contrary to the Gates Commission studies, little or no association was found between rates of enlistment and average wages for unskilled males in a county.

It seemed reasonable that both unemployment and area wage levels would become stronger determinants of enlistment as this country extricates itself from involvement in Vietnam. At the time of the present study serving in the military was associated with a high probability of endangering one's life.

CHAPTER 9

YOUTH SPEAK FOR THEMSELVES

This chapter examines some information that is qualitatively different from that presented in earlier ones. The chapter is concerned with the explanations young men gave for their choice behavior. The first section looks at the reasons they gave for choosing a particular post-high school activity such as college, military service, or a job. The second section focuses on those individuals who did not enlist after high school; it considers the reasons they gave for rejecting military service as an alternative. The last section describes the use that students make of high school counselors—those adults who are assigned the task of facilitating the choice-making behavior of youth.

The data in this chapter are based on an individual's explanation for his own behavior. Such information is always somewhat difficult to interpret. The motivation for most human behavior is very complex, and can seldom be reduced to a single overriding factor. Even when it can, the behaving individual is not always in the best position to identify that factor. The reader is urged to keep these thoughts in mind while reading the chapter.

Explanations for the Choice of a Post-High School Activity

After high school young men select themselves into a variety of activities such as advanced education, military service, or a civilian job. (The distribution of the Youth in Transition sample into these various activities can be found in Figure 2-3.) At the final data collection, which occurred when most boys were one year beyond high school, the interviewer asked the respondent to think back over the past year and indicate what he felt were the most important reasons for choosing the activity he had pursued. The question appears below. [1]

Now we want to get back to what you've been doing this past year. Here is one way of thinking about why a person does things like working, furthering his education, or entering the military service—

There are pressures in life, some of which push a person towards doing something, while others push him away from doing the same thing. Some

139

examples of pressures are: the wishes of parents and other people, attractive opportunities that come along, money concerns, and the need for change.

What are some of the pressures which led you into what you have been doing this past year?

In coding the responses, 59 different types of answers were identified. For analysis purposes, these were collapsed into seven broad categories. (1) *Money* includes the mention of immediate financial needs like money for a car or living expenses. It also covers longer range financial pressures such as the one expressed in this response of a college student: "so I can get a good job and make a good living." (2) *Self-development* covers the expression of needs for advancement and personal development, excluding the explicit mention of higher income. Here are some typical responses placed in this category:

> Felt I had to go to school
> Felt the need for more education
> The job I want requires more education
> Chance to improve myself
> Trying to get ahead

(3) *Excitement* refers to those responses which contain the idea of wanting a chance to live a little, to have some excitement and travel. (4) *People* covers the mention of some person as influencing the choice. Pressure from parents is included, but it is also reported separately so that one can see the extent to which parents dominate the people-pressure category. (5) *Draft* includes the specific mention of the draft or such answers as "get my service time over with" and "the war." The answer had to have a clear connotation of responding to a pressure that was evaluated negatively by the individual. Thus, "serve my country" which connotes a positive evaluation of the war or the draft would not be included in this category. (6) *Other pressures.* This category includes a variety of responses, none of which were mentioned by a large number of respondents.

> Nature of pressure unclear
>
> > It seemed like a good idea
> > It was what I had always wanted to do
> > I had to do something
> > I wasn't sure what I wanted to do
> > I was tired of going to school
> > Social pressure
>
> Circumstances
>
> > No jobs available
> > Couldn't get into college; applied too late; grades not good enough

Couldn't get into the service
I was in an accident (implied: this is why I'm not working)

Miscellaneous

Wanted to fight for my country
Doubted the value of more education
Help other people
Get out of the house

(7) *No pressures.* Finally, there were those respondents who indicated that they felt no pressures at all.

Up to three responses were coded for each respondent. However, only the first response will be examined here. This response was considered to be the one most important to the individual as an explanation for his behavior. In Table 9-1 the most important reason is shown for each of four major post-high school activities. Those in technical or vocational schools were distinguished from those in other types of advanced education, because their answers show some interesting contrasts with both job and college groups. Since the focus of this study is on the choice of a first activity after high school, the table excludes several hundred respondents whose answers applied to the pressures they experienced at the time of choosing their second major activity. For example, some went to college, flunked out, then enlisted; the pressure they reported was for enlisting.

The Pressures That Were Reported. Money pressures were identified as most important by over half of those who took a job, and practically all of these expressed immediate money needs such as payments on a car, living expenses, and marriage. Very few in the other activity categories identified money needs at all. This is not surprising; schooling has no immediate financial payoff and military pay at the time of this study was less than $100 per month. Those among the schooling groups that did indicate money pressures were mostly those who expressed longer-range financial betterment; e.g., "I needed it to get a better job." Note that the percentage of tech/voc youth who identified the money pressure was twice that of the college youth.

The self-development needs were very prominent among the advanced schooling groups; over one-quarter indicated this as the most improtant reason. A much smaller proportion of the military or job groups identified this pressure. Recall that the self-development needs included such mentions as "I felt the need for more education" as well as "trying to get ahead." One could argue that this type of answer is related to social advancement and ultimately to financial concern. Regardless of the goal, it is clear that many of the college youth see continued education, and not on-the-job training or experience in the military, as the best way to achieve the goal.

The findings on pressures from people are interesting.[2] One-quarter of the college youth thought of pressure from people as the major reason why they chose to go to college. Almost all of these indicated that their parents were the source. It seems reasonable (although there are no data in this study

TABLE 9-1

Most Important Reason Given for Pursuing First Major Post-High School Activity

First Major Activity After High School	Money	Excitement; Live a little	Self-development; Need for ed	Pressures: a: everyone b: parents*	Draft; get MS over; the War	Other	No pressures	Total
JOB	54.9 _215_	1.3 _5_	5.6 _23_	a: 10.0 _39_ b: 7.1 _28_	1.8 _7_	15.0 _64_	11.7 _46_	100% _392_
MILITARY SERVICE	6.3 _8_	11.7 _15_	9.3 _12_	a: 13.5 _17_ b: 6.3 _8_	35.2 _45_	18.6 _24_	7.0 _9_	100% _128_
TECHNICAL/ VOCATIONAL SCHOOL	15.1 _11_	5.5 _4_	27.4 _20_	a: 19.2 _14_ b: 12.3 _9_	5.5 _4_	12.3 _9_	15.0 _11_	100% _73_
COLLEGE	8.2 _60_	2.3 _17_	27.1 _196_	a: 25.6 _185_ b: 22.6 _163_	10.0 _72_	12.4 _89_	14.4 _89_	100% _723_

Total N=1316**

5235

*Pressure from parents is included in the a-figure. For example, 10 percent of the job entrants identified pressure from some individual as the most important reason why they took a job. For 7.1 percent, parents were mentioned as the source of pressure.
**This is the number whose response referred to the first major activity after high school. Others answered for the second activity.

to support it) that these parents would be motivated by the desire to see their sons continue their education in order to secure the better job and social position associated with a college degree; thus self-development motives may apply to as many as one-half of the college group. The job and military groups seldom gave first mention to people pressure.

Not surprisingly, the draft is the most prominent reason mentioned by those who enlisted. Over one-third identified this as the most important reason. The draft also affected a number of others: ten percent of the college group felt they were in school to avoid the draft (this study was conducted at the time when it was still possible to obtain a deferment to attend college). One other pressure that was prominent among enlistees was the adventure and excitement associated with a military job. A little over ten percent associated enlisting with a chance to get away from home and see the world.

Explanation for NOT Choosing to Enlist

In a study of enlistment behavior it seemed appropriate to ask some additional questions of those who did not enlist to find out their feelings on military service. Accordingly, those without any military service experience were asked whether they had ever seriously considered enlisting as an alternative to the activity that they had chosen. Some 24 percent of the total sample answered in the affirmative, while another 61 percent indicated that they had never considered it at all. This is shown in Figure 9-1 below. Both of these latter two groups were asked additional questions about their response to the military. Their answers are described in the next two sections.

Those Who Seriously Considered Enlisting at Some Time (24 Percent). This group was asked, "What in particular about military service made you consider it seriously—that is, what were the advantages you saw in military service?" Almost one-half of this group identified educational and training benefits. These included job and skill training, schooling on the job, the G.I. Bill, and career security. Another quarter said they had seriously considered enlisting in order to get their military obligation over with; i.e., to avoid the draft. The remaining quarter identified a number of personal reasons such as "get away from the confusion in my home" and "a chance to grow up." Only three percent felt that they wanted to enlist out of a sense of duty to their country.

This same group was asked what had kept them from enlisting. Their answers are summarized in the left-hand pie chart in Figure 9-2. One-quarter indicated that they thought that school was more important for them. Thus, one of the very reasons given for seriously considering military service was also a reason for rejecting it after comparing the service with other forms of education. Sixteen percent did not think they were qualified, and another 16 percent were convinced by their friends and/or their family to pursue a different course of action. Eighteen percent gave reasons related to the war; how much of this is philosophical opposition to the Vietnam conflict and how much is fear of fighting is not discernible. The remaining one-quarter gave a

FIGURE 9-1

Degree of Interest in Enlistment

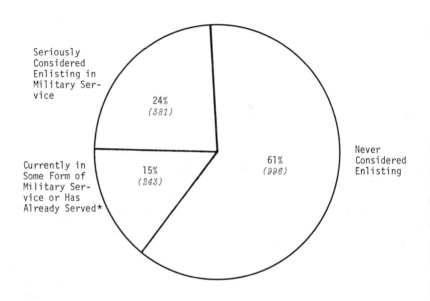

Note: N=1620. This is the size of the entire Time 4 sample.

*See Figure 2-3 for types of military service.

number of different reasons which did not lend themselves to easy categorization. These included such responses as "I got married," "I preferred a job," and "The Army doesn't offer the future I want."

Those Who Never Seriously Considered Enlisting (61 Percent). Respondents in this category were asked, "Why didn't you consider it seriously (as an alternative to what you did last year)?" The responses are summarized in the right-hand pie chart in Figure 9-2. For this group the anti-military/anti-Vietnam response stands out as the most prominent reason. Forty-three percent gave this answer. It appears that the outcome of a decision such as whether to enlist or not is affected by the social context in which that decision is made. To the extent that there is strong anti-war or anti-military sentiment

FIGURE 9-2

Reasons Given for Not Choosing to Enlist After High School

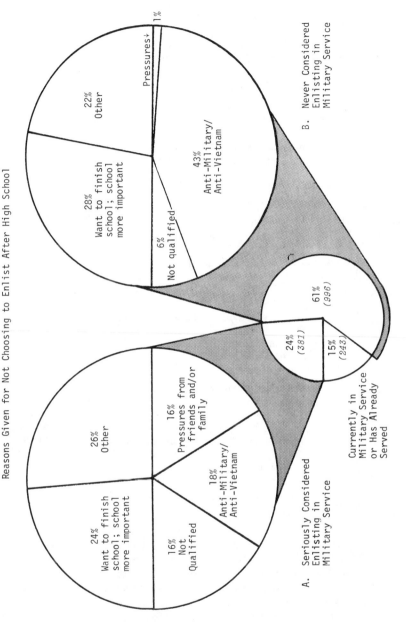

in this country, enlistments are bound to be lower than might otherwise be the case.

Over one-quarter of this group indicated that school was more important for them. This is about the same proportion found in the previous group that had considered enlisting, but did not follow through. It appears that military service does not fulfill the needs of those students who are bound for some form of advanced education.

Only one percent of the "never-considered-it" group identified pressures from other people as the reason. This is not surprising; it is unlikely that family or friends would have spoken out strongly against an individual enlisting unless he had given some indication of being inclined to do so. The impact of other people on the decision is probably captured in the anti-war sentiment, much of which is probably influenced by the opinions and attitudes of others.

The remaining quarter with "other" reasons indicated that they had interests that simply did not fit with the life of an enlisted man. These include marriage and specific job or career plans.

The "never-considered-it" group was also asked, "Are there (other) things about military service, in particular, that led you to reject it as an alternative for *you*?" Their responses are shown below.

3%	Pay is too low
3%	Length of service too long; not enough opportunities for advancement; miscellaneous
5%	Fear of being harmed or leaving home
12%	Anti-Vietnam sentiment
27%	Anti-military sentiment
13	too much discipline; spit and polish; don't like taking orders; not free to do as much.
7	general dislike for military service; I don't want to go; I don't see any benefits; I don't want to be in the 'green machine'
8	general anti-war feelings: I'm against fighting; against killing; I don't believe in the military system; I'm against the glorification of warfare
8%	Other
42%	No other reason given
100%	Never considered enlisting

Half of the "never-considered-it" group could think of nothing else or gave some unique response. Among those who did think of something else, a general dislike for military life was the most prominent reason. Things such as the discipline, spit-and-polish, and restricted life-style are prominent in their answers. Mixed in with this is sentiment against not only this particular war (Vietnam), but war in general. The fact of the matter is, the object of military activity and the style of life lived by a soldier are very repugnant to a large number of male youth. In contrast to this, a small proportion of young men (6 percent) identified less basic issues such as pay and length of service as the critical negative features. This is not to say that others would not be influ-

enced by pay increases. But it does not appear that this alone would be sufficient without a simultaneous withdrawal from Southeast Asia and/or some
changes in the conditions of military service.

School Counseling and Military Service

When the Youth in Transition panel members were interviewed at the
end of their senior year in high school, they were asked a number of questions
about contacts with counselors during their last year. The questions asked
how many times they had seen a counselor and how much time had been
spent discussing each of a number of different topics. These included:
—course selection
—coursework problems
—trouble in school
—personal problems
—military plans and obligations
—plans for education or training
—career or job choice
—procedures and applications for getting a permanent job after high
   school
In the above list there is some overlap in topics covered, so it is not possible to
simply sum the times to get a total time spent with a counselor. But, with
some interpolation, it appears that, on the average, a student saw his counselor about three times during senior year, for a total time of two to four
hours. About an hour of time was spent discussing education or training
after high school, or talking about longer-range career plans. Of those who
saw a counselor during this year, 59 percent never discussed military plans;
the average time for those who did was something less than one-half hour.
These data are presented here because they identify a source of influence on
individual decision-making which did not appear in any of the measures described earlier in this study. It appears that, if the military can offer something that is attractive and helpful to individual vocational concerns (training, money for later education, etc.), then school counselors might be utilized
more frequently as sources of dissemination. To do this counselors would
need to have the necessary information and, more importantly, be supportive
of the enlistment alternative for the youth they counsel. This theme will be
developed more fully in the "Summary and Policy Implications" chapter.

Summary

This chapter focuses on explanations given by youth for their choice of a
post-high school activity. The first section examined the reasons for choosing
as they did; the second section looked at the reasons for *not* choosing to enlist
in the service.

The reasons given for choice of a post-high school activity varied according to the activity pursued. The most commonly expressed reason given by
those who took a job was immediate financial gain. Those who pursued ad-

vanced education emphasized pressures for self-development and advancement, or pressure from parents to continue their education. It was argued that the motive of parents would also be for self-development and advancement, wanting to have their sons achieve a job and status that go along with an advanced degree. Those who were in military service mentioned the draft most frequently. Other reasons included the influence of other people (not always one's parents) and the excitement of travel and adventure.

Those who were not in the service were asked if they had ever seriously considered enlisting. Twenty-four percent of the sample had done so. Most frequently the characteristics of military service that had attracted them were training and education. The reasons given for not enlisting included: school was more important, pressure from family and friends not to enlist, anti-war feelings, or not being qualified.

Sixty-one percent of the sample indicated that they had never seriously thought of enlisting. The most prominent reason mentioned was anti-military and anti-Vietnam sentiment. Next most frequently mentioned was the idea that school was more important. When pressed further, many of this 61 percent indicated a strong distaste for the military life style and its emphasis on fighting and killing.

A brief look at how these youth made use of their high school counselors during senior year showed that an average of almost one hour was spent on vocational matters, but very little time was spent discussing military service plans. It was suggested that the school counselor might be an appropriate person to convey the pros and cons of service in the military.

---

[1] Boys who were overseas in the military were asked the same question with minor modifications for use in a self-administered questionnaire.

[2] The data for the Chapter 7 discussion of influence-sending came from a series of questions that followed the question being discussed here. In the present question an open-ended response was asked for. In the later questions respondents were asked about the pressures exerted by each of a list of people.

CHAPTER 10

WHY YOUNG MEN ENLIST AFTER HIGH SCHOOL — A REVIEW OF THE FINDINGS FROM THIS STUDY

One of the most important tasks facing a young man in high school is the choice of which activity to pursue after leaving high school. Basically, he has three alternatives: find a job, join the military, or continue his education. The central purpose of this study was to discover what factors influence a young man to select the alternative of military service.

The study is longitudinal in design, covering a span of four years in the lives of a panel of young men. The span corresponds to the period between the beginning of tenth grade and a point one year after most of the panel graduated from high school. During that time extensive information was collected on each individual's background, personality, intellectual ability, attitudes, and behaviors. The problem was to discover whether any of these measures, either singly or in combination, was strongly associated with the choice of enlisting. This chapter summarizes the findings.

The Study (Chapters 1 and 2)

The Youth in Transition project began collecting data on a nationwide representative sample of 2213 young men as they began tenth grade in the fall of 1966. The panel was re-interviewed at three points in time: the end of eleventh (1968) and twelfth grades (1969), and one year after graduation from high school (1970). Those who dropped out of school after the initial data collection were retained in the sample and many continued to participate in the research.

Plans and Later Behavior (Chapter 3)

Data from the most recent interview provided information as to which post-high school activity had been chosen by the young men in the sample. The definition of "activity chosen" is the one engaged in during winter/

spring of the year following graduation. For purposes of this study, the activities chosen were limited to three categories: work, military service, and advanced education. Plans during high school for a post-high school activity were similarly categorized.

In every grade during high school, advanced education was the most frequently mentioned plan, with two-thirds to three-quarters of the sample expressing this preference in tenth, eleventh, and twelfth grades. Preference for a civilian job declined during the high school years from a high of 20 percent in tenth grade to 12 percent in twelfth grade. The percent with plans to enlist varied over the years, but never exceeded nine percent.

After high school one-half of the sample actually continued their education, while one-third went to work. Fourteen percent entered some form of military service. The 14 percent includes enlistees, draftees, National Guard and Reserves; less than 12 percent enlisted for active duty in a regular branch of the service.

Focussing on the post-high school behavior groups, it was noted that very few of those in jobs or in the military service had expressed earlier plans to follow these pursuits; but the advanced education group had persistently planned from the tenth grade on to enter advanced education. From these data it was concluded that the decision to go to college is made fairly early; however, the decision to get a job or enter the service is typically made very late in high school, for many not until after graduation. In sum, it appears that advanced education is the most popular first choice early in high school. Military service and work usually become first choices only after it is realized that continued education is an unsuitable or impossible goal to achieve.

The group that enlisted after high school was examined in detail. Figure 10-1 shows what their plans were at the end of twelfth grade. Only one-half of them had expressed the choice of military service by this point in time. Another one-third were still expecting to pursue some form of advanced education. From these data and others, a "time-of-commitment" scale was constructed. This is shown in Figure 10-2. The scale shows that by the end of eleventh grade the choice of enlisting was a firm commitment for only 10 percent of the group that later enlisted, and that another 39 percent developed this commitment during twelfth grade. This leaves over one-half of the enlistees making a firm decision between the end of high school and the actual time of enlistment some months later.[1]

The examination of plans and behaviors suggested the time when the choice is made, but said nothing about the reasons for the choice. The next part of this chapter summarizes the findings from the search for correlates of the enlistment choice.

Predicting to Attempted Enlistment After High School (Chapters 4-8).

The criterion for the predictive study was a single measure which indicated whether or not a young man attempted to enlist at any time during the first year after high school. Because this is a study of choice behavior, those

FIGURE 10-1

Plans at the End of 12th Grade of Those Who Enlisted
During the First Year After High School (1969-1970)*

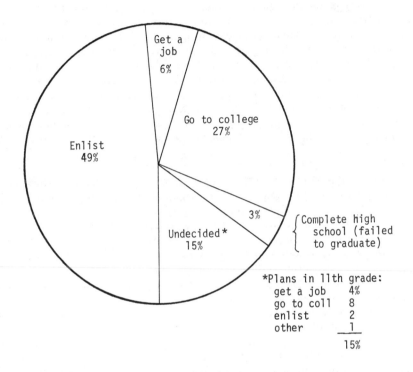

*Plans in 11th grade:
get a job   4%
go to coll   8
enlist   2
other   1
                15%

FIGURE 10-2

For Those Who Enlisted, the Point at Which the
Commitment to Enlist Became Firm

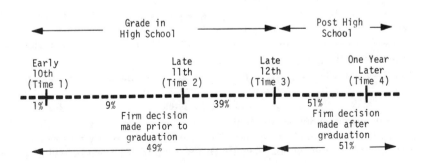

who attempted to enlist but were rejected were included among the enlistees. Young men who were drafted or who entered the National Guard or Reserves were excluded from the analyses (Chapter 2 presents the rationale for this exclusion).

The predictors that were investigated include a wide range of characteristics of the person and his environment (see Table 10-1). Among these are intelligence, school performance and attitudes, draft status, vocational maturity, attitude toward the service, socioeconomic level (and other characteristics of the family), feelings of friends and relatives toward enlistment, and area employment opportunities. Each characteristic was related to the criterion of attempted enlistment. The question to be answered in each case was whether the *rate* of enlistment differed for various levels of the characteristics. For example, to see whether intelligence was related to attempted enlistment, we looked to see if the proportion (rate) that attempted to enlist from the lowest I.Q. category differed from the proportion enlisting out of the middle or top I.Q. categories.

Dispositions or Motives for Enlistment (Chapter 4). Several variables in this study were highly associated with attempted enlistment. The strongest measures were those categorized as specific motives or dispositions for enlistment. Table 10-1 shows the scheme used to categorize the predictors, including the distinction between motives and conditioning factors.

Draft status, from which one can infer a motive of draft avoidance, was the most powerful predictor. This was true when it was used by itself to predict to enlistment; it was also true when it was used in conjunction with other predictors to be described later. In the latter case, draft status usually "dominated" the other predictors and reduced their effect. This is to say that most frequently, a young man's draft status was the most important single piece of information for predicting whether or not he tried to enlist after high school.

Almost as strong a predictor as draft status was a young man's perception of how well his personal job needs fit with his perception of characteristics of a military service job. The better the perceived fit with military service, the more likely he was to enlist. It was thought possible that this finding might be nothing more than a dissonance reduction phenomenon in which a young man, recognizing the inevitability of being drafted, imagined that he fit well into such a job in order to make the inevitable more tolerable. However, several analyses indicated that perceived fit had at least some of its effect independent of draft status, and therefore served as a motive in its own right.

The measure of fit was compared with a measure of simple preference for a military job over a civilian job. The two measures were so strongly related that it was concluded that youths develop at some time in their lives a generalized feeling about service life and the type of job a serviceman performs. It is this image which influences the choice. There were no data in this study to indicate how this image develops.

The one other measure that was classified as a disposition for enlistment was vocational indecision. Indecision over long-range vocational plans was

Table 10-1

Variables Examined as Potential Predictors of the Choice of
Enlisting After High School

I. Motives or Dispositions to Enlist

Perceived "fit" with (affinity for) military service life
Vocational indecision
Draft status (draft avoidance)

II. Conditioning Factors

Background
    Cultural
        Race
        Geographical region
        Urbanicity
    Family
        Broken home
        Family size
        Parental punitiveness
        Social class and richness of home environment
        Father's military experience
        Brother's military experience

Influence sending
    Anticipated response of parents, peers, friends, and school
        officials to possibility of enlisting

Aptitude
    Intelligence (GATB Test)

School factors
    Average classroom grades
    Attitudes toward school
    Rebellious school behavior
    Educational attainment (dropping out)
    Failing a grade prior to high school
    High school curriculum

Attitudes toward jobs

Political attitudes
    Toward Vietnam
    Trust in government

Economics
    Area Unemployment
    Area Wages

---

not associated with higher rates of enlistment; however, indecision over shorter range plans, such as what to do immediately after high school, was moderately related to enlistment. This provides some support for the notion that some young men enlist because a term in the service provides a period of time during which future plans can be thought through. The fact that short-range indecision did not relate more strongly to enlistment probably indicates that many other activities can fill this same need. For example, college attendance does not require much commitment to any well-defined plan; and many initial jobs are little more than exploratory adventures into the world of work.

Conditioning Factors (Chapters 5-8). A search for additional correlates of the enlistment decision was carried on among various categories of variables termed conditioning factors; these were so-called because they were hypothesized to predispose an individual to enlistment, although they could not be thought of as immediate causes of the decision.

To interpret the findings, one must appreciate the fact that a strong relationship was found to exist between a number of the more stable traits and characteristics of the individual and the choice of advanced education. As a result of this relationship, these same traits predicted inversely to enlistment. For example, intelligence and family socioeconomic level predicted strongly to both a young man's planning to go to college and his later entering college: high intelligence, high SEL students were most likely to continue their education after high school instead of taking a job or entering the service. A similar finding held for scholastic performance: good grades were associated with entering college. As a result of this pattern of association, these same factors predicted inversely to enlistment: i.e., *lower* levels of intelligence, SEL, and school grades were associated with enlistment. But when the analyses were repeated, excluding from the sample those who later entered college, the background and scholastic ability characteristics did not distinguish enlistees from those who chose civilian jobs. Thus, *among those who did not go on to college,* the rate of enlistment was virtually the same for all levels of intelligence, SEL, and classroom grades. This was seen as evidence that enlistees were very similar to the job-bound when it comes to background and ability.

Enlisting as an Escape. A major motivational theme which was explored was that of escape and opportunity. It was thought that those who could be classified as being deprived in some way would be more highly motivated to enlist in order to improve their condition. Three different groups were selected as being in some way deprived: blacks, the poor, and rural youth. It was found that young men from all three groups did enlist, but not at higher rates than their "non-deprived" classmates. Thus, while escape and opportunity may be an important reason why some young men enlist, it is only one of many motives which prompt young men to choose a term of service.

It was also hypothesized that those who did very poorly in school and who disliked the school environment would be more highly motivated to leave their home community and make a fresh start; i.e., this group would be more inclined to enlist. This was not the case at all. In fact, slightly higher motivation for enlistment was associated with having received average grades, having held fairly positive attitudes about the value of school, and having been among the less delinquent in school. Such a conclusion is based on relatively small tendencies in the data; nonetheless, it is contrary to what was hypothesized.

Job and Political Attitudes (Chapter 5). An individual's attitude toward jobs is related to enlistment. Two dimensions of job ambition were identified: desire for a job that pays off (e.g., good pay, chance to get ahead, opportunities to learn new skills) and desire for a job that is easy and undemanding (e.g., easy work, little responsibility, no demands to learn new skills). Job payoff was unrelated to enlistment, but job ease was related: those looking for an easy job were much less likely to enlist than those who were relatively unconcerned about this aspect of a job. This was especially true within the noncollege subsample. The data suggest that tolerance for hard work predisposes young men toward military service.

Two other attitudinal measures associated with enlisting are attitude toward the war in Vietnam and trust in government (Chapters 5 and 12). As would be expected, those most strongly against the war were least likely to enlist, and those most trustful of the federal government were most likely to enlist. These and related findings suggest that a "Middle American" value set predisposes an individual to the choice of enlisting.

Influence Sending (Chapter 7). An individual's perception of what other people think he should do—called influence sending—is another important factor in an enlistment decision (Chapter 7). The sources of influence sending examined in this study included parents, siblings, peers, and school officials. If a young man perceived that these people were supportive of his enlisting, then he was much more likely to enlist. Especially important was the opinion of parents. On the other hand, school teachers and counselors seem currently to be a neutral force in decisions to work or enter military service. Related to influence sending was the expected behavior of classmates. If a young man reported that a number of his close friends were planning to enlist, then he was more likely to enlist himself.

Economics (Chapter 8). Early studies done for the Defense Department reported that increased unemployment in the civilian labor market is related to higher rates of enlistment. More recent studies done for the Gates Commission have not supported this finding. Similarly, the present study found very little association between rates of unemployment among unskilled males in a county-wide area and rates of enlistment in the same area. An exception to this occurred when the unemployment rate exceeded six percent. Above this, the enlistment rate was double that for areas with lower rates of unemployment. It appears that enlistment becomes a more prominent alternative for a young man only if he is faced with very severe difficulties finding a job in the civilian work force.

Contrary to the Gates Commission studies, little or no association was found between rates of enlistment and average wages for unskilled males in a county.

It seems reasonable that both unemployment and area wage levels will become more strongly associated with enlistment as this country extricates itself from involvement in Vietnam. At the time this study was conducted, serving in the military was associated with a high probability of endangering one's life, thus reducing the attractiveness of a military job as an alternative to any type of civilian employment.

Youth Speak for Themselves (Chapter 9). A separate chapter was devoted to explanations of the respondents themselves for their particular choice of a post-high school activity. They were asked for this information one year after high school. The reader should exercise caution interpreting the data because of the problems inherent in self-reports of motivation.

The explanations given varied according to the activity pursued. The most commonly expressed reason given by those who took a civilian job was immediate financial gain. Those who pursued advanced education emphasized pressures for self-development and advancement, or pressure from parents to continue their education. It seems likely that these parents were motivated by an interest in their sons' advancement, wanting their sons to acquire the jobs and status that go along with an advanced degree.

Those who were in military service most frequently mentioned pressure from the draft. Other reasons included opinions of other people (not always parents) and the excitement of travel and adventure.

Those who were not in the service were asked if they had ever seriously considered enlisting. Twenty-four percent of the sample said they had done so (see Figure 10-3). They were then asked what aspects of military service had attracted them. Most frequently they mentioned the opportunity for training and education. Interestingly, among the reasons given for *not* enlisting, the one mentioned most frequently was that "school was more important." Also mentioned were such things as pressure from family and friends not to enlist, strong anti-Vietnam sentiment, and feeling unqualified for service.

Sixty-one percent of the sample indicated that they had never seriously thought of enlisting. The most prominent reason mentioned was anti-military or anti-Vietnam sentiment. Next most frequently mentioned was the idea that school was more important. When pressed further, many of these sixty-one percent indicated a strong distaste for the military life style and its emphasis of fighting and killing.

A brief look at how these youth made use of their high school counselors during senior year showed that an average of almost one hour was spent discussing vocational matters, but very little of that time was spent discussing military service plans. It was suggested that the school counselor might be an appropriate person to convey the pros and cons of service in the military.

Summary

It appears that even prior to entrance into tenth grade many young men are "keyed" to the choice of advanced education after high school. Such a choice is highly predictable from aptitude and family background. The same

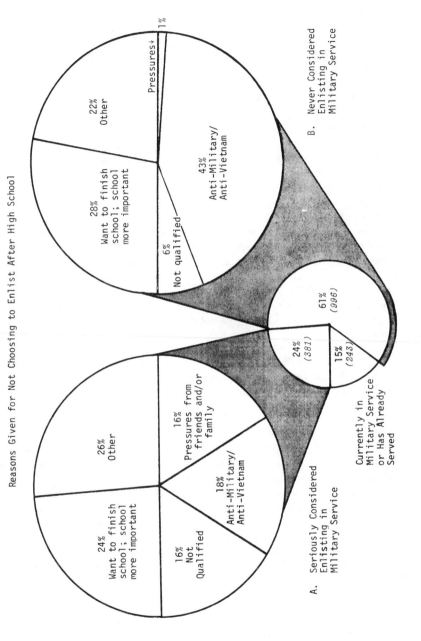

FIGURE 10-3

Reasons Given for Not Choosing to Enlist After High School

is not true for a work or military service choice. In our study of "the class of '69," those who entered work or military service adopted those choices only in the later years of high school, and then somewhat reluctantly. There were almost no background characteristics which distinguished enlistees from those who took jobs. Only ideology—including attitudes toward jobs, school, and the Vietnam War—was associated with higher-than-average enlistment rates.

The emphasis on higher education is not surprising; the environment of an adolescent is strongly oriented to school. The curricula in high schools throughout the country are fairly uniform in their emphasis on academic achievement. It is also apparent that a majority of young men perceive that parents, teachers, sibs, and peers are most supportive of the advanced education choice and least supportive of other alternatives, especially military service.

For those in the study who did not continue their education beyond high school, the high school years were characterized by much indecision and change of plans. However, toward the end of high school and even shortly after graduation, the reality of college admissions standards, the requirements and demands of the world of work, and the threat of the Selective Service system gradually imposed themselves on individuals and forced many to compromise their preferences in the light of personal ability and "market" demands.

The process did not seem entirely outside the individual's control; there were elements of individual choice as well. In selecting among the non-college alternatives, youth matched personal needs with their image of the jobs available (military and civilian) and attempted to maximize the fit. In this process it appears that choices were affected by the influence-network of parents, siblings, and peers, both through the opinions these people expressed and the examples they set.

In the first part of this report we have attempted to explain why some young men in the class of 1969 chose to enlist after high school while others did not. The analysis has focused on the plans, attitudes, and behaviors of young men under conditions that prevailed in 1969-1970. But conditions have changed considerably since then. In the next part of the report we turn to a consideration of what these same youth said they would do if the conditions of enlistment were somewhat different—if various incentives were available to those who enlisted. It is this part of the study which should prove most valuable to those concerned with the implementation of an All-Volunteer Armed Force.

---

[1]Young men may be *predisposed* to an enlistment choice at some earlier point in time, but other alternatives (college, work) are stronger until the point indicated on the scale.

PART II

CONSCRIPTION VS. AN ALL-VOLUNTEER ARMED FORCE

CHAPTER 11

THE NATIONAL DEBATE OVER AN ALL-VOLUNTEER ARMED FORCE

During much of the last decade, the United States has been engaged in a vigorous debate concerning the merits of the draft as a source of military manpower. The great urgency of this debate has derived from the Vietnam War, but the basic issues transcend this particular war and go to the heart of the role of military forces in a free society.

Highlights of the Debate

The military draft, never very popular during the post-World War II era, came under increasing fire in the 1960s. By 1966 there were widespread student demonstrations against the draft and its inequities. On July 1 of that year, President Johnson appointed a National Advisory Commission on Selective Service (the Marshall Commission) charged to ". . . consider the past, present, and prospective functioning of selective service and other systems of national service in the light of the following factors: fairness to all citizens; military manpower requirements; the objective of minimizing uncertainty and interference with individual careers and education; social, economic, and employment conditions and goals; budgetary and administrative consideration . . ." (Tax, 1967, p. 466).

Shortly before the Marshall Commission was appointed, the University of Chicago began plans for a national conference on the draft. The conference took place in December of 1966, under the chairmanship of Sol Tax. It brought together a wide range of participants including social scientists, legislators, military leaders, and also the executive director of the Marshall Commission, Bradley H. Patterson, Jr. Mr. Patterson attended the conference for the explicit purpose of insuring that the Marshall Commission had full benefit of the ideas and recommendations generated in the Chicago Conference. A variety of viewpoints were expressed in prepared papers and in several days of careful discussion. Indeed, the great majority of ideas that have been the focus of discussion in more recent years were represented in the

1966 Chicago Conference. No genuine consensus emerged from the conference; nevertheless, there did appear a considerable depth and range of support for an all-volunteer armed force as an alternative to the draft.[1]

In March of 1967 President Johnson proposed that Congress enact a four-year extension of the authority to induct men into the Armed Forces. His proposal also included a number of reforms in the Selective Service system intended to make the system more fair and less disruptive to young men; by now most of these reforms have been implemented. The President's message to Congress stated a clear *preference* for a force based entirely on volunteers, but concluded that unfortunately this was not feasible for two reasons: most important, the President felt that an all-volunteer force could not be expanded quickly to meet a sudden challenge; in addition, it would probably be very expensive.

Support for an all-volunteer force continued to grow, however, and in 1969 President Nixon announced the appointment of an Advisory Commission on an All-Volunteer Armed Force, chaired by former Secretary of Defense Thomas S. Gates, Jr. In 1970 the Gates Commission submitted its report to the President. The following excerpt captures much of the substance and spirit of the report:

> . . . However necessary conscription may have been in World War II, it has revealed many disadvantages in the past generation. It has been a costly, inequitable, and divisive procedure for recruiting men for the armed forces. It has imposed heavy burdens on a small minority of young men while easing slightly the tax burden on the rest of us. It has introduced needless uncertainty into the lives of all our young men. It has burdened draft boards with painful decisions about who shall be compelled to serve and who shall be deferred. It has weakened the political fabric of our society and impaired the delicate web of shared values that alone enables a free society to exist.

> These costs of conscription would have to be borne if they were a necessary price for defending our peace and security. They are intolerable when there is an alternative consistent with our basic national values. (United States President's Commission on an All-Volunteer Armed Force, 1970, pp. 9-10)

The Gates Commission proposed an all-volunteer force as the alternative, and recommended three basic steps as necessary to attain it: raise pay, improve conditions of service and recruiting, and establish a standby draft system. The Commission also dealt specifically with many of the questions and objections raised in opposition to an all-volunteer force. We review some of the most important of these issues in the next section, often relying on excerpts from the Commission's report.

President Nixon accepted the major conclusions of the Gates Commission. In a message to Congress in April of 1970, he stated his objective of reducing draft calls to zero, and outlined a series of pay increases and other steps designed to reach that objective. He addressed the Congress again in

January of 1971, proposed further steps to move toward the goal of an all-volunteer force, but also requested an extension of the draft. The President requested only a two-year extension of induction authority, and coupled this request with proposals for reform of the draft. The question of extending the draft for even two years was debated vigorously, but eventually the extension was enacted. Later in 1971, Congress also voted substantial increases in military pay. While these were not as high as the Gates Commission recommended, they did almost double the average monthly pay for new recruits.

Major Issues in the Debate

Two major questions had been raised about the feasibility of an all-volunteer armed force.

1. *Does an all-volunteer force lack the flexibility to expand quickly to meet a sudden challenge?* President Johnson had stated in 1967 that this lack of flexibility was his most important reason for not recommending an all-volunteer force. In fact, however, this appears to be a false issue, as Friedman (1967) and later the Gates Commission pointed out:

> Military preparedness depends on forces in being, not on the ability to draft untrained men. Reserve forces provide immediate support to active forces, while the draft provides only inexperienced civilians who must be organized, trained, and equipped before they can become effective soldiers and sailors—a process which takes many months. (U.S. President's Commission . . ., 1970, p. 13)

The argument seems compelling—a draft would be far too cumbersome to provide genuine flexibility to meet a sudden challenge. Thus it cannot be said that national security requires the continuing presence of the draft. (But just for good measure, the Gates Commission developed machinery for a "standby draft" which could go into effect immediately, provided the Congress gave its approval.)

2. *Can the nation afford the cost of an all-volunteer force?* This was the second reason President Johnson had given for not recommending an all-volunteer force. But later the Gates Commission pointed out that the real issue boils down to *who* should bear the costs of the armed forces. A draft system which pays draftees (and draft-induced volunteers) less than would be required to induce truly voluntary service, involves what has been termed a "conscription tax."[2]

> Men who are forced to serve in the military at artificially low pay are actually paying a form of tax which subsidizes those in the society who do not serve . . . . This cost does not show up in the budget. Neither does the loss in output resulting from the disruption in the lives of young men who do not serve, but who rearrange their lives in response to the possibility of being drafted. Taking these hidden and neglected costs into account, the actual cost to the nation of an all-volunteer force will be lower than the cost of the present force. (U.S. President's Commission . . ., 1970, p. 9)

This distinction between real costs and those which show up in a budget was not originated by the Gates Commission; the point had been made sharply and clearly at the 1966 University of Chicago Conference on the Draft by a number of participants, particularly economists Milton Friedman (1967) and Walter Oi (1967). It is thus a matter of no small interest that President Johnson, in his 1967 message urging the extension of the draft, chose not to acknowledge that the reason an all-volunteer force involves a higher military budget is primarily because it eliminates the unfair (and hidden) conscription tax.

In his 1970 message to the Congress, President Nixon spoke directly of the financial inequities borne by draftees. "These men, in effect, pay a large hidden tax—the difference between their military pay and what they could earn as civilians. Therefore, on the grounds of equity alone, there is good reason to substantially increase pay." (Nixon, 1970)

Summarizing our discussion thus far, we see that two major questions which had been raised about the *feasibility* of an all-volunteer force were anticipated in the 1966 Chicago Conference, and were again answered very effectively in the report of the Gates Commission. 1. The flexibility to meet a sudden challenge depends upon the forces presently under arms, rather than forces which could be called up by means of a draft. 2. An all-volunteer force would actually have a lower real cost to the nation; moreover, the cost would be visible rather than hidden, and would be equitably shared among all taxpayers. But there remain other, perhaps more fundamental, issues in the debate over whether we should have a draft or an all-volunteer force. Many of these issues were raised in the 1966 Chicago Conference and then treated also by the Gates Commission.

3. Would an all-volunteer force attract disproportionate numbers of the poor and blacks? Would it fail to attract a sufficient number of skilled and highly qualified men? These several issues all hinge on some labor-market assumptions about how a volunteer force would be recruited. The main assumption is that pay would be raised just enough to insure a sufficient number of volunteers. It is further assumed that this would make military service most attractive to those whose civilian opportunities are most limited— particularly those disadvantaged by a background of poverty or racial discrimination.

The Gates Commission countered this argument in several ways. First, it argued that if we continue to have a mixed force of conscripts and volunteers, the majority of servicemen are likely to be "true volunteers" (i.e., volunteers not motivated by the draft). Thus a conversion to a fully volunteer force would not drastically alter the manpower composition of the armed services.

Second, the commission argued that military pay is already relatively attractive to those who have the poorest civilian alternatives. Raising pay levels ". . . will increase the attractiveness of military service more to those who have higher civilian earnings potential than to those who have lower civilian potential" (U.S. President's Commission . . ., 1970, pp. 16-17).

4. Would an all-volunteer force encourage a separate military ethos, and thus constitute a political threat? It is often maintained that the presence of draftees—civilians who serve only temporarily and do not really consider themselves a permanent part of the military establishment—provide a form of insurance against a further growth of military power, autonomy, and adventurism.

The Gates Commission again took the position that an all-volunteer force would not really be very different from the present *largely* volunteer force, especially since the officer corps is already overwhelmingly staffed by true volunteers. Milton Friedman made the same basic point in the Chicago Conference, but in a less sanguine tone. His statement is worth quoting at length:

> There is little question that large Armed Forces plus the industrial complex required to support them constitute an ever-present threat to political freedom. Our free institutions would certainly be safer if the conditions of the world permitted us to maintain far smaller armed forces.
>
> The valid fear has been converted into an invalid argument against voluntary armed forces. They would constitute a professional army, it is said, that would lack contact with the populace and become an independent political force, whereas a conscripted army remains basically a citizen army. The fallacy in this argument is that the danger comes primarily from the officers, who are now and always have been a professional corps of volunteers . . . .
>
> However we recruit enlisted men, it is essential that we adopt practices that will guard against the political danger of creating a military corps with loyalties of its own and out of contact with the broader body politic . . . .
>
> For the future, we need to follow policies that will foster lateral recruitment into the officer corps from civilian activities—rather than primarily promotion from within. The military services no less than the civil service need and will benefit from in-and-outers. For the political gain, we should be willing to bear the higher financial costs involved in fairly high turnover and rather short average terms of service for officers. We should follow personnel policies that will continue to make at least a period of military service as an officer attractive to young men from many walks of life. (Friedman, 1967, pp. 206-207)

One theme in Friedman's statement needs special emphasis here. It need not necessarily follow that an all-volunteer force will be staffed by career men with long-range commitments to the military establishment. On the contrary, the United States can (and in Friedman's view, should) design policies that will encourage greater turnover, especially in the officer corps—provided, of course, that the nation is willing to pay the financial costs in an open and above-board system of accounting.

To summarize the discussion about the nature of an all-volunteer force, it has been argued fairly effectively by the Gates Commission that the volunteer force it proposed would not differ greatly from the mixed force of volunteers and draftees we have today—especially since our present force is directed by a professional officer corps, with upper levels staffed entirely by career men. This conclusion may be accurate in large measure; nevertheless, it is not entirely satisfactory. Recent disclosures of widespread corruption, deception, and atrocities involving our present military force are not likely to put its critics at ease about the prospects of continuing "business as usual" if we convert to an all-volunteer force. Friedman's argument in favor of greater turnovers remains very persuasive. The nature of an all-volunteer force may depend heavily upon whether we are willing to spend the money and effort necessary to develop incentives that bring to officer as well as enlisted ranks a wide cross-section of citizens for relatively short tours of military duty.

Some Working Assumptions Growing Out of the Debate

The debate over the draft versus an all-volunteer force has been summarized here for two reasons. First, it provides an important background for understanding the changing attitudes of youth toward the draft and military service. More important, it provides the broad context in which the research reported here must be considered.

In our view, the United States is presently moving toward an all-volunteer armed force. Available data (summarized in the next chapter) indicate that young people have come to favor this alternative, and have grown less willing to tolerate the draft no matter how much it is reformed. As more and more young people and teachers and parents come to realize that our present draft system imposes an unfair conscription tax on a fraction of our young ablebodied males, it seems inevitable that we will finally rise above the problem of a larger budget. The question is no longer whether we can afford an all-volunteer force, for we have come to realize that we surely can. The fundamental question is what *kind* of voluntary force do we want, and what kinds of incentives will be most likely to produce it.

The arguments summarized in this chapter suggest that the nation will be best served by a military force with the following manpower characteristics: (1) There should be wide variety of abilities and socioeconomic backgrounds. We should not have a "one class" armed force. (2) A broad range of political views should be represented, including some who are willing to make independent judgments about our military actions. If we have an armed force manned only by those who uncritically follow the call, "My country, right or wrong," we increase the risk that our country will indeed be wrong. (3) There should be a substantial proportion of *non*-career men at all levels—men who see themselves as essentially civilians spending a few useful years in military service before returning to civilian life.

All of the manpower objectives noted above are attainable within a voluntary framework, given an appropriate system of incentives. In a later chapter we will consider some specific examples of such incentives. But first it will be useful to consider some data bearing on the way young people, especially young men, feel about national issues in general, and about the draft and military service in particular. We turn to these topics next.

---

[1]The products of the University of Chicago Conference on the Draft, both position papers and transcripts of the discussions, are contained in a volume edited by Tax (1967).

It should be noted that an all-volunteer force is not the only alternative which has been proposed to take the place of the present draft system. Other possibilities include Universal Military Training, or mandatory National Service (which provides both military and non-military alternatives for serving the national needs). Such alternatives have not been examined here because they seem much less likely to become a reality, given the current commitment of the government to the all-volunteer force concept.

[2]Indeed, the commission estimated that the conscription tax paid by draftees amounts to a tax burden more than three times that paid by comparable civilians. A commission staff report on the conscription tax put the matter succinctly: "As a tax, conscription under Selective Service is brutally inefficient—virtually in a class by itself." (Sjaastad and Hansen, 1970, pp. IV-1-34)

CHAPTER 12

YOUTH VIEWS ON VIETNAM, THE ESTABLISHMENT, AND MILITARY SERVICE

In earlier chapters we established that the threat of being drafted was an important factor in a young man's decision to enlist. Other important factors included personal attitudes toward military life, views about the war in Vietnam, and perceptions of how others—peers as well as parents—feel about such things. In an all-volunteer setting there will be no draft to induce young men to "Go Army!" Attitudes about national military policies, as well as perceptions of the serviceman's life-style, will probably become increasingly important in determining a young man's response to military service. For this reason, we turn our attention now to a description of the ways in which young men's attitudes on these issues have been changing, and the implications such changes might have for recruitment in a no-draft environment.

National Issues

Vietnam. As early as 1966, when they were starting tenth grade, a few of the respondents in the Youth in Transition study (7 percent) mentioned the draft or the Vietnam War in response to the open-ended interview question, "Can you tell me some of the problems young men your age worry about most?" The 7 percent figure in 1966 grew to 38 percent in 1968, and 75 percent in 1970. The 1970 data collection included an item used in several Gallup Polls, which gave respondents a choice among four plans for dealing with the war; 25 percent favored "immediate" withdrawal, 34 percent favored withdrawal "by the end of 18 months" (i.e., by the end of 1971), 25 percent favored withdrawal taking as long as needed to turn the War over to the South Vietnamese, and 12 percent favored a step-up in the fighting. The attitudes of the young men in the Youth in Transition sample were slightly more "dovish" than those of males in the Gallup Polls, but the differences were by no means large; moreover, there is evidence that the percentage of adults favoring rapid withdrawal was also growing during that time (Bachman and Van Duinen, 1971).

The data collections in 1969 and 1970 included a "Vietnam Dissent Index" based on six questionnaire items. (See Chapter Five for a description of this measure.) In the spring of 1969 there seemed to be more support for the War than dissent against it, although a large group gave a mixed picture of some support and some dissent. A clear shift was evident by the late spring and early summer of 1970; the number of dissenters increased, while the supporters decreased. Closer inspection of the data revealed that the changes occurred largely among those who spent the year in college. This is illustrated in Figure 12-1 which shows the shifts in mean Vietnam dissent for various subgroups. Just before high school graduation in 1969, those bound for college differed little from their classmates in Vietnam Dissent; after their first year of college, they were on the average noticeably more critical of United States policy in Vietnam. Only those who spent the year in military service became less critical of this policy.

A survey by Yankelovich (1971) also found that there was a sharp increase in Vietnam-related dissent among college students from spring of 1969 to spring of 1970. He reported that strong agreement to the statement "The war in Vietnam is pure imperialism" increased from 16 percent in 1969 to 41 percent in 1970, based on two cross-sectional studies of college students in the United States. These and other results led Yankelovich to conclude that the continuation of the War has increased alienation of college students and reinforced their doubts about the system. Some findings based on Youth in Transition data lend further support to this conclusion, as we shall note a bit later.

Trust in Government and "The System." All four data collections of the Youth in Transition project included a series of questionnaire items dealing with trust in the government and political leaders. Responses to these items show a steady decline in trust from 1966 through 1970, with the largest shifts occurring between 1969 and 1970. For example, those feeling that the government wastes "a lot" or "nearly all" of the money paid in taxes increased from 30 percent in 1966 to 56 percent in 1970. When asked how much they could "trust the government in Washington to do what is right," 72 percent of the respondents in 1966 answered "often" or "almost always," but by 1970 only 53 percent showed that same level of trust.

An index was created of the above two items and one more which asked respondents whether they thought "the people running the government are smart people who usually know what they are doing." The index is called Trust in Government and is used in Figure 12-1 to demonstrate the shifts in trust which occurred during the first year after high school. It is apparent that Trust in Government declined for the entire sample during this one-year period, but the decline was especially steep among those who attended college.

Further evidence indicates that this drop in trust cannot be written off as something limited to those going through a particular stage of development,

FIGURE 12-1

Comparison of Change Scores in Vietnam Dissent
and Trust in Government for
Selected Subgroups

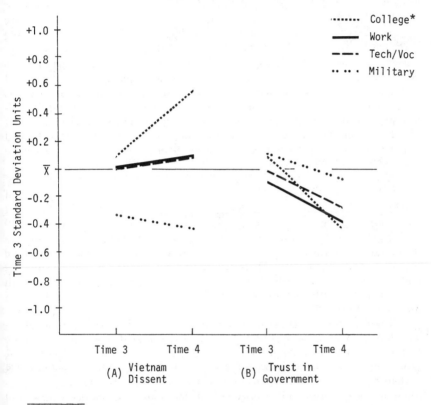

NOTE: Time 3 corresponds to the end of twelfth grade (June, 1969);
Time 4 to one year later (June, 1970). X̄ marks the mean score for
the total Time 3 sample; all other scores are normalized on the
Time 3 mean and standard deviation for the total sample. Those
unemployed (N=73) and continuing high school (N=49) are not included
in the figure.

*College: includes university, four-year liberal arts, junior college
and community college.

nor is it evidence of a generation gap between youth and their elders. Voter studies conducted by the Political Behavior Program at the Institute for Social Research found that the same questions showed a sharp decline in trust among adults between 1964 and 1970; moreover, the overall level of dissatisfaction among adults in 1970 equalled or exceeded that shown by the Youth in Transition sample of young men.

These findings are by no means unique, as an earlier report indicated (Bachman and Van Duinen, 1971, pp. 25-28):

> Our findings of dissatisfaction with government are corroborated by findings from other studies. Thirty-nine percent of Ohio high school students agree that the government does a "bad job" of representing the views and desires of the people. Even more striking are the responses to this statement, "The form of government in this country needs no major changes." Forty-eight percent disagreed, whereas only 31 percent agreed (Bryant, 1970). The Harris poll in *Life* (1971) found similar results to the question, "How much confidence do you have in the government to solve the problems of the 70's?" Twenty-two percent of the 15-21 year olds said "hardly any"; 54 percent said "some but not a lot"; and only 20 percent said "a great deal." Similar results were found in the Purdue study of high school students. Forty-eight percent of the sample of twelfth-graders felt that "there are serious flaws in our society today, but the system is flexible enough to solve them"; the remainder were divided equally between complete endorsement of the present American way of life, calls for radical change, and undecided (Erlick, 1970).

The Role of the Military in National Affairs. Two questions in the 1969 Youth in Transition data collection dealt with the role the military plays in the United States. The first question asked, "Do you think military personnel have too much or too little influence on the way the country is run?" Twenty-five percent answered "too much" or "far too much," 17 percent checked "too little" or "far too little," while 56 percent considered the influence "about right." The second question asked, "Do you think the U.S. spends too much or too little on the military?" Those who indicated we spend "too much" or "far too much" totaled 42 percent, while 18 percent felt we spend "too little," and 39 percent considered the level of military spending to be "about right."

These questions were not included in the 1970 data collection; had they been repeated, they probably would have shown an increased inclination to limit the role of the military, especially among college students. Yankelovich (1971) reports that college students urging "fundamental reform" in the military increased from 50 percent in 1969 to 56 percent in 1970, while those taking the more radical view that the military should be "done away with" increased from 5 percent to 10 percent.

Threat of Nuclear War. Certainly the Vietnam War is a basic cause of discontent with the role of the military in our society, but perhaps another reason that some would be willing to limit military influence and spending is that there is less perceived threat of all-out war than might have been expected among youth raised in the "nuclear era." When the 1970 Youth in Transition interview asked respondents to rate the importance of a number of problems facing the nation, the "chance of nuclear war" was rated as "very important" by a much smaller number than were problems of population, pollution, race relations, crime and violence, hunger and poverty. Many young men stated explicitly their view that a nuclear stalemate had been reached and, as one respondent put it, "no one is stupid enough to kill everyone." When asked what they thought should be done to avoid nuclear war, 8 percent said they didn't think it was much of a problem or threat, and 9 percent said nothing more could (or should) be done. About 5 percent proposed relatively "hard-line" solutions such as strengthening our arms, anti-ballistic missiles, bomb shelters, or civil defense measures. In contrast, a total of 35 percent urged banning nuclear weapons, negotiations with other countries, improving foreign relations, and simply "making peace." (The remaining respondents gave vague, uncodeable answers, or could offer no opinion on how to avoid nuclear war.) An earlier report summarized these findings in the following terms:

> The present generation of young men have strong concerns, and express growing opposition, when it comes to the war in Vietnam. The larger threat of nuclear war, however, does not alarm them nearly as much as may have been expected. Perhaps this is simply a contrast effect; Vietnam is a clear and present danger, especially for young men, whereas the danger of a nuclear holocaust is more abstract and remote. On the other hand, it may be the demise of the foreign policy of "brinkmanship" which is responsible for this feeling that nations can and will avoid the use of nuclear weapons. These young men have seen the bomb shelters come and go; since 1962 (the time of the Cuban missile crisis) there has been a more-or-less steady movement away from nuclear threat and counter-threat. In short, the overall trend of experience for young men (in contrast to that of their parents) has been gradual reduction in emphasis on nuclear war.

> Whatever the reasons may be, the dominant attitude among young men seems clearly to be that a stalemate has been reached. They feel that the major powers are sufficiently aware of the potential for total destruction in a nuclear war that they will not start one. (Bachman and Van Duinen, 1971, pp. 80-82)

Interrelations Among Views. The views on national issues outlined above do not exist in isolation from each other. In particular, the Vietnam War has often been cited as a major cause of eroded trust in government and the military. This assertion is supported by the correlational data presented in Table 12-1. Vietnam Dissent is negatively related to Trust in Government, and positively related to statements that military influence and spending are excessive.

Since Vietnam Dissent and Trust in Government were measured in 1969 and again in 1970, we can note their stability across time. The stabilities are fairly high (.56 for Vietnam Dissent and .48 for Trust in Government), espe-

Table 12-1

Correlations Among Views on National Issues*

	(1)	(2)	(3)	(4)	(5)
(1) Vietnam Dissent, 1969					
(2) Vietnam Dissent, 1970	.56				
(3) Trust in Government, 1969	-.29	-.22			
(4) Trust in Government, 1970	-.35	-.46	.48		
(5) Military has too much influence in U.S., 1969	.30	.27	-.11	-.17	
(6) U.S. spends too much on military, 1969	.36	.33	-.14	-.20	.42

*Table entries are product-moment correlations based on approximately 1600 to 1800 cases. All are statistically significant beyond the .001 level. More extensive descriptions of the Vietnam Dissent and Trust in Government scales are provided in Chapter 5 and in Bachman and Van Duinen (1971).

cially when we consider that the scales are very brief (six items and three items, respectively). Many young men shifted their views on these dimensions between 1969 and 1970, but the overall ordering remained pretty much the same—those dissenting in 1969 were likely to be among the most dissenting in 1970.

The cross-time data may be used in another way to provide further clues about the causal relationship between Vietnam Dissent and Trust in Government. Figure 12-2 presents the necessary data in schematic form using a technique which Campbell and Stanley (1963) have termed "cross-lagged panel correlation." We should note first that the negative correlation between Vietnam Dissent and Trust in Government increased from —.29 in 1969 to —.46 in 1970, suggesting that the two dimensions became more closely interrelated during the intervening year. More important, we can see that the two "causal" arrows are unequal in strength: it appears that 1969 Vietnam Dissent "caused" a decrease in 1970 Trust in Government (r=—.35) to a dis-

Figure 12-2

Cross-Lagged Panel Correlation
between Vietnam Dissent and Trust in Government*

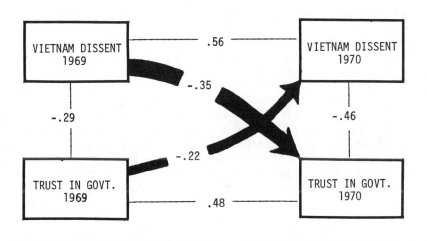

---

*The values displayed in this figure are product-moment correlations
taken from Table 1.

tinctly greater degree than 1969 Trust in Government influenced 1970 Vietnam Dissent ($r=-.22$). In short, our cross-time data provide some empirical support for the widespread view that dissatisfaction with the Vietnam War is among the basic factors eroding confidence in government among youth.

What are the implications of these findings for recruiting under an all-volunteer system? Increasing dissatisfaction with the Vietnam situation, declining trust in government, and a feeling that military power should be curbed are not the kinds of trends likely to increase enthusiasm for serving in an organization that is an arm of the government and its foreign policy. This should be especially true among those who have gone to college. If their alienation, which was increasing at a more rapid rate than others, should continue to increase, then the proportion of college students choosing a term of service is likely to be very low.

Perceptions of Military Service [1]

In the preceding section we examined youth attitudes on a range of important national issues. Now we focus more specifically on the perceptions of young men when asked to consider military service as a short-term or long-term occupation. The material for this section comes primarily from the data collected in 1969 and secondarily from the measurement in 1970.

Military Versus Civilian Career Opportunities. In the spring of 1969, when most Youth in Transition respondents were about to graduate from high school and many were looking forward to entering the world of work, they were asked to compare military and civilian career opportunities along a number of dimensions. The mean responses to those questions are summarized in Figure 12-3. At the top of the figure appear those opportunities which most respondents associated primarily with military service. Some of the perceived advantages of military service fit the traditional stereotype of military life—good habits and self-discipline, a chance to prove oneself a man and become a leader. Perhaps less expected, in the light of the findings in the previous section, is the fact that a majority felt that a military career offered a superior opportunity for making the world a better place to live and serving one's country well. These data were collected in 1969, and current high school seniors might show a somewhat less idealized conception of military service. Nevertheless, these data suggest that there has been a good deal of positive feeling about military service, and that the armed forces do not have a totally negative image in the eyes of young men.

Of course, there are a number of areas in which a civilian career is generally viewed as superior to military service, as shown in the lower portion of Figure 12-3. Advancement, income, and utilization of skills and abilities are thought by most to be better on the civilian side. And when it comes to independence—being one's own boss and controlling one's personal life—a civilian career is considered superior by the overwhelming majority of respondents.

Some additional evidence that young men underrate the more tangible rewards of military service came from the direction of wrong answers to a test of "Military Knowledge." Relatively few high school seniors in 1969 had accurate knowledge of military pay and benefits; most of their wrong answers were underestimates. Similarly, perceptions of military working conditions, hours and vacation allowances tended to err on the unfavorable side (Johnston, 1970).

On the other hand, several other questionnaire items reveal that most respondents felt that the armed services provide relatively good opportunities for the poor and blacks.

In sum, military service was perceived by high school seniors (and dropouts) in 1969 as providing relatively less personal rewards and freedom than civilian jobs. On the other hand, the military was viewed as a good place for the disadvantaged to succeed, and a place for one to develop manhood, leadership, and serve one's country.

Feelings About the Draft and an All-Volunteer Force. The Youth in Transition questionnaire in 1969 asked respondents, "If you were drafted, which of the following would be most true of you?" Twenty-two percent

Figure 12-3

Comparison of Military and Civilian Careers

Section H, Question 21

Suppose that at the end of your education you are trying to
decide between a career in the military and a civilian job.
Which would be better for the following things?

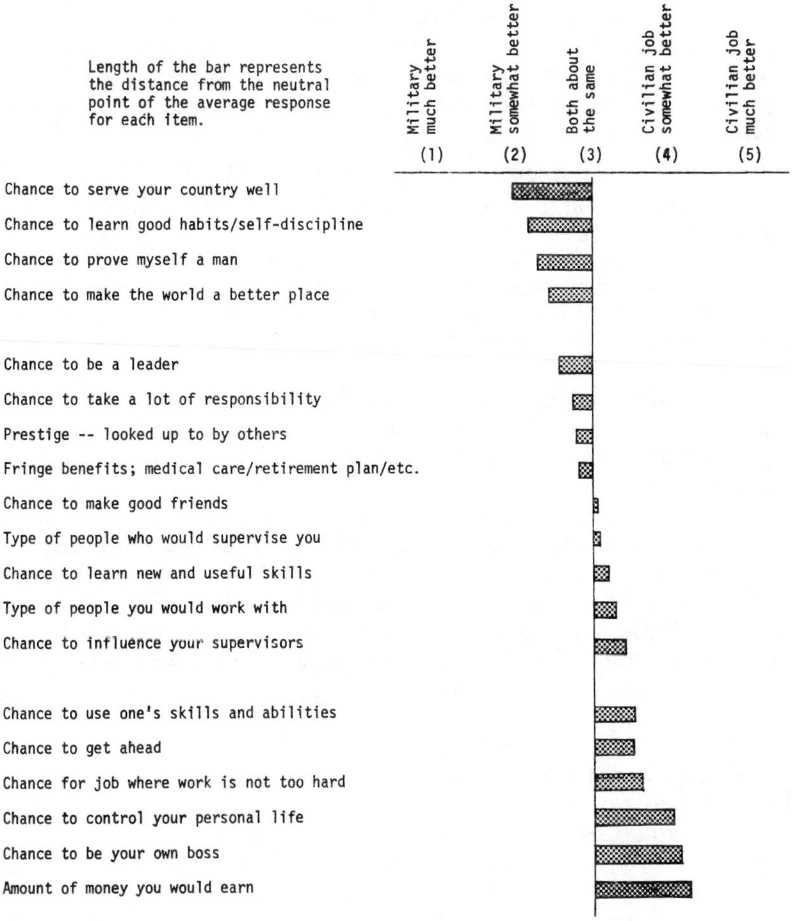

Length of the bar represents the distance from the neutral point of the average response for each item.	Military much better	Military somewhat better	Both about the same	Civilian job somewhat better	Civilian job much better
	(1)	(2)	(3)	(4)	(5)

Chance to serve your country well

Chance to learn good habits/self-discipline

Chance to prove myself a man

Chance to make the world a better place

Chance to be a leader

Chance to take a lot of responsibility

Prestige -- looked up to by others

Fringe benefits; medical care/retirement plan/etc.

Chance to make good friends

Type of people who would supervise you

Chance to learn new and useful skills

Type of people you would work with

Chance to influence your supervisors

Chance to use one's skills and abilities

Chance to get ahead

Chance for job where work is not too hard

Chance to control your personal life

Chance to be your own boss

Amount of money you would earn

NOTE: The number of missing data cases for these items ranges from one to three percent.

Source: Johnston and Bachman (1970, p. 15)

checked the statement, "I'd serve if I had to, but I wouldn't like it," while another 4 percent took the more extreme alternative, "I'd refuse to serve; go to jail or leave the country instead." Thus about one quarter of the respondents took a clearly negative view of the prospect of being drafted. The response "I'd be happy to serve," was checked by 13 percent. (And it should be noted that another 11 percent were not asked the question because they had earlier indicated their plans to enter the service within a few months.) The remaining half of the respondents selected the neutral answer to the question about being drafted, saying simply "I'd serve." As would be expected, scores on the Vietnam Dissent scale tended to be high among those individuals who said they would resent or resist being drafted.

Some additional data concerning attitudes about the draft come from a recent report on the attitudes of entering college freshmen. Based on three large national surveys, the American Council on Education found the following trend:

> . . . there was a steady increase in the proportion of freshmen who favored an all-volunteer army: from 37 percent in 1968, to 53 percent in 1969, to 65 percent in 1970. This trend may be attributable in part to growing disdain for the Vietnam war and for the military in general and in part to an optimism engendered by recent changes in the draft system and by statements from the Federal government indicating that an all-volunteer army is a workable alternative. (Bayer, et al., 1971, pp. 56-57)

This dramatic shift in support of an all-volunteer force represents a great deal of change in a span of only two years, but a change that was paralleled by changes in national policy about staffing the military. During that time, the draft lottery was introduced and Congress debated extensively the wisdom of extending the draft at all. At the same time, President Nixon put the administration on record as favoring an all-volunteer force and even proposed a series of pay increases to help make it possible. Youth and the country's leaders seemed to be coming to an agreement on at least one issue: the all-volunteer force is more desirable than the draft. But the question remains: is it feasible to staff our military forces entirely with volunteers?

---

[1]Many of the findings in this section are summarized from earlier reports by Johnston and Bachman (1970) and Johnston (1970).

CHAPTER 13

MANPOWER FOR AN
ALL-VOLUNTEER ARMED FORCE

The feasibility of an all-volunteer armed force rests largely on the ability of various incentives to attract young men to enlist. It is often assumed that the paramount incentive is increased pay, but there is no reason to limit our consideration to that rather obvious approach. Instead, in this chapter we will consider a number of different alternatives, and ask what sort of young men each incentive is likely to attract. But before discussing several incentives, let us take a moment to put the matter in its proper context.

Some discussions of incentives have implied that staffing an all-volunteer force is simply a matter of supply and demand—of setting wages that will be competitive in the marketplace. To put the matter very bluntly, the notion is that enough men can be brought in to do anything provided the price is right. Perhaps it is this way of looking at things which has sometimes led to the criticism that an all-volunteer force would be staffed by "mercenaries."

Our own view is that incentives such as wages are certainly important—indeed, under most conditions some minimal level of such incentives is a necessary condition for military service. But while incentives are *necessary*, they are not *sufficient* to insure service. Thus we must keep clearly in mind the kinds of issues discussed in the preceding chapter. The conditions of military service—the actual activities of being a serviceman—must be sufficiently attractive (or at least tolerable); otherwise, we assume that monetary or other "external" inducements will not be effective.

Still more important, we make the assumption that a man's views about national military policy—about what impact for good or ill the military service is having in the world—will be fundamental to an enlistment decision. During World War II tens of thousands of men volunteered out of their belief in the rightness and necessity of the nation's military action. (We still use that war as a reference point today, when we ask respondents whether they would be willing to serve if the nation were under the kind of attack experienced then.) At that time, the external incentives such as pay were relatively less important and matters of belief, ideology, and patriotism were overriding considerations.

Such matters can work both ways. Just as under some conditions men will give relatively little consideration to personal hardships and dangers, so under other conditions they may refuse an attractive offer because it conflicts with their values (and the values of their friends and associates). Perhaps this represents one of the distinctive characteristics of an all-volunteer force: it must operate within a context of some minimal level of agreement with national military policies; otherwise, incentives are likely to have little value.

Which Incentives Do Young Men Find Attractive?

We made two efforts to measure young men's responses to various incentives designed to make military service more appealing. Our first attempt took place in 1969, when most respondents were about to graduate from high school. In a fairly extensive questionnaire segment, respondents were asked how attractive they would find each of eleven different incentives, assuming that the Vietnam War had ended and the draft had been eliminated. Our preliminary report of these data expressed a number of reservations about some aspects of the findings:

> Nevertheless, we were singularly impressed by one finding. Considering the first choice of the respondents, one incentive stands out above all others: "The government agrees to pay for up to four years of college . . . in return for four years of active duty." This was selected by a margin of 4-to-1 over the second-ranked incentive, military pay comparable to civilian pay. Each of the remaining incentives was selected as first choice by less than ten percent of those who completed this section. If we look at their top three choices combined, the schooling incentives remain on top. More than three-quarter include government payment for college, technical or vocational school among their top three choices. (Johnston and Bachman, 1970, p. 40)

In 1970, we had another opportunity to explore incentives to enlist, this time using an interview segment rather than items in a paper-and-pencil questionnaire. Most respondents were one year out of high school, and had spent the last year in higher education or on a job. (Those who were already in military service were also asked about enlistment incentives, but their responses are not included in the following discussion.) Our second measurement concentrated on just four incentives which had proved to be among the most important in the 1969 data: higher pay, guaranteed assignment, paid schooling, and a shorter enlistment period. The four incentives are shown in Figure 13-1, using exactly the same wording as was presented to the respondents.

There is one other crucial difference between the 1969 and 1970 questions about incentives. In 1969 we asked respondents to imagine that the Vietnam War and the draft had both ended; in other words, we asked them to conceive of the kind of situation in which a volunteer armed force seemed

Figure 13-1

Incentives to Enlist

A. <u>Higher</u> <u>Pay</u> - Military pay starting at $5,000 per year and reaching $7,200 for the fourth and last year. You would pay for your own food and lodging.

B. <u>Guaranteed</u> <u>Assignment</u> - *Before you enlist,* you are given a guaranteed job assignment, including necessary training, in the military specialty of *your choice.* Before enlisting you would be tested to see if you could meet the requirements of your specialty choice. Here are some examples of specialties: draftsman, electronic technician, bulldozer driver, paratrooper, auto or aircraft mechanic, foreign language expert, pilot.

C. <u>Paid</u> <u>Schooling</u> - The government agrees to assume the cost, including living expenses, for up to four years of schooling at a college or technical/vocational school to which you can get accepted. In return, you serve on active duty for four years. You must *enlist first,* but the schooling could come either before or after you serve.

D. <u>Shorter</u> <u>Enlistment</u> <u>Period</u> - An enlistment period of only two years.

most feasible. By 1970 we decided to omit these conditions for two reasons. First, we found the highly hypothetical questions difficult to interpret and were frankly concerned about their validity. Second, and even more important, it seemed clear by early 1970 that the nation would most likely move *gradually* toward an all-volunteer force, testing out incentives during a transitional period with the draft still in force.

The 1970 questions about incentives were asked of 1273 respondents (representing all participants except those already serving in the military and those who felt sure they were permanently disqualified from military service). Respondents were asked to examine the incentives shown in Figure 13-1 and select the one change which would make military service most attractive to them. Then they were asked this question: "Taking into account other things that you are involved in, and given only this change, how likely is it that you would enlist?" Responses ranged on a scale from "definitely enlist in the next six months" to "definitely not enlist in the next 5 years." The first-choice responses to the incentives and the likelihood of enlisting are summarized in Table 13-1. Note that the higher pay incentive was attractive to the smallest number (14.7 percent), while guaranteed assignment was the most frequently chosen (37.3 percent). On the other hand, when we consider whether incentives are attractive enough so that respondents say they would definitely enlist, then the paid schooling seems to be the most effective.

The data in Table 13-1 are presented primarily to indicate the relative attractiveness of different incentives under conditions present in mid-1970; it

Table 13-1

Responses to Incentives

Incentive Chosen as Most Attractive	Likelihood of Enlisting Given First-Choice Incentive*					
	Definitely enlist in the next 6 months 1.	Definitely enlist in the next 5 years 2.	Probably enlist in the next 5 years 3.	Probably not enlist in the next 5 years 4.	Definitely not enlist in the next 5 years 5.	TOTAL
A. Higher Pay	0.8	0.9	3.5	3.9	5.5	14.7 *187*
B. Guaranteed Assignment	1.0	2.1	9.6	12.8	11.8	37.3 *474*
C. Paid Schooling	2.2	2.4	6.2	8.0	5.5	24.5 *312*
D. Shorter Enlistment Period	1.0	1.2	4.7	7.3	9.4	23.6 *300*
TOTAL	5.1 *65*	6.6 *84*	24.1 *307*	32.0 *407*	32.2 *410*	100% *1273*

*Cell entries are percentages based on a total of 1273 young men from the Youth in Transition study (Summer 1970). Italic entries are for frequencies.

is not suggested that the responses are an appropriate basis for projecting *how many* would actually volunteer given one or another incentive. Furthermore, the effectiveness of any incentive will depend heavily upon the context in which it is offered. A shorter enlistment period may be attractive as an incentive only when there is a threat of being drafted; it is difficult to imagine that offering a shorter enlistment period is likely to be a very positive attraction to an all-volunteer armed force. Similarly, it may be the case that the guaranteed assignment incentive would be most appealing to young men who are draft-motivated; a guaranteed assignment no doubt has a special appeal when contrasted with an uncertain (but almost surely less attractive) assignment under the draft. But if the draft were removed the guaranteed assignment might not, taken by itself, prove to be a very effective incentive. Of course, this discussion is necessarily rather speculative; nevertheless, of the four incentives we have examined, it seems reasonable to suppose that two are most likely to retain their attractiveness after the draft is removed—higher pay and paid schooling. Accordingly, we will focus much of our attention on these two alternatives as we examine the differences among young men who are attracted to different incentives.

To Whom Do the Incentives Appeal?

In Chapter 11 we noted that some people fear an all-volunteer force based on higher pay will appeal mostly to the disadvantaged, the less skilled, and perhaps the less ambitious. We can now ask whether those who respond positively and negatively to different incentives really do differ along these and other dimensions; moreover, we can compare them with other respondents in the Youth in Transition study who had already entered military service by the summer of 1970. For each of the four incentives, we will distinguish between "positive responders"—those who said they probably or definately would enlist (in the next five years or earlier) given their first choice incentive, and "negative responders"—those who said they probably or definitely would not enlist even if they were given their first choice incentive.

Background, Ability, and Personality. Would an all-volunteer force appeal primarily to the poor? The data in Figure 13-2 suggest that there may be some truth to that assertion, if the volunteer force is to be attracted primarily on the basis of increased pay. Those who say they would probably or certainly volunteer given the incentive of higher pay are lower in average socioeconomic level than others. (See Chapter 7 for a discussion of socioeconomic level.) On the other hand, their family socioeconomic level is not much lower on the average than that of young men already in military service. Those who respond positively to the schooling incentive are somewhat higher on the average (almost one-half standard deviation) than those attracted by pay or those already serving. For both incentives, it is true that those who respond positively to the incentive average a bit lower than those who think they would not serve. (Table 13-2X in Appendix G presents the data from which this figure was constructed. It includes as well data for positive and negative responders to the other two incentives, guaranteed assignment and shorter enlistment period.)

Test scores of intelligence and verbal skills (measured in tenth grade) are shown in Figure 13-3. It can be seen that the pay incentive attracts those who average lowest in general intelligence, while the schooling incentive attracts those who are much higher. The median for the positive responders to pay is 16, while that for the schooling group is 20. This is a difference of almost two-thirds of a standard deviation.

It may be helpful to translate these distributions into the proportions that fall into the various Mental Groups used by the military to classify servicemen. The appropriate cutoff points are marked below the axis. Those in Group V are unacceptable, while those in Group IV are considered somewhat marginal, because they have proved to be somewhat more difficult to train.[1] Groups I-III are all acceptable. About 16 percent of the positive re-

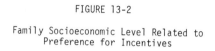

FIGURE 13-2

Family Socioeconomic Level Related to
Preference for Incentives

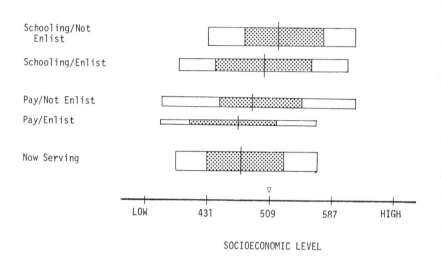

SOCIOECONOMIC LEVEL

———————
5475

NOTE: The height of the bar is proportional to the number of cases in that category. The length of the bar represents the range of scores of those between the 10th and 90th centiles; the length of the shaded portion represents the range of those between the 25th and 75th centiles; the center line corresponds to the median. The inverted triangle (▽) above the main axis is the median for those who responded to the incentives question plus those now serving in the military.

sponders to pay fall in the unacceptable category, Group V. Another 28 percent are in Group IV. By comparison, only six percent of the positive responders to schooling are in Group V, and another 19 percent are in Group IV. Clearly, the schooling incentive is attractive to the more intelligent young men.

Several other characteristics distinguish between those attracted by higher pay and those attracted by paid schooling. It is not surprising to find that a higher proportion of those attracted by paid schooling were already involved in post-high school education (58 percent) than was the case for those attracted by the higher pay incentive (38 percent). Among those who preferred the paid schooling incentive but would not be likely to enlist, the proportion already in higher education was still greater (73 percent).

On measures of ambitious job attitudes and status of aspired occupation, those attracted by paid schooling average one-half standard deviation

FIGURE 13-3

Intelligence Related to Preference for Incentives

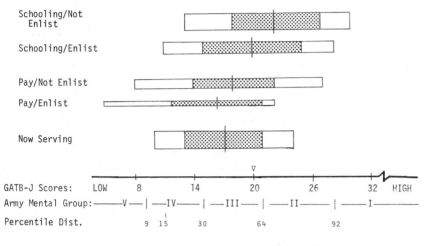

TEST OF VERBAL INTELLIGENCE (GATB-J)

5475

NOTE: The height of the bar is proportional to the number of cases in that
category.   The length of the bar represents the range of scores of those between the 10th and 90th centiles; the length of the shaded portion represents
the range of those between the 25th and 75th centiles; the center line corresponds to the median.   The inverted triangle (∇) above the main axis is the
median for those who responded to the incentives question plus those now serving in the military.

higher than those drawn by higher pay.[2] When asked what they expected to
be earning twenty years later (in the civilian occupation to which they aspired), the average response for those attracted by higher military pay was
about $10,000, whereas for those attracted by paid schooling the average re-
sponse was about $15,000. (The expected pay question used a series of dollar
ranges rather than exact amounts; thus the figures given here can only be
approximations.) The higher long-range financial expectations by the paid
schooling group were not reflected in assessments of immediate earning potential; when asked what they could probably earn in the civilian job market
next year, the answers of both groups averaged slightly below $6000 for the
year.

Some further distinctions may be drawn between those attracted by
higher pay versus paid schooling. Self-esteem, needs for self-development,

and needs for self-utilization all average about one-third of a standard deviation higher for those who favor paid schooling ($p < .05$). Another difference which falls slightly short of statistical significance is nonetheless interesting; those who are attracted by the higher pay incentive are a bit below average in their feelings of internal control or personal efficacy.

In sum, we find that background, ability, and personality differences do exist among those attracted by different incentives. In particular, those who say they would probably enlist given their first choice incentive of higher pay are a bit lower on the average than those attracted by paid schooling, along the following dimensions: family socioeconomic level, test scores, occupational ambition, self-esteem, and needs for self-development and self-utilization.

For each of the dimensions noted above, the mean scores of those respondents already in military service lie between the means for the two contrasting incentive groups. This suggests that the use of a higher pay incentive might tend to attract those slightly lower in ability and aspirations than the men presently serving, while the use of the paid schooling incentive might lead to average increases along these dimensions. Our data do not suggest large differences; nevertheless, the direction of the differences is consistent with concerns raised by critics of a volunteer force recruited primarily by the incentive of higher pay. The incentive of paid schooling, on the other hand, might lead to an all-volunteer force with higher levels of ability and ambition than is found in our current force. A mixture of both incentives might result in the broadest mix of these characteristics.

Is Response to Incentives Related to "Political" Attitudes? One of the major concerns about an all-volunteer force is that it might encourage a separate military ethos and thus constitute a political threat. Accordingly, it is of some considerable interest to know whether those responding positively and negatively to different incentives show some difference in attitudes about national issues—particularly along dimensions which might indicate a willingness to make critical, independent judgments about our military actions. Certainly one such dimension is the Vietnam Dissent Index discussed in Chapter 5. Figure 13-4 relates responses on that index (in 1970) to preferences for different incentives.

Several conclusions can be drawn from the data in Figure 13-4:

1. There are only small and rather unimportant differences among those who respond *positively* to the pay and schooling incentives.

2. Vietnam Dissent is stronger among those who respond negatively to the incentives; moreover, it is particularly strong among those who list paid schooling as their first-choice incentive but say they still would not enlist.

3. Vietnam Dissent is, as we noted in earlier chapters, lowest among those already serving in the armed forces.

The differences in Vietnam Dissent as of 1969 were not as strong as the 1970 differences shown in Figure 13-4; nevertheless, the 1969 data pattern is essentially the same. Recall from Chapter 12 that while Vietnam Dissent increased somewhat from 1969 to 1970 for the sample taken as a whole, it re-

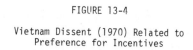

FIGURE 13-4

Vietnam Dissent (1970) Related to
Preference for Incentives

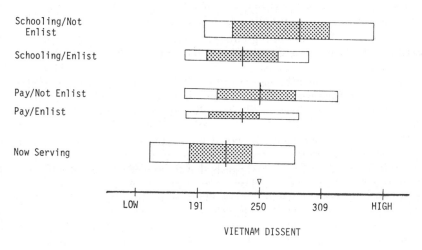

5475

NOTE: The height of the bar is proportional to the number of cases in that category. The length of the bar represents the range of scores of those between the 10th and 90th centiles; the length of the shaded portion represents the range of those between the 25th and 75th centiles; the center line corresponds to the median. The inverted triangle (∇) above the main axis is the median for those who responded to the incentives question plus those now serving in the military.

mained consistently low for those who were in the military service as of 1970. Since most of these respondents entered the service between the 1969 and 1970 data collections, this suggests that the military has been tending to attract those who are least skeptical about United States policies in Vietnam.

A number of other dimensions are related to Vietnam Dissent, as indicated earlier in Chapter 12; and these dimensions are also related to responses to incentives. As might have been expected, those who (in 1969) considered military spending and influence too high were more likely (in 1970) to say that they would not respond positively to incentives. The measure of Trust in Government also was related to response to incentives, but in a more complex way. The "positive" and "negative" responders showed little overall difference in trust back in 1969 when most were about to graduate from high school. But by 1970 those who were the "negative" responders had experienced a relatively sharp drop on the Trust in Government scale. The largest drop (three-fifths of a standard deviation) occurred among those who picked paid schooling as their first-choice incentive but said that they still

188   YOUTH IN TRANSITION

would not be likely to enlist. This shift suggests that growing dissatisfaction with the government, caused in large measure by the Vietnam War, may be a major deterrent to enlistment for these young men. Perhaps in a climate of less dissent and dissatisfaction a good many of these young men would react more positively to the incentive of paid schooling.

Higher Pay Versus Paid Schooling—Contrasting Incentives

Of the four incentives considered here—higher pay, paid schooling, guaranteed assignment, and a shorter enlistment period—the first two seemed most likely to retain their attractiveness in a voluntary system in which no one would enlist to avoid the draft. Accordingly, these have been examined in some detail.

It appears that paid schooling would be attractive to a higher percentage of young men than the alternative of higher pay (Table 13-1). Perhaps more important are the differences in the kinds of young men attracted by the two incentives. Those attracted by paid schooling averaged higher in intelligence, verbal skills, occupational ambitions, and self-esteem.

But what about those who were not sufficiently attracted by the incentives to say that they would enlist? As Figure 13-3 indicates, some of the most intelligent respondents preferred the paid education incentive but still said they would not enlist. Must we assume that such individuals will simply be absent from any all-volunteer force? We think that the answer depends to a considerable degree upon existing patterns of military activity and national opinion about that activity. As we stated at the outset of this chapter, we do not expect incentives to be effective when they come into direct conflict with deeply held values. Again looking at those individuals who stated a preference for paid education but said they still would not enlist, we find that they were well above average in their disagreement with U.S. policy in Vietnam. For many of these young men, the education incentive may have been highly attractive, but not attractive enough to override their objections to current military policies and practices.

If this analysis is at all accurate, then it may be that in the future, given a different and less negative climate of national opinion concerning the military and its activities, the paid schooling incentive would be even more appealing than our present findings show—and its appeal would be strong among some of the brightest of our young men, as well as those who are presently most critical of our involvement in Vietnam.

Do we want such individuals in our military service? Insofar as intelligence is concerned, the answer may be fairly straightforward: a modern military force requires many able individuals. But when we come to the matter of potential for dissent, the issue must be decided in terms of our values, and our views on the proper role and character of servicemen. If our aim is to staff the military with individuals who are guided by the "My country, right or wrong" principle, then perhaps it would be just as well to avoid a greater emphasis on educational incentives. On the other hand, if our aim is to raise the likelihood that at least some of our servicemen will be willing to raise questions, to disagree, and perhaps even to refuse to follow orders that they hold to be contrary to conscience or international law, then educational incentives may be of particular value.

Of course, the use of educational incentives in recruitment will not appeal only to potential dissenters; nor can we be sure that many or even a few dissenters will translate their feelings into effective action, should a situation demand it. But if none are disposed to disagree or dissent, then it seems certain that no one will act.

An Experiment With Educational Incentives. The United States is in a transitional period, moving from conscription toward an all-volunteer force. During this transition, a variety of plans for increasing enlistments are being tried. Some such efforts will appear successful and be retained, while others will be discarded.[3] We have urged the expansion of educational incentives for enlistment, and have outlined in Appendix D a specific "four-for-four" plan involving four years of paid education in return for four years of service. There is no reason why this plan, like others, could not be tried out on a small-scale experimental basis (although some new legislation would be required to implement it). Perhaps the "four-for-four" plan could be offered in a few areas of the nation on a limited-enrollment basis (first-come, first-served). Such an experiment would indicate much more clearly and dramatically than any surveys, the types of young men who would in reality be attracted by educational incentives. A few years ago the Army inaugurated "Project 100,000" in which many men (eventually more than 350,000) who fell below the usual minimum mental standards for military service were nevertheless permitted to enlist. A similar effort with the "four-for-four" plan could tell us a great deal about the effectiveness of educational incentives. Such an experiment would, of course, cost some money; but the investment would be relatively small compared with the level of spending routinely devoted to exploring new weapon systems. And even if the educational incentives were not later adopted on a full-scale basis, the experimental funds spent on higher education could hardly be viewed as wasted. Clearly, if we can afford to explore all sorts of new weapons, we should also be able to afford an exploration of new and potentially better ways of staffing our armed forces.

Note . . . Number 1 footnote follows on page 190.

[2]Most of the dimensions mentioned in this section are described extensively in Bachman, et al. (1967) and Bachman (1970). Some are also discussed in Chapters 5-7 of the present monograph.

[3]Of course, there remains the problem of "draft motivation" noted in earlier chapters—the fact that some "volunteers" enlist because they expect otherwise that they will be drafted. The new draft lottery system removes such effects of "draft motivation" for those with high lottery numbers. Thus when these young men (who are certain they will not be drafted) volunteer in considerable numbers, then we can feel confident that the incentives really are effective.

[1]The standards for induction vary somewhat by service, and are changed as the needs of the services change. But these general rules applied in Spring, 1972.

Mental Group	Percentile Distribution on intelligence (AFQT Test)	Approximate Score Range on GATB-J Test	Standards
I-III	31-99	16-44	All are acceptable
IVa	21-30	14-15	Acceptable if a high school graduate; otherwise only if candidate shows special aptitude in one of seven AQB areas such as infantry, electronics, maintenance, clerical, etc.
IVb	16-20	12-13	High school grads must show special aptitude in two AQB areas; others also have to show minimal proficiency in all other areas
IVc	10-15	10-11	All candidates must show special aptitude in two areas and minimal aptitude in the remaining five areas.
V	0-9	0-9	Not acceptable

PART III

SUMMARY AND POLICY IMPLICATIONS

CHAPTER 14

SUMMARY AND POLICY IMPLICATIONS

During the last few decades, very few young men in the United States have grown to maturity without having to come to grips with the possibility of serving in the armed forces, and perhaps becoming involved in armed conflict. The Youth in Transition project would thus be incomplete if it failed to examine this central factor in the thinking and planning of virtually all young men in the nation.

But there are many additional considerations underlying the research reported in this volume. For a number of years the nation has been engaged in a vigorous debate concerning military manpower policies—much of it centered on the proposal that we abolish the draft and rely upon an armed force made up entirely of volunteers. This proposal has far-reaching implications for recruitment policies and for the conditions of military service; more important, it has implications for the abilities, personalities, and perceptions of the men who serve in the armed forces. Is there a "military type" of individual who enlists in the present armed forces, and would this represent a problem in an all-volunteer force? Would an all-volunteer force appeal only to the poor and the disadvantaged? Would enough capable individuals enlist to meet the needs of an increasingly technological armed force? Is the nation best served by an armed force of "career men," or does it require a substantial proportion of "citizen soldiers" who think of themselves as basically civilians who are spending a few years in the service?

Such questions are not concerned exclusively, or even primarily, with *numbers* of men who enlist or might enlist. Rather, they reflect an assumption which has guided each phase of this research on young men and military service: Not only the number of recruits, but also the types of individuals who are recruited and the means of recruiting them, must all be consistent with the larger aims of society.

This volume approaches the problem of military recruitment from two distinct but interrelated perspectives. Part I deals with enlistment under existing conditions (as of the end of the 1960s). It is a predictive study which attempts to discover some of the correlates of the decision to enlist in military service after high school. The results of this study are detailed in Chapters 1-9 and summarized in Chapter 10. Part II deals with the possibilities for enlistment in the future. It reviews the debate over an all-volunteer force (Chapter 11), examines attitudes of youth toward military service and the nation (Chapter 12), and describes young men's responses to a number of possible incentives for enlistment (Chapter 13). This present chapter presents some of the highlights of the findings from both parts and considers possible implications these might have for future policy.

As this summary chapter is written, the future is already upon us, to at least a degree. There is a growing acceptance of the all-volunteer force concept; and one of the key requirements for its implementation, higher pay for first-term servicemen, is already reflected in new legislation. Given the rate of change in national policy and practice toward military recruitment, there is a danger that this sort of volume will be out-of-date by the time it appears in print. We have tried to take account of that problem throughout this book, but particularly in this summary chapter we try to focus on those findings which have broadest implications for future military manpower policies.

The data for this volume came from a nationwide study called Youth in Transition which followed a sample of over 2000 young men from the start of tenth grade to a time nearly four years later. When the study began in 1966 all of the young men were in school; by the time it ended in 1970 some had dropped out, most had graduated, and quite a few had gone on to college or entered military service.

Conclusions Based on Recent Enlistment Patterns (Part I)

When this research began it was thought highly possible that a "military type" of individual would be discovered—that those in the sample who enlisted could be characterized as different in many ways from their non-enlisting counterparts. After examining the data, we come to two general conclusions about the kinds of young men who enlist. First, it does not appear that there is a single "military type;" enlistees are not characterized by any particular "profile" of background, ability, or personality which sets them clearly apart from other young men their age. Some small exceptions have been noted with respect to attitudes about jobs (Chapter 5), and feelings about the value and worth of school (Chapter 6). However, the relationships are not large and do not imply any very substantial personality differences between enlistees and non-enlistees. A more important difference has to do with ideology—particularly attitudes about the Vietnam war (Chapters 5 and 12.)

Our first conclusion is that there is no single "military type;" but our second conclusion is that one major group is systematically under-represented in the military service—the young men who enter college. And this means that those factors associated with college entrance—high socioeconomic status, academic ability, and past scholastic success—are all under-represented among enlistees. This is a source of some concern. One of the major questions surrounding the feasibility of an all-volunteer force is whether it can attract sufficient numbers of qualified individuals to staff an increasingly complex and technological military operation. An equally important consideration is that the manpower for such a force be somewhat representative of a cross-section of American society. For both of these reasons it would appear that the college-bound ought to be the object of special recruitment efforts.

It is appropriate to ask what would make enlistment attractive to this group. It appears from the data in Chapter 9 that the college-bound are not strongly motivated by immediate monetary needs in the way that the job-bound are; so pay incentives alone are unlikely to be the dominant factor in their decisions about post-high school activities. Of greater interest to the college-bound are those aspects of self-development and personal advancement which are associated with advanced education and the opportunities it opens up for the individual. Of those who seriously considered enlisting after high school as an alternative to their present activity, one-half rejected military service because the alternative of advanced education was more attractive to them. It seems clear that to attract the more able individuals the military must offer either more in the way of educational alternatives or more assistance to individuals to pursue education on their own. There are several possibilities here. One involves a change in the present incentives for enlistment to include a broad-reaching subsidy for advanced education in exchange for a term of service. Such a plan is introduced in Chapter 13 and will be discussed later in this chapter; a more detailed outline of the plan is presented in Appendix D. Another possibility takes account of the fact that few young men are aware of what is already available in the way of educational benefits for those who enlist (Appendix E). It seems appropriate to stress the extent to which the present G.I. Bill will subsidize advanced education, since this is one of the big benefits to come from a term of service, and certainly one that would be attractive to academically capable young men.

Timing of Recruitment Efforts. The findings from this study suggest two recommendations for the timing of a recruitment message. It is assumed that the time when information about military service would be most relevant is the point when a decision is made about which post-high school activity to pursue (see Chapter 3). For those not going to college, this period includes twelfth grade and the first few months after graduation. If the services have something to offer to the non-college bound, this is the time to have the message visible for their consideration.

Recruitment efforts emphasizing educational incentives, on the other hand, might be initiated as early as eighth or ninth grade. Such efforts would not, of course, be directed toward enlistment commitments; rather, they would take the form of information-giving, with emphasis on the ways in which military service can help pay for higher education. One advantage of an early (i.e., junior high school level) consideration of the paid education incentive is that some young people could use the information to plan and work toward higher educational possibilities which would otherwise be beyond their financial reach. Plans for college are often well established by the end of ninth grade. During the later high school years most boys who are going to college decide which institution to attend. At this point the full cost of advanced education becomes more clearly apparent, and decisions may be influenced by the extent of available resources—including the possibility of using a term of service to pay for education.

The Recruiter and School Counselors. Only a small fraction of the total time a youth spends with his counselor is devoted to discussing military plans and obligations. One of the reasons for this may well be that guidance counselors do not look favorably on enlistment for those capable of going to college. On the other hand, those in the Youth in Transition sample who did enlist reported that they talked over these plans with their counselors for something approaching an average of one-half hour. It seems a waste of valuable resources to ignore the role which a counselor could play in presenting the advantages and disadvantages of a term of service, especially if the counselors themselves had a clear understanding of the advantages and limitations. To accomplish this, recruiters would do well to spend some time discussing service options with school counselors.

The Social Context of Enlistment Decisions. We noted in a number of chapters that enlistment decisions are made in the context of parental pressures, opinions of friends, and the broader climate of public opinion. In the recent past, including the period in which our data were collected, the Vietnam War has been the dominant feature in this social context—and it has become a more and more negative feature. Some enlistment decisions have been made in spite of Vietnam, and many nonenlistment decisions have been made because of it.

Some of the current effects of social context seem fairly obvious, but implications for the future are less clear, and we speculate in this area with some caution. It seems quite likely that an all-volunteer force will be more readily attainable as Vietnam becomes a less acute national issue. Conversely, it seems likely that the supply of volunteers in the future would be threatened by other military involvements resembling the one in Vietnam. If this is so, it suggests that reliance on an all-volunteer force would actually tend to discourage large-scale military adventures in the future.

Manpower for the Future (Part II)

The debate concerning an all-volunteer force is reviewed in Chapter 11, and evidence bearing on its feasibility and desirability is presented in Chapter 13. In our view the balance of the evidence lies in favor of an all-volunteer force, particularly if incentives are geared to match the full range of military manpower needs.

The Case for an All-Volunteer Force. Any system involving compulsory service is likely to conflict with the principles of freedom, but in the recent history of the military draft this problem has been exacerbated by further and unnecessary inequities. An unduly heavy financial burden has been borne by draftees and draft-motivated enlistees, who were required to serve at much lower pay than they would have received in comparable civilian jobs. Until recently, the government refused to acknowledge this so-called "conscription tax" and argued that the nation could not afford to pay the price of an all-volunteer armed force. To the more perceptive among our young people, this argument and many of the others which were used to extend the draft must have seemed shallow if not cynical. A nation which can afford vast expenditures for military hardware can surely afford to pay its military manpower costs fairly and above-board.

An all-volunteer force is affordable, but is it desirable? Critics have argued that a strictly voluntary system might appeal primarily to the poor and the less able, and perhaps to those susceptible to a sort of "military mentality" which could eventually pose a political threat. The report of the Gates Commission has argued that an all-volunteer force attracted primarily by higher pay would not really be very different from the present mixed force of volunteers and conscripts, especially given the fact that we already have a professional officer corps staffed largely with career military men. That argument is not entirely convincing. It may be that even a small minority of conscripted civilians provide a corrective against military excesses. It requires only a few individuals to "blow the whistle" on corruption or atrocities, as recent events have shown. It can be argued that an all-volunteer force would fail to include such individuals, and thus make a bad situation worse. We should think twice before adopting a military manpower system which does not include at least some individuals who see themselves as civilians whose military service is only temporary. Perhaps any all-volunteer system should include mechanisms to insure some greater degree of turnover, especially in the officer corps.[1]

The discussion above illustrates a fundamental point: the desirability of an all-volunteer force should not be considered in the abstract, apart from the question of what changes will be made in order to attract volunteers. It is generally agreed that enlistment may be encouraged by less emphasis on "spit-and-polish," more attractive living conditions, and fewer unnecessary restrictions on personal freedom. Such changes seem desirable in any case. But these alone are unlikely to attract sufficient volunteers to staff the armed forces. Greater financial incentives are surely necessary if we are to have an all-volunteer force. It has often been assumed without question that such financial incentives should take the form of higher pay. Our own view is that the inclusion of other incentives as well may better serve the nation's needs.

Paid Schooling in Return for Military Service. Appendix D proposes a program which offers up to four years of paid schooling in return for four years of military service (before or after the schooling). Such an incentive for enlistment has a number of attractive features:

1. It appeals to the more able and ambitious of our young men.

2. It has the *potential* of appealing to those young men who, judging from their attitudes, are more likely to exercise independent and sometimes critical judgment about military activities, those better equipped to act as "watchdogs" against excessive militarism in a "professional army." (This

point is not self-evident; the argument is developed and discussed in Chapter 13.)

Apart from the question of *whom* it would attract, the paid schooling incentive has some built-in advantages:

3. Those electing to serve their four years first and go to school afterward would help insure a healthy rate of military turnover and a supply of young servicemen who see their primary, long-term commitments as being outside the military.

4. Those going to college first and then entering the service would help meet military needs for skilled and educated manpower. Moreover, it seems likely that the broadening and liberalizing effects of college, plus the maturity of additional years, would make these men less malleable, more confident and self-reliant, and better able to handle responsibilities than those recruited at an earlier stage of education and maturity. We view these characteristics as distinct advantages to the military service and to the nation in general. But it should be noted that some military leaders do not share this viewpoint; they state a preference for the young and impressionable high school graduate rather than the older, cautious, more questioning college graduate.

5. Apart from its effects on the military establishment, the use of an educational incentive for enlistment would have almost entirely positive by-products throughout the civilian society. Vast numbers of servicemen have already received lasting educational benefits under the G.I. Bill; and surely society as a whole gained from their increased level of education. What we are proposing here really represents an enlargement and extension of those educational opportunities which have been available to most veterans over the last three decades.

Concluding Comments

> Since the founding of the republic, a primary task of the government of the United States has been to provide for the common defense of a society established to secure the blessings of liberty and justice. Without endangering the nation's security, the means of defense should support the aims of the society. (U.S. President's Commission . . . ., 1970, p. 5)

This volume has explored present enlistment practices and has examined some possibilities for more effective recruiting in the future. We have offered suggestions for improvement in recruiting practices because we share the fundamental assumption that ". . . the means of defense should support the aims of the society."

Our suggestions, summarized earlier in this chapter, have been concerned with the *means* of securing military manpower; but such efforts must take place within the larger context of the *ends* toward which military forces are employed.

One of the concerns sometimes raised about an all-volunteer force is that it might foster military adventurism, whereas the draft system is presumed to be a source of restraint. Recent history hardly supports this contention. The nation has been involved in its longest and most unpopular war, and much of the fighting has been done by draftees.

The most important reason given by President Johnson for extending the draft in 1967 was that ". . . the sudden need for more men than a volunteer force could supply would find the nation without the machinery to respond." But as we noted in Chapter 11, the draft does not really provide a basis for quick response to threat. Moreover, in the event of a genuine threat requiring large-scale mobilization of manpower (a condition increasingly difficult to imagine in a nuclear age), the Congress could quickly reinstate the draft. It seems that there may be only one sort of flexibility which would be lost under an exclusively voluntary system—Presidential options to threaten military action knowing that such threats are backed up by a capacity to draft men for long-term struggles, even in the absence of a Congressional declaration of war. In our view, this is a type of flexibility which the nation can well afford to lose.

The lessons of Vietnam have been incredibly costly. To a considerable degree, trust in government has been one of the casualties of the war. It is likely to take a long time to rebuild. A conversion to an all-volunteer armed force can play a positive role in such a rebuilding of trust, especially among young people. One of the first steps has been the national commitment to pay a fair price for military manpower; the end of the inequitable and deceptive conscription tax was long overdue. Another step should be a searching examination of the role of the military in a free society, with emphasis on insuring a broad base of civilian control. Then we can proceed to establish a system of incentives that will meet our military manpower needs, and serve other national needs as well, within a voluntary framework.

----

[1]It should be noted that the Gates Commission report supported a change in the system of retirement benefits for military men. The present system requires almost twenty years of service before any benefits can be realized. An alternative system of providing both officers and enlisted men with the same retirement arrangements as civil service employees would do away with this unnecessary emphasis on twenty years of service.

APPENDICES

APPENDIX A

RESPONSE OF COLLEGE STUDENTS TO ROTC PROGRAMS

During the first year after high school, about one-half of the respondents in the Youth in Transition study pursued some form of advanced education.[1] They attended institutions which ranged in type from universities to vocational schools; about one-half of the students were in schools that offered ROTC. What can be called their "response" to ROTC is summarized in Figure A-1. Six percent were enrolled in ROTC and another nine percent said they would enroll if it were offered at their school. The remaining 85 percent were uninterested in this kind of training.

This appendix is divided into three parts. First, within the sample that attended schools offering ROTC, we compare the characteristics of those enrolled in ROTC with those not enrolled; this enables us to see how the two groups compare in "quality" and to see if there is anything in their family backgrounds which suggests a reason for their choice. In the second part we compare the characteristics of those enrolled in ROTC with those who would like to enroll, but who attend schools that do not offer ROTC. The findings suggest whether it would be reasonable to recruit officer candidates from a broader range of schools than currently is the case. Finally, we will examine the reasons the young men themselves give for their response to ROTC.

The reader is reminded that the comparisons which are made here must be considered suggestive, since the numbers are small and the Youth in Transition sample was not designed to represent all young men in college (see Chapter 2 for a discussion of the sample design). Nonetheless, the sample is adequate to suggest trends and relationships which could be confirmed in other studies.

---

[1]This appendix is based on data collected from that portion of the YIT panel which participated in the final data collection (see Chapter 2). Total N in data collection = 1620; pursuing advanced education and answering ROTC questions N = 821. An additional 17 respondents were students, but they indicated earlier in the interview that they were definitely ineligible for military service.

FIGURE A-1

College Students* and ROTC
a)projected behavior of those in schools that do not offer ROTC
b)actual behavior of those in schools that offer ROTC

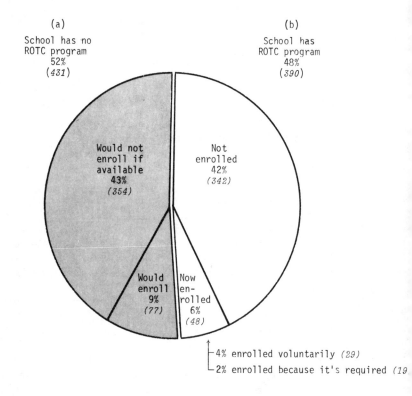

(a)   (b)
School has no   School has
ROTC program   ROTC program
52%   48%
(431)   (390)

Would not
enroll if
available
43%
(354)

Not
enrolled
42%
(342)

Would
enroll
9%
(77)

Now
en-
rolled
6%
(48)

⌐4% enrolled voluntarily (29)
└2% enrolled because it's required (19

5443

*N=821; this is the number pursuing advanced education minus 17 who
indicated to the interviewer that they were definitely disqualified
from military service duty.

ROTC Students Compared with Others in Schools Offering ROTC Programs

Ability, performance, and aspirations. Before comparing these two groups, the ROTC group was divided up, separating out those who said they enrolled only because it was required from those who enrolled voluntarily. This resulted in the following groups.

> 29 Enrolled voluntarily
> 19 Enrolled because it is required
> <u>342</u> Did not enroll
> 390 Total number in schools offering ROTC

First of all, it should be noted that ROTC is offered only at the "better" schools, i.e., ones that admit the higher ability students from among all those who continue their education beyond high school. The average GATB-J intelligence scores (see Chapter 6) for those in schools offering ROTC is 23.6; the range covers the top two Mental Groups in the Armed Forces classification scheme. Table A-1 shows the GATB-J scores for those in ROTC compared with those not in ROTC. The mean score of those who enrolled voluntarily (column 2) is virtually identical with the mean for those not enrolled (column 3); while those who are enrolled because it is required are about one-quarter of a standard deviation lower than the others. (This score of 21.9 is near the bottom of the range for Mental Group II.) Looking at other characteristics, the voluntary enrollees look very much like those not enrolled. They had a slightly higher grade average in senior year of high school (B+ vs. B), but had identical grade averages in their freshman year of college. The future jobs to which they aspired are also very similar, being in the professional and business/managerial categories. For college majors, the distribution of those in ROTC spans the entire range, including the social sciences, liberal arts (English, foreign language, history, etc.), the natural sciences, and engineering.

Background. In terms of family background the similarities are more outstanding than the differences. About one-half of those in ROTC have fathers with jobs in the professional and business categories. The socioeconomic level of their families (see Chapter 7) is only slightly lower (one-fifth of a standard deviation) than those not enrolled—not large enough to be important. The father's military experience is also not very important, although there is a small tendency for boys whose fathers have more than eight years of military service to enroll in ROTC. But such youth make up only 14 percent of those in ROTC; so military background does not appear to be an important determinant of the ROTC choice.

The most striking difference is associated with the region from which an individual comes. The proportion of the entire college sample that comes from the South is 30 percent, yet 59 percent of those who enrolled voluntarily in ROTC came from the South. Urbanicity of the area does not seem to be important, so it is the region itself which is associated with the preference for

TABLE A-1

Response to ROTC Compared With Selected Characteristics

	ROTC Program is available			ROTC Program not available			
	Enrolled/ required (19)	Enrolled/ voluntar. (29)	Not enrolled (342)	Would enroll (77)	Would not enroll (354)	Mean or marg. % (821)	S.D.
1. Type of school							
Univ. & 4-yr. Lib. Arts	100%	100%	93%	41%	49%	69%	--
Junior & Community	--	--	4	29	33	19	--
Tech/Voc, Business	--	--	2	29	16	11	--
2. Degree expected							
BA, BS, etc.	100%	100%	96%	56%	64%	80%	--
AA (2-year)	--	--	3	21	26	14	--
Certificate	--	--	1	23	10	6	
3. Ability--intelligence							
GATB-J	21.9	23.6	23.7	19.3	20.6	21.9	6.2
4. Ave. classroom grades							
Senior yr. of h.s.	B	B+	B	B-	B-	B	A-toC+
Freshman yr. of coll.	C+	B-	B-	B-	B-	B-	B+toC
5. Status of aspired occ.	76	77	73	63	67	70	19
6. Socioeconomic level	509	536	550	502	531	536	74
7. Father's job							
Professional	--	21%	19%	1%	16%	11%	--
Mgrs., off., prop.--bus.	42%	28	24	17	20	18	--
Clerical, sales	11	7	10	8	9	7	--
Skilled wrkers & foremen	21	14	19	25	20	24	--
Unskilled/operators	11	7	11	20	19	19	--
Lab./farm & non-farm	5	7	3	4	4	5	--
Farmer, farm mgr.	11	3	6	10	3	6	--
Military service	--	3	1	3	1	1	--
No father, unemp., MD	--	10	8	13	9	10	--
8. Father's military exp.							
None	44%	24%	33%	30%	31%	32%	--
< 8 years	50	62	64	60	65	63	--
> 8 years	6	14	3	10	4	5	--
9. Region of res. in h.s.							
West	11%	14%	12%	10%	17%	14%	--
North Central	--	17	35	21	31	31	--
Northeast	11	10	22	26	30	25	--
South	79	59	31	43	22	30	--
10. Urbanicity							
Rural	37%	21%	15%	27%	18%	18%	--
< 15,000	11	10	20	21	20	19	--
15,000 - 50,000	16	17	12	12	15	14	--
Suburbs	10	28	27	17	23	24	--
> 50,000	26	24	27	23	24	25	--

officer training.

It is not within the scope of this appendix to explain why this relationship holds. Janowitz (1964) reports that there has been a long tradition of the South being overrepresented among the high-ranking officers in the services. He bases this on a detailed investigation into the background of those officers who were in power through the year 1950. His explanation of this phenomenon may be helpful in understanding the ROTC findings on region. Janowitz explained the "southern preference" in terms of two factors, both associated with the lack of industrialization of the South compared with other regions of the country. The background of southerners is much more rural than other parts of the country, and there is an integral association between rural existence and military institutions. "The out-of-doors existence, the concern with nature, sport, and weapons which is part of rural culture, have a direct carry-over to the requirements of the pretechnological military establishment" (p. 86). If this rural background is associated with being from the South, then this cultural influence would be a part of a young man's family and social environment as he grew up, whether or not his place of residence were rural or urban. The second factor is the issue of career opportunities. In an under-industrialized area there are fewer opportunities for the ambitious to find positions in business. As support for this interpretation, Janowitz notes the overrepresentation of the South among military leaders and the underrepresentation of this region among the top business leaders at mid-century. This interpretation is interesting, especially in the light of findings reported earlier (Chapter 7) that there was no tendency for boys from the South to enlist more frequently after high school. If the "southern preference" is linked to career opportunities, it would appear to be restricted to the opportunities available for jobs at the business and managerial levels—jobs associated with a college degree.

ROTC Students Compared with Those Who Would Like to Enroll, But ROTC is not Offered at Their School

Two approaches could be taken to increase enrollments in ROTC. One is to attract more students at institutions already offering ROTC. Another is to increase the number of institutions which offer ROTC. To evaluate the latter approach we must ask what the qualifications are of those who would enroll from these other institutions. Would they make good officers? While this question cannot be fully answered with the data in this study, it is possible to suggest what some of their characteristics would be.

Ability, performance, and aspirations. Nine percent (77) of the young men pursuing advanced education said they would enroll in ROTC if it were offered at their school. Comparing columns two and four in Table A-1 it can be seen that only 40 percent of these ROTC aspirants were in universities or four-year liberal arts colleges. About 29 percent were in junior or community colleges, and the remaining 29 percent were in technical, vocational, or business schools. A number of these latter two groups aspired to a bachelors degree, with the result that 56 percent of the ROTC aspirants thought of themselves as four-year collegians, while the remainder viewed themselves as being in a two-year or less program of training. Looking at their aptitude we find that their GATB-J scores are almost one-half a standard deviation below the mean of those in post-high school education. This mean score is roughly equivalent to Mental Group III, with the range extending down to Group IV and up to Group II. Table A-2 displays the mean GATB-J score for various subgroups in the YIT sample and may be helpful in making comparisons.

TABLE A-2

GATB-J Scores for Selected Subgroups
of the Youth in Transition Sample

Activity during year after high school (1969-1970)	Mean GATB-J Test Score	
University	24.1	
Liberal Arts	21.7	
Junior	20.3	
Community	21.1	
Technical/Vocational	18.1	
High School*	16.5	Mean = 19.6
Military Service	17.2	S.D. = 6.5
Job	17.1	N = 1576
Unemployment	15.0	

*This group failed to graduate with the class of 1969.

The grade average of ROTC aspirants in senior year of high school was lower than average, B— ; but so was the average of all those students who later attended colleges that did not have ROTC programs. Considering average grades for the first year of advanced education, ROTC aspirants were at the mean for the entire education group; but this measure is less meaningful as an indicator of achievement. A grade of B at a business college is not the same as a grade of B from Harvard.

Background. The aspirants to ROTC come from somewhat different family backgrounds than those enrolled in ROTC. It was noted earlier that one-half of those already enrolled in ROTC came from families in which the father was a professional, businessman, or official. Of the ROTC aspirants, only 18 percent have fathers employed in these categories. Twenty-five percent have fathers who are skilled workers. This is reflected in the socioeconomic level of the family which is appreciably lower than the average for all students and even lower than students in similar schools. There is a slight tendency for ROTC aspirants to have fathers with more than eight years military experience.

Again, there is a tendency for a relatively high proportion of southerners to want to enroll. Thirty percent of the sample were located in the South during their high school years, but 43 percent of those aspiring to ROTC come from this region. There is a small tendency for these individuals to be from rural areas.

Explanations for ROTC Choices

Positive response to ROTC. Those in schools offering ROTC were asked to explain why they did or did not choose to enroll in an officer training program. Of the 48 respondents who were enrolled in ROTC, 19 gave the reason that it was required by the school, implying that they would not have joined had it not been required. Another 15 respondents (one-half of the voluntary enrollees) said they were attracted by the "chance to be an officer, get a commission." The real meaning of this response is not clear. Some may have assumed, because of the draft, they would have to serve at some time and they preferred to serve as an officer. Others may have been more genuinely interested in a military career and through ROTC would be taking the necessary steps to achieve that goal. The remaining 14 boys in ROTC gave a variety of responses, ranging from "I like military service," to "it provides me with a deferment for college." Only three individuals indicated that it would help them pay for their schooling. This is not surprising; payment for participation in ROTC does not begin until the summer after sophomore year. But it needs to be established that ROTC entrants did not appear to be motivated by anticipated economic advantages.

Those who were in schools that did not have ROTC, but who said they would join if it were offered (N=77), gave responses similar to those who were already enrolled. Thirty-five of the ROTC aspirants (almost one-half) said, "Chance to be an officer, get a commission." The remainder gave a variety of answers all of which could be classified as showing a general interest in military life or the skill training available to those in the service.

Negative response to ROTC. Those who were not enrolled in ROTC, although there was an available program, numbered 344. The reasons given for not choosing ROTC can best be described as statements of noninterest in military life. They include such things as "Don't believe in it; don't agree with the program" (137); "no future for me in military service; not interested in military service" (57); and "don't want to have to serve in the military" (16). Such answers are not very helpful to anyone interested in evaluating present ROTC programs. However, it does appear that the young men are not criticizing the way that ROTC is run. Rather, they do not find it relevant to their lives, especailly when becoming an officer is associated with going to Vietnam to serve.

Those in schools not offering ROTC, who would not be interested in enrolling if it were, gave the same answers to explain their preference.

Summary

The boys who were enrolled in ROTC look like intelligent students, with diverse interests and high aspirations. More than one-half of them are from the South. Those who would like to enroll, but are not in schools offering ROTC, are somewhat less intelligent, although their average test scores are above those for youth who are working, serving in the military, or attending technical school. Whether their abilities are adequate to the job of being an officer cannot be discerned from the available data.

The students were asked to explain why they responded favorably or unfavorably to ROTC. Their answers were not very helpful in identifying particular aspects of ROTC which might be changed to make it more attractive. Those who were interested in ROTC were simply attracted to the life and job of a military officer, while those not interested were "turned off" by any and all aspects of military service.

APPENDIX B

CHANGES DURING THE FIRST YEAR
OF MILITARY SERVICE

What happens to a young man's values and attitudes during his first year of military service? Does self-esteem increase or decrease? Are there shifts in aggressive attitudes and behaviors? Do views toward government change? In this appendix we will take a look at some data bearing on such questions. While far from definitive, the data do give some indications of effects that military service may have on an individual's values and attitudes.

We must note at the outset that these findings are excerpted from a much more extensive analysis reported in a forthcoming volume in the Youth in Transition monograph series. That report includes a comparison of a number of different post-high school environments, one of which is military service. Data from Time 3 (Spring, 1969) are compared with data from Time 4 (Summer, 1970), thus providing an indication of changes during the year following high school. The present appendix presents a small portion of these analyses, concentrating on those in military service, and focusing on dimensions which show some difference between servicemen and most other respondents. Some of the dimensions treated here have been discussed elsewhere in this volume, and all are presented and defined in earlier volumes (Bachman, et al., 1967; Bachman, 1970; Bachman, et al., 1971).

Occupational attitudes. Occupational aspirations, measured by asking each respondent what sort of work he planned "in the long run" to do for a living, were scaled according to the Duncan socioeconomic status index (Reiss, 1961). Such measures showed a good deal of stability throughout high school and the year beyond. During the year following high school there was no shift in mean level for all respondents taken together. Moreover, there was great stability in average scores for those in civilian occupations and those in different educational subgroups (e.g., those in universities, liberal arts colleges, community colleges, junior colleges, and technical/vocational schools). Within each such category there were some individuals who increased their aspirations, while others lowered their occupational sights; but

211

such upward and downward changes occurred in roughly equal numbers, so that the net effect was one of stability. This is to say that there was very little environmental effect on occupational aspiration.

Those in military service were an exception to this general pattern of stability, for their mean occupational aspiration rose by about one-third of a standard deviation. As Figure B-1, Part A indicates, this increase in aspiration left them still somewhat below the mean for all respondents; however, they were above the mean level of aspiration for those not in college. It should be kept in mind that the question about occupational plans referred to "the long run," and in most cases this meant a civilian occupation after military service. It is beyond the scope of this appendix to pursue a detailed analysis of the kinds of occupational changes which led to the overall rise in status of aspired occupation for those in military service, but it might be a matter

FIGURE B-1

Comparison of Change Scores in Occupational Aspirations
and Ambitious Job Attitudes for Total Sample
and Military Subgroup

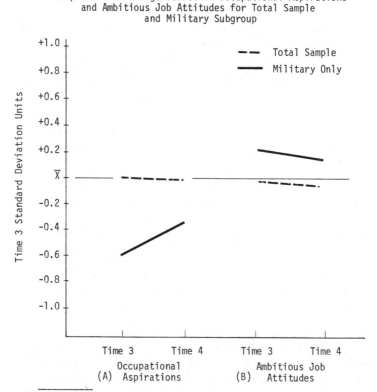

NOTE: Time 3 corresponds to the end of twelfth grade (June, 1969); Time 4 to one year later (June, 1970). X̄ refers to the mean score for the total Time 3 sample; all other scores are normalized on the Time 3 mean and standard deviation for the total sample.

worth pursuing in other research on young men in military service. If other studies were to replicate this finding of higher long-term occupational aspirations after a year or less of military service, it would be useful to know what aspects of the military experience lead to such increases in aspirations.

Another aspect of occupational views is measured by a scale of "ambitious job attitudes." This is a composite index based on the "job that pays off" scale and "job that doesn't bug me" scale discussed in Chapter 5. In effect, the index gives a positive weighting to questionnaire items reflecting a desire for self-development and "getting ahead," and gives negative weighting to items suggesting an aversion to such things as assuming responsibility on the job and working hard on the job. Thus, a high score reflects a set of attitudes which can be described as wanting to get ahead by dint of hard work. Part B of Figure B-1 shows the consistent difference of about one-quarter of a standard deviation between average scores for all respondents and those for young men in the service; the servicemen were above average in ambitious job attitudes both before and during their first year of duty.

Self-esteem and internal control. Figure B-2, Part A indicates that self-esteem scores rose about 20 percent of a standard deviation for those in military service, while scores for the total sample did not shift. Part B shows a nearly identical pattern for the measure of internal control—the feeling that an individual controls his own fortunes and destiny (Rotter, 1963, 1966). In each case the change meant that young men who averaged a bit below the overall mean when they entered the service had reached (and very slightly exceeded) that mean after a year in the military. It appears that a period of time in the service may improve an individual's sense of self-worth and his feeling of being able to control his own destiny. The increase in occupational aspiration suggests that there may be a corresponding increase in the confidence a person has in his ability to secure a good job.

Aggression. Two measures related to aggression are shown in Figure B-3. One is a four-item scale of aggressive impulses (feeling like: swearing, losing one's temper, being rude, picking a fight). The total sample of respondents dropped about 15 percent of a standard deviation along this scale between Time 3 and Time 4; however, those in military service dropped about twice as far, on the average.

The other measure related to aggression is a scale of actual interpersonal aggression (hitting, fighting, etc.). The majority of the total sample reported zero instances of such aggressive behavior at the Time 4 data collection (their Time 4 reports covered the preceding year, i.e., roughly the period between the end of high school and one year later). Among those in military service, on the other hand, 61 percent reported at least one instance of interpersonal aggression during the year preceding Time 4, a noticeable increase from the 51 percent who reported such aggressive behavior in the period prior to Time 3.[1]

---

[1]Because of problems of confidentiality, servicemen in Vietnam (N=48) were not asked at Time 4 (Spring, 1970) to report on instances of aggression or delinquent behavior. This group is not included in the mean scores for Time 3 or Time 4 interpersonal aggression.

   Increases in *actual* aggression may lead to a reduction in *impulses* toward aggression; however, that simple explanation does not fit all the facts. If we limit our consideration to those in the military, we find that those who reported higher aggressive impulses also were more likely to report actual aggressive behavior during the preceding year. (This same sort of positive correlation between impulse and action was also found within other categories, such as those in universities, colleges, civilian employment, etc.)

   Thus while individuals with more aggressive impulses are more likely to be the ones actually committing aggressive acts, it remains the case that *on the average* those in military service reported lower aggressive impulses but more actual instances of aggressive acts. Perhaps the increased instances of

FIGURE B-2

Comparison of Change Scores in Self-Esteem
and Internal Control for Total Sample and
Military Subgroup

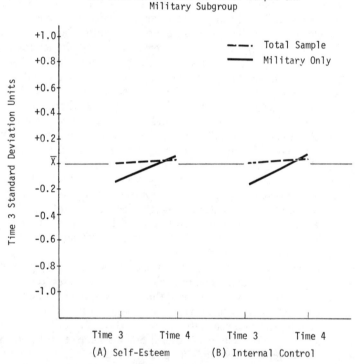

NOTE: Time 3 corresponds to the end of twelfth grade (June, 1969);
Time 4 to one year later (June, 1970). X refers to the mean score
for the total Time 3 sample; all other scores are normalized on
the Time 3 mean and standard deviation for the total sample.

APPENDIX B   215

actual aggression occurred under conditions in which the usual restraints
against aggression were somewhat relaxed, possibly during some of the
stresses involved in the early weeks of service.

Trust in government and Vietnam dissent. We noted in Chapter 12 that
trust in government was negatively related to Vietnam dissent, and that the
pattern of cross-time correlations suggested that Vietnam dissent was among
the causes of reduced trust in government. Figure B-4, Part A shows that
young men in military service were relatively low in Vietnam dissent at Time
3; and at Time 4, when dissent had increased among many respondents,
those in the service were even lower in dissent. (The decrease in dissent was by
no means unanimous among those in the service; while 36 percent showed at

FIGURE B-3

Comparison of Change Scores in Impulse to Aggression
and Interpersonal Aggression for Total Sample
and Military Subgroup

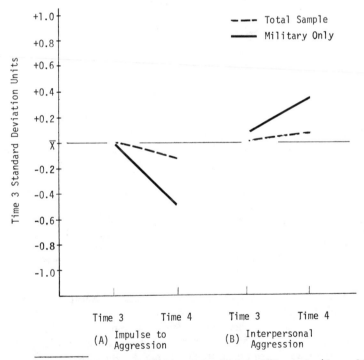

NOTE: Time 3 corresponds to the end of twelfth grade (June, 1969);
Time 4 to one year later (June, 1970). X̄ refers to the mean score
for the total Time 3 sample; all other scores are normalized on
the Time 3 mean and standard deviation for the total sample.

FIGURE B-4

Comparison of Change Scores in Vietnam Dissent
and Trust in Government for Total Sample
and Military Subgroup

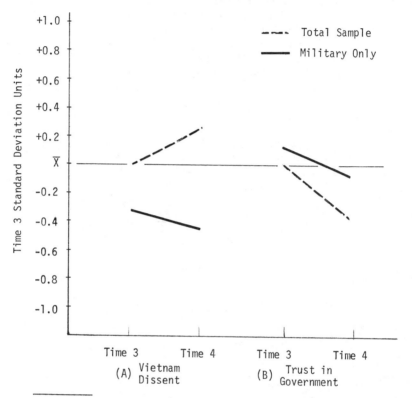

NOTE: Time 3 corresponds to the end of twelfth grade (June, 1969); Time 4 to one year later (June, 1970). X̄ refers to the mean score for the total Time 3 sample; all other scores are normalized on the Time 3 mean and standard deviation for the total sample.

least a half standard deviation decrease in dissent, another 24 percent showed a half standard deviation or more increase.)

That those in military service should show some overall decrease in Vietnam dissent could have been anticipated on several grounds, including reduction in cognitive dissonance after enlistment. Once committed to military service, it may be easier if one is not critical of current military policies. But it is interesting to note that while Vietnam dissent decreased somewhat among those in the service, there was no corresponding increase in trust in government. On the contrary, those in military service showed some drop in government trust, albeit not as large a drop as appeared for the total set of respondents.

A forthcoming publication from the Youth in Transition project (Lloyd Johnston, *Drugs and American Youth*. Ann Arbor: Institute for Social Research, 1972) provides some interesting information on drug use among first-year servicemen who were assigned to military bases in the United States. Some of the findings are in contrast to the more positive effects of military service enumerated above. Excerpts from Chapter Six of the drug report are included here; the interested reader should secure the complete report to fully appreciate the dimensions of the drug problem.

> Recently a great deal of public attention has been focused on the incidence of illegal drug use in the armed services. While most of the emphasis has been directed toward heroin use by servicemen in Vietnam (a population on which we unfortunately do not have drug data[2]), there has also been speculation that drug use is more prevalent in the service generally than in other sectors. While our data on young men in the military are based on a rather limited number of cases (N=144), they certainly tend to support that speculation.
>
> Some 41% of these young men in service in the continental United States [tried] one or more illegal drugs in the year after high school [see Figure B-5]. This is a substantially higher proportion . . . than we found among those in civilian employment (32% users) and a 4% higher usage rate than we found among college students. Furthermore, 25% of the military group had used amphetamines, barbiturates, and/or hallucinogens during that year, a quite substantial jump from 14% during high school. This 25% rate is also considerably higher than the 18% of employed young men or 16% of young men in college who used any of those drugs during the same period. In fact, the military group shows the second highest rate of conversion of non-users to the use of illegal drugs (including marijuana) and by far the highest rate of conversion to the more serious illegal drugs (except heroin)."

Data on conversion rates are presented in Table B-1.

> Our sample in the military did, however, show the highest rate of conversion to regular drinking of any of the five groups examined. Fifty-five percent reported drinking regularly (weekly or more often) and sixty percent smoking regularly (daily), making military men the heaviest users of cigarettes and alcohol of any of the groups; and while they started out with higher rates of usage than most other groups, they also showed the highest rate of conversion of nonusers.

Conclusions. The first year of military service does not produce many really dramatic changes in the attitude and personality dimensions employed in the Youth in Transition study. Nevertheless, there were some shifts in scores suggesting that during the first year of military service young men

---

[2]It was not felt that confidentiality could be insured for the 48 overseas military respondents who participated in the interview by mail.

showed some increases in occupational aspirations and ambitions, along with a rise in self-esteem and feelings of personal efficacy (internal control). These findings should be replicated, preferably with much larger samples of servicemen, before firm conclusions are drawn. For the present, it is sufficient to say that the direction of change among these personality dimensions seems positive.

Clearly on the negative side, we noted that one year in military service was associated with a high rate of conversion to the use of illegal drugs (mari-

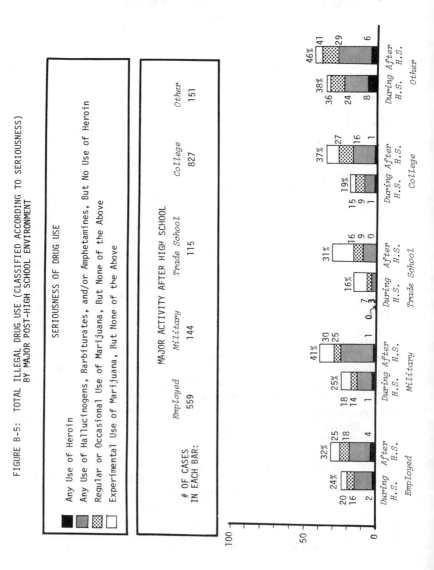

FIGURE B-5: TOTAL ILLEGAL DRUG USE (CLASSIFIED ACCORDING TO SERIOUSNESS) BY MAJOR POST-HIGH SCHOOL ENVIRONMENT

TABLE B-1

Net Conversion Rates* Associated With
Major Post-High School Environments

	NET CONVERSION TO:			
	Regular Smoking	Regular Drinking	Any Illegal Drug Use**	Any Use of More Serious Illegal Drugs***
Employed	4%	15%	11%	2%
Military	13	20	21	13
Trade School	10	17	18	7
College	7	18	22	8
Other	9	10	13	7

*Net conversion rate is defined as the decrease in the total number of non-users during the year after high school, stated as a percent of the total number of non-users during high school.

**Marijuana, amphetamines, barbiturates, hallucinogens, and/or heroin.

***Amphetamines, barbiturates, hallucinogens, and/or heroin.

juana, hallucinogens, barbiturates, and amphetamines). This effect of environment was not limited to the illegal drugs, but was also associated with a large proportion adopting habits of regular smoking and drinking.

It is more difficult to draw conclusions based on Vietnam dissent or trust in government. It is, of course, not surprising that those in the military service would be least critical of United States policy in Vietnam, nor is it startling that they remained quite low in criticism during a year when others became more critical. Perhaps this serves to illustrate one of the dangers sometimes attributed to a military force made up largely of "career men"—it is relatively unlikely that those presently in military service are going to challenge national military policies. On the other hand, it is worth remembering that one-quarter of those in the service showed a half standard deviation or more *increase* in Vietnam dissent during their first year of service.

APPENDIX C

A PROFILE OF DROPOUTS
WHO ENTERED MILITARY SERVICE

Throughout this volume we have concentrated much of our attention on young men who enlisted after high school graduation. We have also focused on those respondents whose participation in the longitudinal research effort extended through the third and fourth data collections (1969 and 1970). In so doing, we omitted from consideration a group of young men who dropped out of high school and then entered military service. Now in the present appendix we turn to that group of young men and present a profile of the high school dropout who entered military service.

The background of this analysis. We first became aware of the special characteristics of this group—dropouts who entered the service—during the course of an analysis of the causes and effects of dropping out of high school. We discovered that a number of young men who had participated in our initial data collection had not continued their participation in the research through the third data collection; but although they had not remained in the panel, we were aware in many cases that they had dropped out of high school (because the interviewers were able to ascertain this from friends, parents, etc.). In a number of such cases we were also aware that the young men had entered military service after they had dropped out of school.

One of the early phases of our research on dropouts involved a comparison between dropouts who had continued their participation in the research and other dropouts who had not continued their participation. The latter group was further subdivided according to whether respondents had entered military service. (Indeed, such involvement in the service was often the reason for an inability to participate further in the research—many individuals were stationed out of reach of our interviewing staff, etc.) The early analyses of these several groups were intended to determine whether various sorts of nonparticipants among the dropouts were different from those dropouts who did continue their participation in the Youth in Transition research. Our general conclusion, as reported in our volume on dropouts (Bachman, et al., 1971),

221

was that the non-respondents among the total set of dropouts were not greatly different *on the average* from the other dropouts, and thus we felt that our major conclusions about dropouts were basically sound. Nevertheless, we did find that those dropouts who entered military service were different from other dropouts in a number of respects. For those who wish to examine some of these differences as displayed in the original analyses, the information is presented in Table C-1, which contrasts three dropout subgroups and also presents data from three sets of comparison of "control" respondents matched according to socioeconomic level, school, and race. Our present purposes do not require a further discussion of these data except to note again that the one group which seemed to stand apart were the dropouts who entered military service.

High school dropouts in the military—a comparison with other groups. Table C-2 presents a comparison among three military groups: dropouts who enlisted (column 1), high school graduates who enlisted (column 2), and those whose military service involved national guard, reserves, or being drafted (column 3). Also included in Table C-2 for comparison purposes are three civilian groups: dropouts—mainly employed but including some unemployed (column 4), high school graduates who did not enter college—also mostly employed (column 5), and finally those who went on to post-high school education—mostly college and university (column 6).

The row entries in Table C-2 represent a variety of personal characteristics, *all of which were measured at the first data collection* (Fall, 1966) when respondents were beginning tenth grade. The personal characteristics shown in the table include ability and intelligence, family background dimensions, attitudes, behaviors, and aspirations. The particular dimensions listed will not be discussed in any detail in this appendix, but some have been discussed earlier in the present volume and all are discussed in earlier volumes of the Youth in Transition series (Bachman, et al., 1967; Bachman, 1970; and especially Bachman, et al., 1971.)

On the whole, the intelligence and verbal skill levels of dropouts who entered the military were not inferior to those of the high school graduates who entered the service (column 1 versus columns 2 and 3). On the other hand, the dropouts in the military were noticeably higher (40 to 50 percent of a standard deviation) on these dimensions than civilian dropouts (column 1 versus column 4). A similar pattern appeared for socioeconomic level, although the difference was not as large (less than one-quarter of a standard deviation).

The other family background measure shown in the table, family relations, shows that dropouts who entered the service reported poorer family relations than any other group. They were nearly half of a standard deviation below other military groups along this dimension, and a quarter of a standard deviation lower than other dropouts.

Dropouts who entered the service had been (at the start of tenth grade) below average in measures of self-esteem and happiness, compared with others in military service (columns 2 and 3) and also compared with other dropouts (column 4). Dropouts who entered the service were also high in

TABLE C-2

Environmental-Status/Educational Attainment
Compared With Selected Characteristics

	MILITARY			CIVILIAN				
	Enlist/Dropout (43)	Enlist/HS Grad (181)	RES, NG, Drafted/HS Grad (63)	Other (Work)/Dropout (211)	Other (Work)/HS Grad (606)	Coll/HS Grad (891)	Grand Mean (1996)	S. D.
1. Intell.--Verbal Skills								
Quick Test	108.7	107.9	105.3	103.2	105.6	113.2	109.0	12.1
GATB-J	16.9	17.5	17.5	14.4	17.4	22.1	19.2	6.5
Gates Reading Test	35.3	36.1	34.9	32.3	35.0	38.5	36.4	5.9
2. Family Background								
Socioeconomic Level	478	481	477	461	479	537	504	79
Family Relations	3.19	3.44	3.43	3.32	3.48	3.61	3.51	.54
3. Self Esteem	3.44	3.63	3.64	3.62	3.70	3.87	3.75	.52
4. Affective States								
Neg. Affective States	2.77	2.62	2.74	2.78	2.63	2.54	2.61	.54
Happiness	3.51	3.77	3.79	3.66	3.72	3.84	3.77	.62
5. Independence as a Value	3.63	3.47	3.51	3.56	3.52	3.42	3.48	.51
6. Impulse to Aggression	2.77	2.54	2.67	2.76	2.54	2.41	2.51	.80
7. Delinquent Behavior								
Total Delinquency	2.07	1.65	1.44	1.96	1.63	1.50	1.61	.51
Delinquent Beh in Sch	2.15	1.53	1.33	2.03	1.54	1.31	1.49	.60
Aggression in School	2.57	2.23	2.18	2.48	2.19	2.05	2.17	.70
8. Rebellious Beh in School	2.36	2.11	2.05	2.31	2.06	1.91	2.03	.54
9. School Performance								
Average Grade (9th)	C(35)	C+(38)	C+(39)	C(35)	C+(38)	B-(43)	C+(40)	(7)
Self-Con of Sch Abil	3.78	3.93	3.89	3.83	3.98	4.44	4.16	.73
10. Occupational Attitudes								
Ambitious Job Att	5.06	5.05	5.02	4.79	4.98	5.24	5.08	.69
Occ. Aspirations	52	56	53	48	55	72	62	26

NOTE: The category "Other (work)" includes all those who were not specifically in
military service or pursuing advanced education of some form. For the most
part, these people are all in the work force. However, there are some whose
educational attainment is known (high school graduation or not) but whose
post-high school activity was unknown; these were placed in this category.

TABLE C-1

Selected Characteristics of
Dropout Matched Groups

	HIGH SCHL DROPOUT			HIGH SCHL STAYIN				
	Respondent (118)	Non-respondent (55)	Non-respondent in M.S. (43)	H.S. Grad./ match group 1 (118)	H.S. Grad/ match group 2 (55)	H.S. Grad/ match group 3 (43)	Grand Mean	S.D.
1. Intell.--Verbal Skills								
Quick Test	102.5	103.7	108.7	106.2	106.1	107.9	105.3	12.5
GATB-J	14.8	15.4	16.9	17.7	18.1	18.9	16.7	6.3
Gates Reading Test	32.8	32.6	35.3	35.0	36.3	35.8	34.4	7.2
2. Family Background								
Socioeconomic Level	453	468	478	454	471	475	462	66
Family Relations	3.42	3.35	3.19	3.38	3.49	3.47	3.39	.56
3. Self Esteem	3.62	3.67	3.44	3.76	3.80	3.67	3.67	.54
4. Affective States								
Neg. Affective States	2.77	2.72	2.77	2.56	2.59	2.61	2.67	.55
Happiness	3.74	3.64	3.51	3.84	3.83	3.75	3.74	.64
5. Independence as a Value	3.52	3.53	3.63	3.54	3.45	3.43	3.52	.51
6. Impulse to Aggression	2.76	2.70	2.77	2.43	2.39	2.49	2.59	.85
7. Delinquent Behavior								
Total Delinquency	1.92	1.97	2.07	1.60	1.49	1.50	1.75	.66
Delinquent Beh in Sch	1.97	2.00	2.15	1.52	1.46	1.35	1.74	.79
Aggression in School	2.41	2.52	2.57	2.15	2.19	2.09	2.31	.78
8. Rebellious Beh in School	2.26	2.31	2.36	2.07	2.08	1.98	2.17	.60
9. School Performance								
Average Grade (9th)	C(35)	C(34)	C(35)	C+(40)	B-(41)	B-(41)	C+(37)	7.36
Self-Con of Sch Abil	3.80	3.82	3.78	3.99	4.15	4.02	3.92	.71
10. Occupational Attitudes								
Ambitious Job Att	4.75	4.82	5.06	4.92	4.97	5.03	4.89	.72
Occ. Aspirations	45	50	52	62	66	56	55	27

---

[*]Individuals in Groups 4-6 were chosen to match, pairwise, individuals in Groups 1-3.
Matching was done for school, race, and socioeconomic level.

stated needs for independence and in aggressive impulses.

It is in the area of delinquent behavior and rebellious behavior in school that dropouts in general stood most clearly apart from those who graduated from high school. Such differences were clearly in evidence by the start of tenth grade (Bachman, et al., 1971). As Table C-2 indicates, dropouts who entered military service were a bit higher than other dropouts in various measures of delinquent and rebellious behavior (column 1 versus column 4), and they were much higher than others who entered military service (column 1 versus columns 2 and 3). Our study of non-military dropouts indicated a consistent pattern of high delinquency both before and after leaving school; unfortunately, the data presently available to us do not indicate whether dropouts who entered the military continued to display high levels of delinquent behavior.

Dropouts who entered military service, like other dropouts, had relatively low grades in school and low estimates of their own ability. This is interesting, given the fact noted above that those dropouts who entered the service actually scored somewhat higher than other dropouts in tests of intelligence and academic skills.

In the area of ambitious job attitudes, dropouts who entered the service were not different from others who joined the armed forces; they were, however, considerably higher on the average than civilian dropouts. They were also slightly higher in status of aspired occupation.

Summary. It should be recalled that the differences among groups which we have noted here were all based upon measures taken at the start of tenth grade—some time before the actions and choices which led some individuals to drop out and others to graduate, some to enter military service and others to remain civilians. Thus we are in no way dealing with the *effects* of dropping out or of military service. Rather, we are noting that those young men who entered the service after dropping out of high school were different in a number of respects from their classmates who graduated from high school before entering the service.

Dropouts who entered the service were brighter than other dropouts, on the average, and generally equivalent in intelligence to those who entered the service after high school graduation. Nevertheless, these young men tended to have histories of poor performance in school and poor self-concepts of their ability. They were also below average in self-esteem and affective states, and above average in aggressive impulses and needs for independence. Their family background included socioeconomic levels equivalent to others who entered the service, and above those of other dropouts. On the other hand, they reported getting along less well with their families than was the case for other dropouts and others who entered the service.

In short, many dropouts who entered the service were, by the time they entered tenth grade, misfits at home and at school. They were performing somewhat below their abilities, disliking school, engaging in delinquent behaviors, and generally dissatisfied with things as they were. Whether these characteristics changed during the years of military service we do not know; such data are, alas, unavailable in the present study.

APPENDIX D

THE "FOUR-FOR-FOUR" PLAN
PAID EDUCATION
AS AN ENLISTMENT INCENTIVE

The paid schooling incentive discussed in Chapters 13 and 14 was outlined in the 1970 interview in the following words:

> The government agrees to assume the cost, including living expenses, for up to four years of schooling at a college or technical/vocational school to which you can get accepted. In return, you serve on active duty for four years. You must *enlist first*, but the schooling could come either before or after you serve.

The statement is fairly clear—as far as it goes. But what is the likely cost of four years of schooling, and how should it be financed? These are questions which go beyond our interview item; and, indeed, they go somewhat beyond the scope of our research effort. Nonetheless, we have felt some compulsion to specify more clearly what the "four-for-four" incentive plan might look like, if for no other reason than to make our general suggestions more concrete.

What follows, then, is a set of guidelines which would be fully consistent with the interview item cited above, and with our suggestions in the text. It must be emphasized that this is not the only possible form which an educational incentive could take, and it may not prove to be the best. But until a better plan is specified, this one seems to us to meet the basic requirements for an educational incentive, and it does so in a manner which is likely to be accepted by both young people and the tax-paying public.

How Would the Costs Be Covered?

Four years of paid schooling including expenses is no small financial matter. Tuition plus room and board can run to $4,000 or more per year in

227

colleges and universities, or a total of more than $16,000 for four years. Would all this represent the cost of "four-for-four" for each serviceman who elected the plan? No indeed, for many would attend less expensive schools, and some would not decide to take advantage of the full four years. Still, we propose that for those who require it there would be approximately $4,000 per year available to cover tuition and living expenses. We propose that the money come from two sources: (a) a modified and expanded G.I. Bill, and (b) savings from military pay (a path made more feasible by the recent pay increases).

A modified G.I. Bill. The G.I. Bill has been a great success. It has provided the benefits of higher education to many veterans who could otherwise never have afforded them. We propose that the tradition of the G.I. Bill be extended and enlarged in three ways:

1. The G.I. Bill should be made a permanent benefit available to anyone serving (four years or more) in the military service, in wartime or peacetime.

2. The funds made available under the G.I. Bill should be increased. The present limit is $175 a month for up to 36 months of full-time education, or $1575 per (9-month) academic year. We propose that the enlarged G.I. Bill should include (a) an allowance of $100 per month to cover a portion of living expenses, and (b) all expenses for tuition, books and fees (up to a limit of perhaps $800 to $1000 per semester) for up to 8 semesters or 36 months.[1]

3. G.I. Bill benefits should be made available *in advance of active duty* for those who enlist and elect the option of four years of college followed by four years of service. Unlike ROTC, the "G.I. Bill in advance" plan would involve no military classes or activities prior to active duty, nor would it commit the enlistee to serve as an officer.

These three modifications would enable the G.I. Bill to cover full tuition, books and fees, and a portion of living expenses, either before or after the required four year period of active duty. The government share of costs would be higher *in some cases,* but the overall expense would be relatively small in contrast to the impact of the recent military pay increases.

Savings from military pay. The paid schooling incentive was offered in our survey of young men as a possible *alternative* to increased military pay. Now that the pay increases are an accomplished fact, it seems reasonable that part of the costs of the paid schooling incentive should be covered by the increased military pay. A serviceman who decided on four years of active duty followed by four years of college under the enlarged G.I. Bill might decide to save $125 per month toward his college expenses, providing a total of more

---

[1] Assuming an allotment of $800 per semester for tuition and fees, plus a living allowance of $100 per month for nine months, the total yearly cost to the government would be $2500. For a full four years the total would be $10,000, or $3700 more than available under the present G.I. Bill. This cost estimate is probably much higher than the average student would require, given that many students would attend state colleges, junior colleges, and community colleges which have lower rates than private institutions, especially for residents of the state. In addition, many programs of study require less than the full four years allotted.

than $6000 (savings plus interest) at the end of his active duty. The amount of $125 might be recommended (but not required) as an automatic payroll deduction and savings program for those entering the service and expecting to go on to college under the G.I Bill. Since this amount is similar in size to the recent pay increase for servicemen, it means that a recruit electing to set aside $125 per month toward his education would be left with a take-home pay roughly the same as the typical take-home pay before the new rates went into effect.

But what about those who elect the college-first service-later option? How can they use savings from military pay which they have not yet earned? Our proposal is that they be permitted to borrow up to $6000 ($750 per semester or $1500 per academic year) as an interest-free loan to be repaid from their military pay during the four years of active duty that will follow their years in college. Many would not need to borrow the full limit of $6000; those who did would have a repayment rate of $125 per month, an amount which would not represent a great hardship given the new military pay scales.

Advantages of the Plan

Use of existing systems. The G.I. Bill and the idea of regular saving through payroll deduction have both been with us for a long time. Thus the plan proposed here requires no massive new bureaucracy to make it function—it simply uses existing systems in new and slightly expanded ways. Even the idea of getting paid education before military service has been used for some time, although it has not been widely applied to those in the enlisted ranks.

Flexibility. The proposed plan is flexible in several ways. There are suggested amounts for savings and an upper limit on loans, but otherwise the amount saved or borrowed is up to the individual to determine according to his educational needs.

For those who serve first and plan to go on to college, there is no loss if they later decide to do something else. Any savings for college set aside from their military pay are available along with interest—there is no requirement that the savings be spent on education.

For those who complete their service and *then* decide to go on to college, the enlarged G.I. Bill benefits remain available and will cover the majority of educational costs. Thus it is possible to decide on using the educational incentive before entering the service, after leaving the service, or any time during service.

Visibility. The idea of four years of fully paid schooling in return for four years of service had strong appeal to many of the respondents in our survey of young men. While we do not wish to encourage a Madison Avenue approach to recruiting ("Today's Army wants to join *you*"), we recognize that some ways of presenting alternatives are more attractive than others. We think the "four-for-four" way of offering an educational incentive for military service is both attractive and honest—and that is the way recruiting efforts ought to be.

APPENDIX E

KNOWLEDGE OF CURRENT INCENTIVES (1970)[1]

In Chapter 13, we discussed young men's responses to various incentives designed to make military service more attractive. The section of the interview which presented these incentives also asked for responses to some questions which disclose how much the young men actually knew about what the military already offered along these lines. One of these questions asked the respondent to estimate his civilian earnings for the year to come. We were trying to see if the higher military pay incentive was competitive with what these young men thought they could earn in a civilian job. The question read:

Now, I would like you to imagine that you are going to be working at some full-time job for the next 12 months, whether or not you are doing so presently. Given your present skills, how much do you think you could earn during these 12 months? A rough estimate is all right.

$_____FOR THE NEXT 12 MONTHS
(BEFORE TAXES)

For those respondents who answered this question[2] the mean projected earnings were $6300, however the range was very broad.[3] So, although the mean is higher than the military pay incentive for the first year, the range would indicate that many of the respondents do not feel they could earn much more than reflected in the proposed incentive of $5000 (see Chapter 13).

Table E-1 shows the parallel figures for those who say they would enlist if military service pay were higher. The average estimate ($5700) is lower for

---

[1]This appendix was written by Diane Davidson, Survey Research Center.

[2]The answers of young men who were already in the military are not included in this section in order to parallel the sample used in Chapter 13.

[3]The standard deviation was $3500.

TABLE E-1

Expected Income on a Civilian Job

A. For those in the total sample	B. For those who say they would enlist given pay as their first choice of incentives
N = 1273	N = 64
Mean = $6300.00	Mean = $5700.00
S.D. = $3500.00	S.D. = $2600.00
Median = $6000.00	Median = $5350.00

this group by $600 per year and the range (standard deviation) is much narrower.

Another question aimed at the respondents' knowledge of military offerings asked about the idea of a guaranteed assignment:

Recall the Guaranteed Assignment change—that is, where there is a guaranteed job assignment to the specialty of your choice. As far as you know, does the military already offer things similar to this?

Sixty-seven percent (834) of the respondents answered "Yes" or "I think so; not sure" to this question. However, when asked "Can you tell me what you know about this?" only 22 percent answered that there was indeed such a thing as a guaranteed assignment—that a young man could get an assignment to the field of his choice; a few qualified their answers saying that if there were no openings you would not get the job of your choice. Fourteen percent were not sure if there were such a thing as guaranteed assignment. Finally, 18 percent answered that there really was not any guaranteed assignment—the military assigns people to whatever field they qualify for. Some indicated that the military *says* there is such a thing, but in fact a person cannot be assured of any job choice—the implication being that the military will promise a job but one cannot count on them following it up. In effect, less than one-quarter think that an enlistee can be guaranteed an assignment before he enlists.

The last question involving knowledge of incentives referred to education:

How about the change involving support for schooling—that is, where the government agrees to assume the cost of some further education. As far as you know, does the military already offer things similar to this?

Eighty-nine percent (1115) of the respondents answered "Yes" or "I think so; not sure" to this question. But only thirty-six percent could give us any correct answer when asked "Can you tell me what you know about this?" (By correct we mean an accurate description of such educational benefits as the G.I. Bill, or ROTC, or in-service vocational training.) Twenty-four percent of the respondents answered that there was the G.I. Bill which offered post-service support for schooling. Seven percent mentioned ROTC as a means of government-sponsored schooling for boys in the military service. Four percent said that the service was a place to receive vocational education/training. The remaining one percent mentioned both the G.I. Bill and ROTC.

A subset of the group discussed above said that their first choice of incentives was education. It is worth noting in Table E-2 that of those who say they would enlist given the education incentives, only 27 percent actually knew anything about what the military presently offers educationally.

TABLE E-2

Response to Educational Incentives Compared
with Knowledge of Present Military Educational Benefits

	Enlist or Not	Knew Nothing about Present Military Educational Offerings	Knew Something about Present Military Educational Offerings	Total
1st Choice is Educ. Incentive	Would Enlist	101/72.7%	38/27.3%	139/100%
	Would not Enlist	107/58.5%	76/41.6%	183/100%

APPENDIX F

ESTIMATES OF SAMPLING ERROR*

As reported in Bachman, et al., (1967, pp. 21-24, 123-129), the sample for this study was selected in three stages. Stage one consisted of the Survey Research Center's national sample of counties and metropolitan areas selected from each of 88 strata. Stage two involved selecting one school from each such county or metropolitan area. (In one area several attempts were unsuccessful in locating a school willing to participate; therefore, it was necessary to omit this area and proceed with 87 schools.) Finally, stage three consisted of randomly selecting about 25 boys from each school.**

Given this type of clustered and stratified sample design, it is not appropriate to apply the standard, simple random sampling formulas to obtain estimates of sampling errors. The use of these formulas will almost always understate the actual sampling errors.

One measure of this understatement is the design effect (DEFF). For each sample estimate, the design effect is the square of the ratio of actual standard error to the expected standard error of the estimate from a simple random sample of the same size.

$$\text{DEFF (sample estimate)} = \left[\frac{\text{actual standard error of the estimate}}{\text{expected standard error of the estimate if the sample were simple random of the same size.}} \right]^2$$

For most of the *simple means* in this monograph, our estimates suggest that design effects will be under 3.

We recommend that an assumed value of DEFF = 2.8 be used in computing standard errors for the proportions (p) presented in Chapters 4 - 8. Estimate s.e. (p) by

$$(1) \quad \text{s.e.}(p) = \sqrt{\frac{\text{DEFF } p(1-p)}{N}} = 1.7 \sqrt{\frac{p(1-p)}{N}}$$

---

*This appendix was written by Martin Frankel, Sampling Section, Survey Research Center.
**We are grateful to Leslie Kish and Irene Hess for developing the sampling procedure used in this study.

Although the clustered nature of the data collection (sampling) introduces correlation between observations, we feel that the sampling error of a difference between two proportions p_1 and p_2, based on subclass sizes of N_1 and N_2 respectively, may be conservatively estimated as

$$(2) \quad \text{s.e.}(p_1\text{-}p_2) = \sqrt{\text{DEFF}\left[\frac{p_1 (1\text{-}p_1)}{N_1} + \frac{p_2 (1\text{-}p_2)}{N_2}\right]} = 1.5\sqrt{\frac{p_1 (1\text{-}p_1)}{N_1} + \frac{p_2 (1\text{-}p_2)}{N_2}}$$

Even when design effects for *simple means* are rather large, there exists a good deal of evidence to indicate that design effects for more complex statistics (e.g., regression and MCA coefficients, correlation coefficients, MCA Etas and Betas) are significantly lower (Kish and Frankel, 1970; Frankel, 1971).

The table below presents what we feel are conservative estimates of the standard errors for the Etas of Chapters 4 - 8. These standard errors are based on a sample size N=1600 and a Design Effect (DEFF)=2.3 using the approximation

$$(3) \quad \text{S.E. (ETA)} = \sqrt{\frac{\text{DEFF } (1\text{-ETA}^2)^2}{N}}$$

Value of ETA	S.E. (ETA)
> .10	.038
.15	.037
.20	.036
.30	.034
.40	.032
.50	.028
.60	.024
.70	.019
.80	.014

The user is cautioned against using these standard errors for computing "exact" significance levels, confidence (or credible) intervals. These standard errors as well as the necessary normal distributional assumptions are approximations. For further discussion of some of the issues raised in this appendix, see Kish (1967), Kish and Frankel (1970), Frankel (1971).

APPENDIX G

TECHNICAL TABLES AND FIGURES

TABLE 2-2X

Branch of Service Entered

	Frequency	
Category	Pre-Time 3	Post Time 3
Army	22	32
Navy	12	67
Marine Corps	10	32
Air Force	2	39
Coast Guard	0	5
Branch Unknown	10	4
Total	56	179

The Relationship of Socioeconomic Level to Attempted Enlistment (Chapter 7)

To investigate further the relationship of SEL to attempted enlistment, a version of SEL was used which made finer distinctions than the six-category version used in Table 7-5. Each of the 20 categories shown in Figure 7-1X represents approximately five percent of the sample. Two dependent variables were used: enlistment after high school and enlistment any time after the beginning of tenth grade. Using the additional breakdown of SEL introduced considerable "noise" into the picture, but overall the relationship with either criterion is strongly linear, with deviations at only two points along the distribution.

The two curves coincide at the high levels of SEL, but diverge at the lower levels. The higher curve for enlistment any time after the beginning of tenth grade results from the fact that SEL is inversely associated with drop-

FIGURE 7-1X

Socioeconomic Level (20-bracket version)
Related to Attempted Enlistment

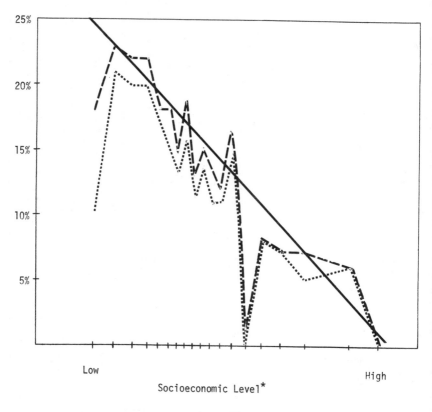

Socioeconomic Level*

······ Attempted enlistment after high school

——·Attempted enlistment any time after the beginning of tenth grade

—— Projection of the true relationship of SEL to attempted enlistment

*Each category contains approximately five percent of the sample, where the
sample includes all respondents at the end of twelfth grade, including
dropouts from the class but excluding those who were drafted or who entered
the National Guard or the Reserves. N=1719

TABLE 7-1X

Race Related to Attempted Enlistment Showing
Educational Attainment and Time of Attempt

Race	Educational Attainment	No Enlistment Attempt	Attempted to Enlist Time 1-3[4]		Time 3-4[4]		Total	Total
White[1]	Dropout	67.3 / 146	21.6 / 47	+	11.1 / 24	=	32.7 / 71	100 / 217
	Graduate	88.5 / 1320	.8 / 12	+	10.8 / 160	=	11.5 / 172	100 / 1492
	Total[2]	85.4 / 1466	3.8 / 66	+	10.7 / 184	=	14.6 / 250[5]	100 / 1716 --- 1716
Black	Dropout	75.5 / 37	18.3 / 9	+	6.1 / 3	=	24.5 / 12	100 / 49
	Graduate	89.3 / 142	2.5 / 4	+	8.1 / 13	=	10.7 / 17	100 / 159
	Total[2]	85.6 / 179	6.7 / 14	+	7.7 / 16	=	14.4 / 30[5]	100 / 209 --- 209 / 1925[3]

[1] Minority groups other than Negro are included in this category. They are not distinguished in this table because their numbers are too small.

[2] Totals are slightly higher than the sum of the dropout and graduate categories because of a small number whose educational attainment is unknown.

[3] This includes all YIT panel members, except those about whom no followup information could be obtained (N=209) and those who were drafted, entered the National Guard or the Reserves, or entered a military academy.

[4] Time 1-2 = 1966-1969, the time when most of the panel was in high school. Time 3-4 = 1969-1970, corresponding to the year after high school for most of the panel.

[5] In this sample, the rates for rejection (attempted to enlist, but turned down) are these: Black: 12/30 = 40%. White: 32/250 = 12.8%.

5482   5412

ping out of high school, so there are more respondents at the lower levels of SEL who both dropped out and, soon after, tried to enlist in the service. This fact helps explain the deviance of the lowest five percent of the cases. Note the difference between the two curves at the lowest point on SEL. Eleven percent enlisted after high school (or the time when the majority of the Class of 1969 would have graduated); but note that the number is much bigger (18 percent) if the criterion is broadened to include enlistments any time after the beginning of tenth grade. The estimate of 18 percent is much closer to the trend line. In addition, there is good reason to believe that the actual rate from this category may be higher. The highest rate of missing data on respon-

TABLE 7-4X

A Selection of Occupations and Their
Duncan S.E.S. Ranking

Bracket Category	Duncan S.E.S. Ratings Included in Category	Exemplary Occupations
1	1-9	Coal Miner (02) Sawyer (05) Janitor (09) Operative in Cement-Making or Textile Manufacturing (03) Construction Laborer (07)
2	10-29	Farmer (14) Blacksmith (16) Carpenter (19) Auto Mechanic (19) Sailor, Dockhand (16) Taxi Driver (10) Newsboy (27) Bus Driver (24) Baker (22)
3	30-49	Plumber (34) Service Station Owner or Mgr. (33) Cashier (44) File Clerk (44) Attendants & Assistants in Dentist & Doctors Offices (38)
4	50-69	Railroad Conductor (58) Prof Athletes (52) Clergyman (52) Secretary (61) Lithographer (64) Social Worker (64) Local Public Administrator (54)
5	70-89	Airplane Pilot (79) Teacher (72) Bank Manager (85) Insurance Manager (84) Federal Official (84) Social Scientist (81) Buyer & Purchasing Agent (77)
6	90-98	Lawyer & Judge (93) Doctor (92)

NOTE: Duncan scale range: 01-98

dents' activities at Time 4 (the last data collection) is associated with this category: 14.8 percent compared to 12.3 percent as the highest rate for any other category. Thus, many from this category who enlisted or tried to enlist may have gone undetected.

Farther up the SEL scale—category 14—there is another extreme deviation from the trend line; but this has to be considered as a chance fluctuation associated with any sampling distribution. There is no reason to suppose that there is anything in the population that is unique about this particular level of SEL that would result in a zero rate of enlistment.

In sum, it is this author's view that the lower rate of enlistment for the bottom SEL category is no more than an artifact, and that in fact the relationship of this measure in the real population is a linear one, with almost 5 percent enlisting from the lowest level of SEL.

TABLE 13-2X

Distribution of Scores on Socioeconomic Level
Related to Preference for Incentives

	10th Centile	25th Centile	Median	75th Centile	90th Centile	N
Pay/enlist	376	418	471	516	567	61
Pay/not enlist	377	446	489	549	619	107
Gtd assmt/enlist	381	436	503	554	588	160
Gtd assmt/not enlist	442	474	521	576	631	302
Schooling/enlist	394	442	504	563	606	134
Schooling/not enlist	432	477	517	578	617	178
Shorter enl/enlist	411	446	502	546	606	83
Shorter enl/not enlist	432	478	526	581	622	214
Now serving (enlist & drafted)	392	431	476	523	571	198
TOTAL of all Respondents	407	457	509	562	614	1437[*]

5475   Total Standard Deviation = 78.3

*Excludes 41 cases for whom socioeconomic level could not be determined.

TABLE 13-3X

Distribution of Scores on GATB-J Test of Intelligence
Related to Preference for Incentives

	10th Centile	25th Centile	Median	75th Centile	90th Centile	N
Pay/enlist	5.0	12.0	16.0	21.0	22.0	64
Pay/not enlist	8.0	14.0	18.0	22.0	27.0	114
Gtd assmt/enlist	9.0	14.0	18.0	23.0	26.0	163
Gtd assmt/not enlist	13.0	18.0	21.0	25.0	29.0	311
Schooling/enlist	11.0	15.0	20.0	25.0	28.0	139
Schooling/not enlist	13.0	18.0	22.0	27.0	30.0	183
Shorter enl/enlist	11.0	15.0	20.0	24.0	28.0	84
Shorter enl/not enlist	13.0	17.0	21.0	26.0	29.0	214
Now serving (enlist & drafted)	10.0	13.0	17.0	21.0	24.0	205
TOTAL of all Respondents	11.0	15.0	20.0	24.0	28.0	1477*

5475

Total Standard Deviation = 6.5

*Excludes one case for whom there was no score on the GATB-J Test of Intelligence.

TABLE 13-4X

Distribution of Scores on Vietnam Dissent
Related to Preference for Incentives

	10th Centile	25th Centile	Median	75th Centile	90th Centile	N
Pay/enlist	179	202	233	250	287	64
Pay/not enlist	177	207	250	283	324	113
Gtd assmt/enlist	173	199	233	263	283	161
Gtd assmt/not enlist	192	217	267	303	342	308
Schooling/enlist	177	199	233	267	294	136
Schooling/not enlist	196	223	283	314	357	181
Shorter enl/enlist	175	204	250	282	300	83
Shorter enl/not enlist	189	217	267	297	333	213
Now serving (enlist & drafted)	146	183	217	243	283	198
TOTAL of all Respondents	182	205	250	283	326	1457*

5475   Total Standard Deviation = 58.8

*Excludes 21 cases for whom score on the Vietnam Dissent Index could not be
determined.

BIBLIOGRAPHY

Abelson, R. P.   Modes of resolution of belief dilemmas. *Journal of Conflict Resolution,* 1959, 3, 343-352.

Altman, S. H.   Earnings, unemployment, and the supply of enlisted volunteers. *Journal of Human Resources,* 1969, 1, 38-59.

Andrews, F. M., Morgan, J. N., & Sonquist, J. A.   *Multiple classification analysis, a report on a computer program for multiple regression using categorical predictors.* Ann Arbor: The University of Michigan, 1969.

Bachman, J. G.   *Youth in transition, volume II: the impact of family background and intelligence on tenth-grade boys.* Ann Arbor: Survey Research Center, Institute for Social Research, 1970.

Bachman, J. G., Green, S., & Wirtanen, I.   *Youth in transition, volume III: dropping out—problem or symptom?* Ann Arbor: Survey Research Center, Institute for Social Research, 1971.

Bachman, J. G., Kahn, R. L., Mednick, M. T., Davidson, T. N., & Johnston, L. D.   *Youth in transition, volume I: blueprint for a longitudinal study of adolescent boys.* Ann Arbor: Survey Research Center, Institute for Social Research, 1967.

Bachman, J. G., & vanDuinen, E.   *Youth look at national problems.* Ann Arbor: Survey Research Center, Institute for Social Research, 1971.

Bachman, J. G.   The draft, military service, and national unity—a contribution to the debate. In Gottlieb, D. (ed.) *Youth in Contemporary Society,* Sage Publications, 1972 (in press).

Bayer, A. E., Astin, A. W., & Boruch, R. F.   College students' attitudes toward social issues: 1967-70. *Educational Review,* 1971, 52-59.

Blau, P., Gustad, J., Jessor, R., Parnes, H., & Wilcock, R.   Occupational choice: a conceptual framework. *Industrial and Labor Relations Review,* 1956, 9, 531-543.

Bryant, B. E.   *High school students look at their world.* Columbus: R. H. Goettler and Assoc., 1970.

Campbell, D. T. & Stanley, J. C.   Experimental and quasi-experimental designs for research on teaching. In Gage, N. L. (ed.) *Handbook of Research on Teaching.* Chicago: Rand McNally, 1963.

Cook, A. A.   Supply of Air Force volunteers. In *Studies Prepared for the President's Commission on an All-Volunteer Armed Force, Volume II.* Washington: U. S. Government Printing Office, 1970.

246   YOUTH IN TRANSITION

Crites, J. O. *Vocational psychology*. New York: McGraw-Hill, Inc., 1969.
Department of Defense. *Reference materials from the Department of Defense study of the draft*. Washington: Office of the Assistant Secretary of Defense, 1966.
Erlick, A. C. *People problems: population, pollution, prejudice, poverty, peace, report of poll #89: the Purdue Opinion Panel*. Lafayette: Purdue University, 1970.
Fechter, A. E. *The supply of first term military officers*. Institute for Defense Analysis. Study S-290, 1968.
Fechter, A. E. Impact of pay & draft policy on army enlistment behavior. In *Studies Prepared for the President's Commission on an All-Volunteer Armed Force*. Volume II. Washington: U. S. Government Printing Office, 1970.
Festinger, L. *A theory of cognitive dissonance*. Stanford: Stanford University Press, 1957.
Flanagan, J. C. & Cooley, W. W. *Project TALENT: one-year follow-up studies*. (Technical report to the U. S. Office of Education, Co-operative Research Project No. 2333), Pittsburgh: University of Pittsburgh Project TALENT Office, 1966.
Flanagan, J. C., Davis, F. B., Dailey, J. T., Shaycoft, M. F., Orr, D. B., Goldberg, I., & Neyman, C. A. *Project TALENT: the identification, development and utilization of human talents. The American high school student*. (Final report to the U.S. Office of Education, Project No. 635), Pittsburgh: University Project TALENT Office, 1964.
French, J. R. P., Jr., Kahn, R. L., & Mann, F. C. Work, health and satisfaction. *Journal of Social Issues*, 1962, 18, 3.
French, J. R. P., Jr., Rodgers, W. L., & Cobb, S. *Adjustment as person-environment fit*. In G. Coelho (ed.), forthcoming.
Friedman, M. Why not a volunteer army? In S. Tax (ed.) *The draft: a handbook of facts and alternatives*. Chicago: The University of Chicago Press, 1967.
Gray, B. C. Supply of first-term military enlistees. In *Studies Prepared for the President's Commission on an All-Volunteer Armed Force*. Volume II. Washington: U. S. Government Printing Office, 1970.
Guide to the use of the General Aptitude Test Battery, (Section III: Development). Washington, D. C.: U. S. Department of Labor, 1962.
Hays, W. *Statistics for psychologists*. New York: Holt, Rinehart and Winston, 1963.
Holland, J. L. *The psychology of vocational choice*. Waltham: Blaisdell Publishing Company, 1966.
Janowitz, M. *The professional soldier: a social and political portrait*. New York: The Free Press, 1964.
Janowitz, M. & Little, R. W. *Sociology and the military establishment*. New York: Russell Sage Foundation, 1965.
Johnston, J. The future soldier: a profile of today's youth. In proceedings of the Army Social Work Current Trends Conference, September, 1970.

(Available from Department of Army Social Work, Fitzsimons General Hospital, Denver, Colorado, 80240).

Johnston, J. *Young men and military service: a study of choice behavior at the end of high school.* Doctoral dissertation, Ann Arbor: University of Michigan, 1971.

Johnston, J. & Bachman, J. G. *Young men look at military service: a preliminary report.* Ann Arbor: Survey Research Center, Institute for Social Research, 1970. (The same report was reprinted in 1971 and an appendix was added entitled "Updated information on Vietnam attitudes.")

Katz, M. *Decisions and values: a rationale for secondary school guidance.* New York: College Entrance Examination Board, 1963.

Life. A new youth poll: change, yes—upheaval, no. (Poll conducted by Louis Harris and Assoc.). *Life,* 1970, 1, 22-30.

Morgan, J. N. & Smith, J. D. *A panel study of income dynamics: study design, procedures and forms: 1969 interviewing year (wave II).* Ann Arbor: Institute for Social Research, 1969. See also same publication for 1970.

Nixon, President Richard M. Message from the President of the United States relative to reforming the draft system. Address to the House of Representatives, 91st Congress 2d Session, April 23, 1970, Document No. 91-324.

Nixon, President Richard M. Message from the President of the United States relative to the military draft. Address to the House of Representatives, 92nd Congress 1st Session, January 29, 1971, Document No. 92-37.

Oi, W. Y. Costs and implications of an all-volunteer force. In S. Tax (ed.) *The draft: a handbook of facts and alternatives.* Chicago: The University of Chicago Press, 1967.

Reiss, A. J., Jr. *Occupations and social status.* New York: The Free Press, 1961.

Roe, A. *The psychology of occupations.* New York: Wiley, 1956.

Rotter, J. B. External control and internal control. *Psychology Today,* 1971, 5, (1), 37-42+.

Sjaastad, L. A. & Hansen, R. W. The conscription tax: an empirical analysis. In *Studies Prepared for the President's Commission on an All-Volunteer Armed Force.* Volume II. Washington: U. S. Government Printing Office, 1970.

Super, D. E. *The psychology of careers.* New York: Harper & Row, 1957.

Super, D. E. The critical ninth grade: vocational choice or vocational exploration. *Personnel and Guidance Journal,* 1960, 39, 106-109.

Super, D. & Bachrach, P. Scientific careers and vocational development theory. New York: Bureau of Publications, Teachers College, Columbia University, 1957.

Super, D. E., Starishevsky, R., Matlin, N. and Jordan, J. P. *Career development: self-concept theory.* New York: College Entrance Examination Board, 1963.

Tax, S. *The draft: a handbook of facts and alternatives.* Chicago: The University of Chicago Press, 1967.

Tiedeman, D. V. & O'Hara, R. P. *Career development: choice and adjustment.* New York: College Entrance Examination Board, 1963.

Thorndike, R. The prediction of intelligence at college entrance from earlier tests. *Journal of Educational Psychology,* 1947, 38, 129-148.

U. S. President's Commission on an All-Volunteer Armed Force. *The report of the president's commission on an all-volunteer armed force.* Washington: U. S. Government Printing Office, 1970a.

—————. *Studies prepared for the president's commission on an all-volunteer armed force.* Volume I. Washington: U. S. Government Printing Office, 1970b.

Wool, H. *The military specialist: skilled manpower for the armed forces.* Baltimore: The Johns Hopkins Press, 1968.

Wrenn, C. G. Intelligence and the vocational choices of college students. *The Educational Record,* 1935, 16, 217-219.

Yankelovich, D. Inc. Youth and the establishment: a report on research for John D. Rockefeller 3rd and the task force on youth. 1971.

INDEX

towards Vietnam, 77-78
military service as an alternative
to, 88, 99, 109
related to grades, 88
related to scholastic aptitude, 86
related to socioeconomic status,
108-110
"Conscription tax," 163, 164, 167,
197
Cook, A., 133, 134, 245
Cooley, W., 131, 246
Cope, R., preface
Costs of conscription, 162, 163
Crites, J., 246
Cultural influences, 101, 126t, 127t,
128t
geographic region, 75, 103, 105t
race, 102-103, 104t
urbanicity, 105, 106t
urbanicity of childhood location, 106
urbanicity related to influence
sending, 128
Dailey, J., 246
Data collections described, 13-16
Davidson, D., preface
Davidson, T., preface, 245
Davis, F., 246
Disadvantaged home life
escape and opportunity, 101,
106, 114, 131, 154, 155
related to enlistment, 101-102
Disruptive behavior in school (see
Rebellious behavior in
school)
Douvan, E., 117
Draft
as a motive for enlistment, 5, 34,
60-70, 140, 143, 152
Draft Status, 62t, 63, 64t, 65-69, 65t,
67t, 82t, 98t
Dropouts who enlist, 92t, 93
Dropping out of high school
alienation hypothesis, 91
related to enlisting, 92t
Economic influences, 133-137
expected civilian earnings, 136
Gates Commission study, 155
unemployment rate, 133-134,
135t, 137, 155
wages, 134, 136t, 155
Enlistment
and job attitudes, 73-75
as an escape from home life,
107-114
conditioning factors for, 4t, 5, 6t

criterion for predictive study,
21t
defined for this study, 19
degree of interest in, 144t
explanations for NOT choosing,
143-144, 145t, 157t
major reason for choice of, 142t
motives or dispositions for, 4t,
4-5, 6t, 52, 153t, 154
related to intellectual ability, 83,
85t, 86t, 88t
related to race, 102-103
related to Vietnam war attitudes, 77, 79t
Erlick, A., 172, 246
Eta statistic, 8-9
Family background influences,
107-118, 126t, 127t, 129t
broken home, 112
family relations; parental punitiveness, 112-113, 113t,
114, 114t
family size, 112
father's and brother's military
experience,   114-115,
115t, 116t
quality of home environment,
108
reactions of family and friends
to enlistment choice, (see
also Influence sending)
118t
S.E.S., SEL, 109-111
socioeconomic status, 107
Fechter, A., 133, 134, 137, 246
Festinger, L., 52, 246
Fit
MIL-FIT, 34-38, 38t, 65-69, 65t,
67t, 68t, 73, 79, 81t, 82t,
98t, 129-130
with job, 34, 35t, 36t, 41t
with military service, 34-52,
65-69
with school, 87, 92
Fit with military service (see also Fit)
as dissonance reduction, 152
concept introduced, 5
Flanagan, J., 3, 131, 246
"Four-for-four" plan, 189
French, J., preface, 34, 246
Friedman, M., 163, 165, 246
Gamma statistic, 9, 10t, 50
GATB-J scores, 84-85, 84t, 85t, 86t
Gates Commission (see U.S. Pres-
ident's Commission on
an All-Volunteer Armed